Robert Cochrane

The Romance of Industry and Invention

Robert Cochrane

The Romance of Industry and Invention

ISBN/EAN: 9783337064761

Printed in Europe, USA, Canada, Australia, Japan

Cover: Foto ©ninafisch / pixelio.de

More available books at **www.hansebooks.com**

THE
ROMANCE OF INDUSTRY
AND
INVENTION

SELECTED BY

ROBERT COCHRANE

EDITOR OF

'GREAT THINKERS AND WORKERS,' 'BENEFICENT AND USEFUL LIVES,' 'ADVENTURE AND ADVENTURERS,' 'RECENT TRAVEL AND ADVENTURE,' 'GOOD AND GREAT WOMEN,' 'HEROIC LIVES,' &c.

PHILADELPHIA
J. B. LIPPINCOTT COMPANY
1897

PREFACE.

Our national industries lie at the root of national progress. The first Napoleon taunted us with being a nation of shopkeepers; that, however, is now less true than that we are a nation of manufacturers—coal, iron, and steel, and our textile industries, taken along with our enormous carrying-trade, forming the backbone of the wealth of the country.

A romantic interest belongs to the rise and progress of most of our industries. Very often this lies in the career of the inventor, who struggled towards the perfection and recognition of his invention against heavy difficulties and discouragements; or it may lie in the interesting processes of manufacture. Every fresh labourer in the field adds some link to the chain of progress, and brings it nearer perfection. Some of the small beginnings have increased in a marvellous way. Such are chronicled under Bessemer and Siemens, who have vastly increased the possibilities of the steel industry; in the sections devoted to Krupp, of Essen; Sir W. G. Armstrong, of the Elswick Works, where 18,000 men are now employed alone in the arsenal; Maxim, of Maxim Gun fame; the rise and progress of the cycle industry; that of the gold and diamond mining industry; and the carrying-trade of the world.

Many of the chapters in this book have been selected from a wealth of such material contributed from time to time to the pages of *Chambers's Journal*, but additions and fresh material have been added where necessary.

LIST OF ILLUSTRATIONS.

	PAGE
The Rush for the Gold-fields................................*Frontispiece*	
Nasmyth's Steam-hammer..	19
Bessemer Converting Vessel..	28
Bessemer Process..	30
Krupp's 15·6 Breech-loading Gun (breech open)......................	47
Josiah Wedgwood...	52
Wedgwood at Work...	56
Portland Vase...	62
The Worcester Porcelain Works..	64
Chinese Porcelain Vase...	71
Wool-sorters at Work..	82
Cotton Plant..	101
The Hand-cradle Method of extracting Gold...........................	103
Welcome Nugget..	106
Hydraulic Gold-mining...	115
Prospecting for Gold..	125
Square-cut Brilliant, Round-cut Brilliant, Rose-cut Diamond...	136
Kimberley Diamond-mine...	139
Some of the Principal Diamonds of the World.......................	145
The *Great Harry*..	153
Gatling Gun on Field Carriage..	163
Nordenfelt-Palmcrantz Gun mounted on Ship's Bulwark........	164
Lord Armstrong..	166
Rifle-calibre Maxim Gun..	178
One of the 'Wooden Walls of Old England'...........................	184
The *Majestic*...	186
Section of the Goubet Submarine Boat..................................	190
The Dandy-horse..	204
The *Great Eastern* and the *Persia*.....................................	232
The *Campania*...	237
Clipper Sailing-ship of 1850–60..	241
La France...	246
The *Great Eastern* paying out the Atlantic Cable.................	281
Edison with his Phonograph...	291

CONTENTS.

CHAPTER I.
IRON AND STEEL.

Pioneers of the Iron and Steel Industry—Sir Henry Bessemer—Sir William Siemens—Werner von Siemens—The Krupps of Essen... 9

CHAPTER II.
POTTERY AND PORCELAIN.

Josiah Wedgwood and the Wedgwood Ware—Worcester Porcelain... 51

CHAPTER III.
THE SEWING MACHINE.

Thomas Saint—Thimonnier—Hunt—Elias Howe—Wilson—Morey—Singer.. 72

CHAPTER IV.
WOOL AND COTTON.

WOOL.—What is Wool?—Chemical Composition—Fibre—Antiquity of Shepherd Life—Varieties of Sheep—Introduction into Australia—Spanish Merino—Wool Wealth of Australia—Imports and Exports of Wool and Woollen Produce—Woollen Manufacture... 81

COTTON.—Cotton Plant in the East—Mandeville's Fables about Cotton—Cotton in Persia, Arabia, and Egypt—Columbus finds Cotton-yarn and Thread in 1492—In Africa—Manufacture of Cloth in England—The American Cotton Plant.......... 91

CHAPTER V.
GOLD AND DIAMONDS.

GOLD.—How widely distributed—Alluvial Gold-mining—Vein Gold-mining—Nuggets—Treatment of Ore and Gold in the

CONTENTS.

PAGE

Transvaal—Story of South African Gold-fields—Gold-production of the World—Johannesburg the Golden City—Coolgardie Gold-fields—Bayley's discovery of Gold there.... 102

DIAMONDS. — Composition — Diamond-cutting — Diamond-mining—Famous Diamonds—Cecil J. Rhodes and the Kimberley Mines.. 135

CHAPTER VI.

BIG GUNS, SMALL-ARMS, AND AMMUNITION.

Woolwich Arsenal—Enfield Small-arms Factory—Lord Armstrong and the Elswick Works—Testing Guns at Shoeburyness—Hiram S. Maxim and the Maxim Machine Gun—The Colt Automatic Gun—Ironclads—Submarine Boats........................ 152

CHAPTER VII.

THE EVOLUTION OF THE CYCLE.

In praise of Cycling—Number of Cycles in Use—Medical Opinions—Pioneers in the Invention—James Starley—Cycling Tours.. 192

CHAPTER VIII.

STEAMERS AND SAILING-SHIPS.

Early Shipping—Mediterranean Trade—Rise of the P. and O. and other Lines—Transatlantic Lines—India and the East—Early Steamships—First Steamer to cross the Atlantic—Rise of Atlantic Shipping Lines—The *Great Eastern* and the New Cunarders *Campania* and *Lucania* compared—Sailing-ships 205

CHAPTER IX.

POST-OFFICE—TELEGRAPH—TELEPHONE—PHONOGRAPH.

Rowland Hill and Penny Postage—A Visit to the Post-office—The Post-office on Wheels—Early Telegraphs—Wheatstone and Morse—The State and the Telegraphs—Atlantic Cables—Telephones—Edison and the Phonograph........................... 247

ROMANCE OF INDUSTRY
AND
INVENTION.

CHAPTER I.

IRON AND STEEL.

Pioneers of the Iron and Steel Industry—Sir Henry Bessemer—Sir William Siemens—Werner von Siemens—The Krupps of Essen.

RANCIS HORNER, writing early in this century, said that 'Iron is not only the soul of every other manufacture, but the mainspring perhaps of civilised society.' Cobden has said that 'our wealth, commerce, and manufactures grew out of the skilled labour of men working in metals.' According to Carlyle, the epic of the future is not to be Arms and the Man, but Tools and the Man. We all know that iron was mined and smelted in considerable quantities in this island as far back as the time of the Romans; and we cherish a vague notion that iron must have been mined and smelted here ever since on a progressively increasing scale. We are so accustomed to think and speak of ourselves as first among all nations, at the smelting-furnace, in the smithy, and amid the Titanic labours of the mechanical workshop, that we

open large eyes when we are told what a recent conquest all this superiority is!

There was, indeed, some centuries later than the Roman occupation, a period coming down to quite modern times, during which English iron-mines were left almost unworked. In Edward III.'s reign, the pots, spits, and frying-pans of the royal kitchen were classed among his majesty's jewels. For the planners of the Armada the greater abundance and excellence of Spanish iron compared with English was an important element in their calculations of success. In the fourteenth and fifteenth centuries, the home market looked to Spain and Germany for its supply both of iron and steel. After that, Sweden came prominently forward; and from her, as late as the middle of the eighteenth century, no less than four-fifths of the iron used in this country was imported!

The reason of this marvellous neglect of what has since proved one of our main sources of wealth lay in the enormous consumption of timber which the old smelting processes entailed. The charcoal used in producing a single ton of pig-iron represented four loads of wood, and that required for a ton of bar-iron represented seven loads. Of course, the neighbourhood of a forest was an essential condition to the establishment of ironworks; but wherever such an establishment was effected, the forest disappeared with portentous rapidity. At Lamberhurst, on the borders of Kent and Sussex, with so trifling a produce as five tons per week, the annual consumption of wood was two hundred thousand cords. The timber wealth of Kent, Surrey, and Sussex—which counties were then the centres of our iron industry—seemed menaced with speedy annihilation. In the destruction of these great forests, that of our maritime power was supposed to be intimately involved; so that it is easy to understand how, in those days, the development of the iron manufacture came to be regarded in the light of a national calamity, and a fitting subject for restrictive legislation! Various Acts were passed towards the end of the sixteenth century prohibiting smelting-furnaces within twenty-two miles of London, and many of the Sussex masters found themselves compelled, in consequence, to break up their works. During the civil wars of the seventeenth century, a severe blow was given to the trade by the destruction of all furnaces belonging to royalists; and after the Restoration we find the crown itself demolishing its own works in the Forest of Dean, on the old plea that the supply of ship-building timber was thereby imperilled. Between 1720 and 1730 the ironworks of Worcestershire and the Forest of Dean consumed 17,350 tons of timber annually, or five tons for each furnace.

'From this time' (the Restoration), says Mr Smiles, 'the iron manufacture of Sussex, as of England generally, rapidly declined. In 1740 there were only fifty-nine furnaces in all England, of which ten were in Sussex; and in 1788 there were only two. A few years later, and the Sussex iron-furnaces were blown out altogether. Farnhurst in Western, and Ashburnham in Eastern Sussex, witnessed the total extinction of the manufacture. The din of the iron hammer was hushed, the glare of the furnace faded, the last blast of the bellows was blown, and the district returned to its original rural solitude. Some of the furnace-ponds were drained and planted with hops or willows; others formed beautiful lakes in retired pleasure-grounds; while the remainder were used to drive flour-mills, as the streams in North Kent, instead of driving fulling-mills, were employed to work paper-mills.' The plentifulness of timber in the Scottish Highlands explains the establishment of smelting-furnaces, in 1753, by an English company at Bunawe in Argyllshire, whither the iron was brought from Furness in Lancashire.

Few of our readers can be unacquainted with the fact that iron-smelting at the present day is performed not with wood but with coal. It will readily, then, be understood that the substitution of the one description of fuel for the other must have formed the turning-point in the history of the British iron manufacture. This substitution, however, was brought about very slowly. The prejudice against coal was for a long period extreme; its use for domestic purposes was pronounced detrimental to health; and, even for purposes of manufacture, it was generally condemned. Nevertheless, as wood became scarcer and dearer, a closer examination into the capabilities of coal came naturally to be made; and here, as in almost every other industrial path, we find a foreigner acting as our pioneer. The Germans had long been experienced in mining and metallurgy; and it was a German, Simon Sturtevant, who first took out a patent for smelting iron with coal. But his process proved a failure, and the patent was cancelled. Other Germans, naturalised here, followed in Sturtevant's footsteps, but with no better results; until at last an Englishman, Dud Dudley (1599–1684), took up the idea, and gave it practical success. The town of Dudley was even then a centre of the iron manufacture, and Dud's noble father, Lord Dudley, owned several furnaces. But here, also, the forest-wealth of the district was fast melting away, and the trade already languished under the dread of impending dissolution. In the immediate neighbourhood, meanwhile, coal was abundant, with ironstone and limestone in close proximity to it. Dud, who, as a child, had haunted and scrutinised his father's ironworks with wondering delight, was placed just at this juncture in charge of a furnace and a couple of forges, and immediately turned his energetic mind to the question of smelting with coal. Some careful experiments succeeded so well that he wrote to his father, requesting him to take out a patent for the process; and this patent, registered in Lord Dudley's name, and dated the 22d February 1620, properly inaugurated the great metallurgic revolution which had made the English iron trade what it now is. Andrew Yarranton was another pioneer in the iron and tin-plate industry, and wrote a remarkable work on *England's Improvement by Sea and Land* (1677-81).

Nevertheless, even with this positive success on record, the inert insular mind long refused to follow the path cleared for it. Dud's discovery 'was neither appreciated by the iron-masters nor by the workmen;' and all schemes for smelting ore with any other fuel than wood-charcoal were regarded with incredulity. His secret seems to have been bequeathed to no one, and for many years after his death the old, much-abused, forest-devouring system went tottering on. Stern necessity, however, taught its hard lesson at last, and a period insensibly arrived when the employment of coal in smelting processes became the rule rather than the exception, and might be seen here and there on an unusually large scale—especially at the celebrated Coalbrookdale works, in the valley of the Severn, Shropshire.

The founder of the Coalbrookdale industries was a Quaker—Abraham Darby (1677-1717). A small furnace had existed on the spot ever since the days of the Tudors, and this small furnace formed the nucleus of that industrial activity which the visitor of Coalbrookdale surveys with such wonder at the present day.

In Darby's time, the principal cooking utensils of the poorer classes were pots and kettles made of cast-iron. But even this primitive ware was beyond native skill, and most of the utensils in question were imported from Holland. Exercising an effort of judgment, which, moderate as it was, seems to have been hitherto unexampled, Darby resolved to pay that country a visit, and ascertain in person why it was that Dutch castings were so good and English so bad. The use of dry sand instead of clay for the moulds comprised, he found, the whole secret.

On returning to England, Darby took out a patent for the new process, and his castings soon acquired repute. The use of pit-coal in the Coalbrookdale furnaces is not supposed, however, to have become general until the worthy Abraham had been succeeded by his son; but when it once did become so, the impetus thereby given to the iron trade and to coal-mining was immense. It is the latter industry which may pre-eminently claim to have called the steam-engine into existence. The demand for pumping-power adequate to the drainage of deep mines set Newcomen's brain to work; and the engine rough-sketched by his ingenuity, and perfected by the genius of Watt, soon increased enormously the production of iron by rendering coal more accessible and the blast-furnace more efficient.

A son-in-law of Abraham Darby's, Richard Reynolds by name, made a great stride towards the modern railway by substituting iron for wood on the tramways which connected the different works at Coalbrookdale; and it was a grandson of the same Abraham who designed and erected the first iron bridge.

England, we have seen, borrowed the idea of her smelting processes and iron-castings from Germany and Holland; but the discovery of that important material, cast-steel, belongs, at least, to one of her own sons. Yet even here the relationship is a merely conventional one, for Benjamin Huntsman (1704-1776) was the child of German parents who had settled in Lincolnshire.

Huntsman's original calling was that of a clock-maker; but his remarkable mechanical skill, his shrewdness, and his practical sense, soon gave him the repute of the 'wise man' of the district, and brought neighbours to consult him not only as to the repair of every ordinary sort of machinery, but also of the human frame—the most complex of all machines! It was his daily experience of the inferior quality of the tools at his command that led him to make experiments in the manufacture of steel. What his experiments were we have no record to show; but that they must have been conducted with Teutonic patience and thoroughness there can be no doubt, from the formidable nature of the difficulties overcome.

England, however, long refused to make use of Huntsman's precious material, although produced in her very midst. The Sheffield cutlers would have nothing to do with a substance so much harder than anything they were accustomed to, and Huntsman was actually compelled to look for his market abroad! All the cast-steel he could manufacture was sent over to France, and the merit of employing this material for general purposes belongs originally to that country. The inventions of Henry Cort (1740-1800) for refining and rolling iron (1785) were the mainspring of the malleable iron trade, and made Great Britain independent of Russia and Sweden for supplies of manufactured iron. One authority has stated that since 1790, when Cort's improvements were entirely established, the value of landed property in England had doubled. But he was unfortunate in business life, and in 1811 upwards of forty iron firms subscribed towards a fund for the assistance of his widow and nine orphan children. David Mushet (1772-1847) did much for the expansion of the iron trade in Scotland by his preparation of steel from bar-iron by a direct process, combining the iron with carbon, and by his discovery of the effect of manganese on steel.

Steel is the material of which the instruments of labour

are essentially made. Upon the quality of the material, that of the instrument naturally depends, and upon the quality of the instrument, that, in great measure, of the work. Watt's marvellous invention ran great risk, at one time, of being abandoned, for the simple reason that the mechanical capacities of the age were not 'up' to its embodiment. Even after Watt had secured the aid of Boulton's best workmen, Smeaton gave it as his opinion that the steam-engine could never be brought into general use, because of the difficulty of getting its various parts made with the requisite precision.

The execution by machinery of work ordinarily executed by hand-tools has been a gigantic stride in the path of material civilisation. The earliest phase of the great modern movement in this direction is represented, probably, by the sawmill. A sawmill was erected near London as long ago as 1663—by a foreigner—but was shortly abandoned in consequence of the determined hostility of the sawyers; and more than a century elapsed before another mill was put up. But the sawmill is comparatively a rude structure, and the material it operates upon is easily treated, even by the hand. When we come to deal, however, with such substances as iron and steel, the benefit of machinery becomes incalculable. Without our recent machine-tools, indeed, the stupendous iron creations of the present day would have been impossible at any cost; for no amount of hand-labour could ever attain that perfect exactitude of construction without which it would be idle to attempt fitting the component parts of these colossal structures together.

The first impulse, however, to the improvement of machine-tools for ironwork was given by a difficulty born not of mass but of minuteness.

Up to the end of the last century, the locks in common

use among us were of the rudest description, and afforded scarcely any security against thieves. To meet this universal want, Joseph Bramah set his remarkable inventive faculties to work, and speedily contrived a lock so perfect, that it held its ground for many a day. But Bramah's locks are machines of the most delicate kind, depending for their efficiency upon the precision with which their component parts are finished; and, at that time, the attainment of this precision, at such a price as to render the lock an article of extensive commerce, seemed an insuperable difficulty. In his dilemma, Bramah's attention was directed to a youngster in the Woolwich Arsenal smithy, named Henry Maudsley, whose reputation for ingenuity was already great among his fellows. Bramah was at first almost ashamed to take such a mere lad into his counsels; but a preliminary conversation convinced him that his confidence would not be misplaced. He persuaded Maudsley to enter his employment, and the result was the invention, between them, of the planing-machine, applicable either to wood or metal, as also of certain improvements in the old lathe, more particularly of that known as the 'slide-rest.'

In the old-fashioned lathe, the workman guided his cutting-tool by sheer muscular strength, and the slightest variation in the pressure necessarily led to an irregularity of surface. The rest for the hand is in this case fixed, and the tool held by the workman travels along it. Now, the principle of the slide-rest is the opposite of this. The rest itself holds the tool firmly fixed in it, and slides along the bench in a direction parallel with the axis of the work. All that the workman has to do, therefore, is to turn a screw-handle, by means of which the cutter is carried along with the smallest possible expenditure of strength; and even this trifling labour has been since got rid of, by making the rest self-acting.

Simple and obvious as this improvement seems, its importance cannot be overrated. The accuracy it insured was precisely the desideratum of the day! By means of the slide-rest, the most delicate as well as the most ponderous pieces of machinery can be turned with mathematical precision; and from this invention must date that extraordinary development of mechanical power and production which is a characteristic of the age we live in. 'Without the aid of the vast accession to our power of producing perfect mechanism which it at once supplied,' says a first-class judge in matters of the kind, 'we could never have worked out into practical and profitable forms the conceptions of those master-minds who, during the past half-century, have so successfully pioneered the way for mankind. The steam-engine itself, which supplies us with such unbounded power, owes its present perfection to this most admirable means of giving to metallic objects the most precise and perfect geometrical forms. How could we, for instance, have good steam-engines if we had not the means of boring out a true cylinder, or turning a true piston-rod, or planing a valve-face?'

It would perhaps be impossible to cite any more authoritative estimate of Maudsley's invention than the above. The words placed between inverted commas are the words of James Nasmyth, the inventor of that wonderful steam-hammer which Professor Tomlinson characterises as 'one of the most perfect of artificial machines and noblest triumphs of mind over matter that modern English engineers have yet developed.'

This machine enlarged at one bound the whole scale of working in iron, and permitted Maudsley's lathe to develop its entire range of capacity. The old 'tilt-hammer' was so constructed that the more voluminous the material submitted to it, the *less* was the power attainable; so that as soon as certain dimensions had been

Nasmyth's Steam-hammer.

exceeded, the hammer became utterly useless. When the *Great Western* steamship was in course of construction, tenders were invited from the leading mechanical firms for the supply of the enormous paddle-shaft required for her engines. But a forging of the size in question had never been executed, and no firm in England would undertake the contract. In this dilemma, Mr Nasmyth was applied to, and the result of his study of the problem was this marvellous steam-hammer—so powerful that it will forge an Armstrong hundred-pounder as easily as a farrier forges a horse-shoe, and so delicately manageable that it will crack a nut without bruising its kernel!

BESSEMER STEEL.

In 1722, Réaumur produced steel by melting three parts of cast-iron with one part of wrought iron (probably in a crucible) in a common forge; he, however, failed to produce steel in this manner on a working scale. This process has many points in common with the Indian Wootz-steel manufacture.

As we have seen, to Benjamin Huntsman, a Doncaster artisan, belongs the credit of first producing cast-steel upon a working scale, as he was the first to accomplish the entire fusion of converted bar-iron (that is, blister-steel) of the required degree of hardness, in crucibles or clay pots, placed among the coke of an air-furnace. This process is still carried on at Sheffield and elsewhere, and is what is generally known as the crucible or pot-steel process. It was mainly supplementary to the cementation process, as formerly blister-steel was alone melted in the crucibles; but latterly, and at the present time, the crucible mode of manufacture embraces the fusion of other varieties and combinations of metal, producing accordingly different classes and qualities of steel.

In 1839, Josiah Marshall Heath patented the important application of carburet of manganese to steel in the crucible, which application imparted to the resulting product the properties of varying temper and increased forgeability. He subsequently found out that a separate operation was not necessary to form the carburet—which is produced by heating peroxide of manganese and carbon to a high temperature—but that the same result could be attained by simply in the first instance adding the carbon and oxide of manganese direct to the metal in the crucible. He unsuspectingly communicated this after-discovery to his agent—by name Unwin—who took advantage of the fact that it was not incorporated in the wording of the patent, and so was unprotected, to make use of it for his own advantage. The result was one of the most remarkable patent trials on record, extending over twelve years, and terminating in 1855 against the patentee—a remarkable instance of the triumph of legal technicalities over the moral sense of right.

A very important development of the manufacture of steel followed the introduction of the 'Bessemer process,' by means of which a low carbon or mild cast-steel can be produced at about one-tenth of the cost of crucible steel. It is used for rails, for the tires of the wheels of railway carriages, for ship-plates, boiler-plates, for shafting, and a multitude of constructional and other purposes to which only wrought iron was formerly applied, besides many for which no metal at all was used.

Sir Henry Bessemer's process for making steel, which is now so largely practised in England, on the continent of Europe, and in America, was patented in 1856. It was first applied to the making of malleable iron, but this has never been successfully made by the Bessemer method.

For the manufacture of a cheap but highly serviceable steel, however, its success has been so splendid that no other metallurgical process has given its inventor so great a renown. Although the apparatus actually used is somewhat costly and elaborate, yet the principle of the operation is very simple. A large converting vessel, with openings called tuyères in its bottom, is partially filled up with from 5 to 10 tons of molten pig-iron, and a blast of air, at a pressure of from 18 to 20 lb. per square inch, is forced through this metal by a blowing engine. Pig-iron contains from 3 to 5 per cent. of carbon, and, if it has been smelted with charcoal from a pure ore, as is the case with Swedish iron, the blast is continued till only from ·25 to 1 per cent. of the carbon is left in the metal, that is to say, steel is produced. Sometimes, however, the minimum quantity of carbon is even less than ·25 per cent. In England, where a less pure but still expensive cast-iron—viz. hæmatite pig—is used for the production of steel in the ordinary Bessemer converter, the process differs slightly. In this case the whole of the carbon is oxidised by the blast of air, and the requisite quantity of this element is afterwards restored to the metal by pouring into the converter a small quantity of a peculiar kind of cast-iron, called *spiegeleisen*, which contains a known quantity of carbon. But small quantities of manganese and silicon are also present in Bessemer steel. The 'blow' lasts from 20 to 30 minutes. Steel made from whatever kind of pig-iron, either by this or by the 'basic' process, is not sufficiently dense, at least for most purposes, and it is accordingly manipulated under the steam-hammer and rolled into a variety of forms. Bessemer steel is employed, as we have said, for heavy objects, as rails, tires, rollers, boiler-plates, ship-plates, and for many other purposes for which malleable iron was formerly used.

Basic steel is now largely made from inferior pig-iron, such as the Cleveland, by the Thomas-Gilchrist process patented in 1878. It is, however, only a modification of the Bessemer process to the extent of substituting for the siliceous or 'acid' lining generally used, a lime or 'basic' lining for the converter. Limestone, preferably a magnesian limestone in some form, is commonly employed for the lining. By the use of a basic lining, phosphorus is eliminated towards the end of the 'blow.' Phosphorus is a very deleterious substance in steel, and is present, sometimes to the extent of 2 per cent., in pig-iron smelted from impure ore.

The four inventions of this century which have given the greatest impetus to the manufacture of iron and steel were —the introduction of the hot blast into the blast-furnace for the production of crude iron, made by J. B. Neilson, of the Glasgow Gas-works, in 1827; the application of the cold blast in the Bessemer converter which we have just described; the production of steel direct from the ore, by Siemens, in the open hearth; and the discovery of a basic lining by which phosphorus is eliminated and all kinds of iron converted into steel. This last was the discovery of G. J. Snelus, of London, and it was made a practical success by the Thomas & Gilchrist process just described. In 1883, Mr Snelus was awarded the Bessemer gold medal of the Iron and Steel Institute 'as the first man who made pure steel from impure iron in a Bessemer converter lined with basic materials.'

SIR HENRY BESSEMER.

Sir Henry Bessemer, the inventor of the modern process of making steel from iron, which has just been described, was the son of Anthony Bessemer, who escaped from France in 1792, and found employment in the English Mint. He was born in 1813, at Charlton, Herts, where his father had an estate, was to a great extent self-taught, and his favourite amusement was in modelling buildings and other objects in clay. He came up to London 'knowing no one, and no one knowing me—a mere cipher in this vast sea of enterprise.' He first earned his living by engraving a large number of elegant and original designs on steel with a diamond point, for patent medicine labels. He found work also as designer and modeller. He has been a prolific inventor, as the volumes issued by the Patent Office show. It has been said that he has paid in patent stamp duties alone as much as £10,000. At twenty he invented a mode of taking copies from antique and modern basso-relievos in such a way that they might be stamped on card-board, thousands being produced at a small cost.

His inventive faculty also devised a ready method whereby those who were defrauding the government by detaching old stamps from leases, money-bills, and agreements, and by using them over again, could be defeated in their purpose.

His first pecuniary success was obtained by his invention of machinery for the manufacture of Bessemer gold and bronze powders, which was not patented, but the nature of which was long kept secret. Another successful invention was a machine for making Utrecht velvet. He also interested himself in the manufacture of paints, oils, and varnishes, sugar, railway carriages, ordnance, projectiles, and the ventilation of mines. In the Exhibition of 1851 he exhibited an ingenious machine for grinding and polishing plate-glass.

Like Lord Armstrong, Bessemer turned his attention to the subject of the improvement of projectiles when there was a prospect of a European war in 1853. He invented a mode of firing elongated projectiles from smooth-bore guns, but received no countenance from the officials at Woolwich.

Commander Minié, who had charge of the experiments which Bessemer was making on behalf of the Emperor of the French, said: 'Yes, the shots rotate properly; but if we cannot get something stronger for our guns, these heavy projectiles will be of little use.' This started Bessemer thinking and experimenting further, and led up, as we will see, to the great industrial revolution with which his name stands identified. He informed the Emperor that he intended to study the whole subject of metals suitable for artillery purposes. He built experimental works at St Pancras, but made many failures, furnace after furnace being pulled down and rebuilt. His prolonged and expensive experiments in getting a suitable ordnance metal were meanwhile using up his capital; but he was on the eve of a great discovery, and began to see that the refinement of iron might go on until pure malleable iron or steel could be obtained. His wife aided and encouraged him at this time as only a true wife can. After a year and a half, in which he patented many improvements in the existing systems of manufacture, it occurred to him to introduce a blast of atmospheric air into the fluid metal, whereby the cast-iron might be made malleable. He found that by blowing air through crude iron in a fluid state, it could thus be rendered malleable. He next tried the method of having the air blown from below by means of an air-engine. Molten iron being poured into the vessel, and air being forced in from below, resulted in a surprising combustion, and the iron in the vessel was transformed into steel. The introduction of oxygen through the fluid iron, induced a higher heat, and burned up the impurities. Feeling that he had succeeded in his experiment, he acquainted Mr George Rennie with the result. The latter said to him: 'This must not be hid under a bushel. The British Association meets next week at Cheltenham; if you have patented your invention, draw up an account of it in a paper, and have it read in Section G.' Accordingly Bessemer wrote an account of his process, and in August 1856, he read his paper before the British Association 'On the Manufacture of Malleable Iron and Steel without Fuel,' which startled the iron trade of the country.

On the morning of the day on which his paper was to be read, Bessemer was sitting at breakfast in his hotel, when an iron-master to whom he was unknown, laughingly said to a friend: 'Do you know that there is somebody come down from London to read us a paper *on making steel from cast-iron without fuel?* Did you ever hear of such nonsense?'

Amongst those who spoke generously and enthusiastically of Bessemer's new process was James Nasmyth, to whom the inventor offered one-third share of the value of the patent, which would have been another fortune to him. Nasmyth had made money enough by this time, however, and declined.

In a communication to Nasmyth, Sir Henry Bessemer thanked him for his early patronage, and described his discovery: 'I shall ever feel grateful for the noble way in which you spoke at the meeting at Cheltenham of my invention. If I remember rightly, you held up a piece of malleable iron, saying words to this effect: "Here is a true British nugget! Here is a new process that promises to put an end to all puddling; and I may mention that at this moment there are puddling-furnaces in successful operation where my patent hollow steam-rabbler is at work, producing iron of superior quality by the introduction of jets of steam in the puddling process. I do not, however, lay any claim to this invention of Mr Bessemer; but I may fairly be entitled to say that I have advanced along the roads on which he has travelled so many miles, and has effected such unexpected results, that I do not hesitate to say that I may go home from this meeting and tear up my patent, for my process of puddling is assuredly superseded."'

After giving an account of his failures, as well as successes, Sir Henry proceeded to say: 'I prepared to try another experiment, in a crucible having no hole in the bottom, but which was provided with an iron pipe put through a hole in the cover, and passing down nearly to the bottom of the crucible. The small lumps and grains of iron were packed round it, so as nearly to fill the crucible. A blast of air was to be forced down the pipe so as to rise up among the pieces of granular iron, and partly decarburise them. The pipe could then be withdrawn, and the fire urged until the metal with its coat of oxide was fused, and cast-steel thereby produced.

'While the blowing apparatus for this experiment was being fitted up, I was taken with one of those short but painful illnesses to which I was subject at that time. I was confined to my bed, and it was then that my mind, dwelling for hours together on the experiment about to be made, suggested that instead of trying to decarburise the granulated metal by forcing the air down the vertical pipe among the pieces of iron, the air would act much more energetically and more rapidly if I first melted the iron in the crucible, and *forced the air down the pipe below the surface of the fluid metal*, and thus burnt out the carbon and silicum which it contained.

'This appeared so feasible, and in every way so great an improvement, that the experiment on the granular pieces was at once abandoned, and as soon as I was well enough, I proceeded to try the experiment of forcing the air under the fluid metal. The result was marvellous.

Complete decarburation was effected in half an hour. The heat produced was immense, but unfortunately more than half the metal was blown out of the pot. This led to the use of pots with large, hollow, perforated covers, which effectually prevented the loss of metal. These experiments continued from January to October 1855. I have by me on the mantelpiece at this moment, a small

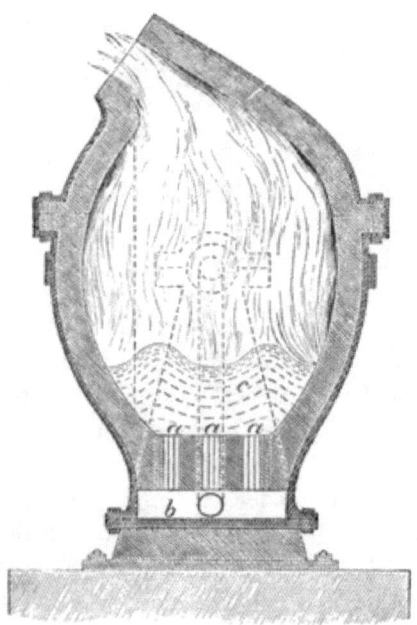

BESSEMER CONVERTING VESSEL:
a, a, a, tuyères ; *b*, air-space ; *c*, melted metal.

piece of rolled bar-iron which was rolled at Woolwich Arsenal, and exhibited a year later at Cheltenham.

'I then applied for a patent, but before preparing my provisional specification (dated October 17, 1855), I searched for other patents to ascertain whether anything of the sort had been done before. I then found your patent for puddling with the steam-rabble, and also Martin's patent for the use of steam in gutters while molten iron was being conveyed from the blast-furnace to a finery, there to be refined in the ordinary way prior to puddling.

Several leading men in the iron trade took licenses for the new manufacture, which brought Bessemer £27,000 within thirty days of the time of reading his paper. These licenses he afterwards bought back for £31,000, giving fresh ones in their stead. Some of the early experiments failed, and it was feared the new method would prove impracticable. These experiments failed because of the presence of phosphorus in the iron. But Bessemer worked steadily in order to remove the difficulties which had arisen, and a chemical laboratory was added to his establishment, with a professor of chemistry attached. Success awaited him. The new method of steel-making spread into France and Sweden, and in 1879 the works for making Bessemer steel were eighty-four in number, and represented a capital of more than three millions. His process for the manufacture of steel raised the annual production of steel in England from 50,000 tons by the older processes to as many as 2,000,000 tons in some years. It was next used for boiler-plates; shipbuilding with Bessemer steel was begun in 1862, and now it is employed for most of the purposes for which malleable iron was formerly used. The production of Europe and America in 1892 was over 10,000,000 tons, of a probable value of £84,000,000, sufficient, as has been remarked, to make a solid steel wall round London 40 feet high, and and 5 feet thick. It would take, according to the inventor, two or three years' production of all the gold-mines in the world to pay in gold for the output of Bessemer steel for one year. The price of steel previous to Huntsman's process was about £10,000 per ton; after him,

Bessemer Process.

from £50 to £100. Now Bessemer leaves it at £5 to £6 per ton. And a process which occupied ten days can be accomplished within half an hour.

In his sketch of the 'Bessemer Steel Industry, Past and Present' (1894), Sir Henry Bessemer says: 'It is this new material, so much stronger and tougher than common iron, that now builds our ships of war and our mercantile marine. Steel forms their boilers, their propeller shafts, their hulls, their masts and spars, their standing rigging, their cable chains and anchors, and also their guns and armour-plating. This new material has covered with a network of steel rails the surface of every country in Europe, and in America alone there are no less than 175,000 miles of Bessemer steel rails.' These steel rails last six times longer than if laid of iron.

Bessemer was knighted in 1879, and has received many gold medals from scientific institutions. In addition he has, to use his own words, received in the form of royalties 1,057,748 of the beautiful little gold medals (sovereigns) issued by her Majesty's Mint. The method chosen by the Americans to perpetuate his name has been the founding of the growing centre of industry called Bessemer in Indiana, while Bessemer, in Pennsylvania, is the seat of the great Edgar Thompson steel-works. Thus the man who was at first neglected by government has become wealthy beyond the dreams of avarice, and his name is immortal in the annals of our manufacturing industry.

SIR CHARLES WILLIAM SIEMENS AND THE SIEMENS PROCESS.

Another pioneer in the manufacture of steel and iron was CHARLES WILLIAM SIEMENS, the seventh child of a German landowner, who was born at Lenthe, near

Hanover, 4th April 1823. He showed an affectionate and sensitive disposition while very young, and a strong faculty of observation. He received a good plain education at Lübeck, and in deference to his brother Werner he agreed to become an engineer, and accordingly was sent to an industrial school at Magdeburg in 1838, where he also learned languages, including English; mathematics he learned from his interested brother. He left Magdeburg in 1841 in order to increase his scientific knowledge at Göttingen, and there he studied chemistry and physics, with the view of becoming an engineer. Werner, his elder brother, was still his good genius, and after the death of their parents counselled and encouraged him, and looked upon him as a probable future colleague. They corresponded with one another, not only about family affairs, but also about the scientific and technical subjects in which both were engrossed. This became a life-long habit with the brothers Siemens. One early letter from William described a new kind of valve-gearing which he had invented for Cornish steam-engines. Then the germ of the idea of what was afterwards known as the 'chronometric governor' for steam-engines was likewise communicated in this way. Mr Pole says that his early letters were significant of the talent and capacity of the writer. 'They evince an acuteness of perception in mechanical matters, a power of close and correct reasoning, a sound judgment, a fertility of invention, and an ease and accuracy of expression which, in a youth of nineteen, who had only a few months' experience in a workshop, are extraordinary, and undoubtedly shadow forth the brilliant future he attained in the engineering world.'

Werner in 1841 had taken out a patent for his method of electro-gilding, while William early in 1843 paid his first visit to England, travelling by way of Hamburg. He took up his abode in a little inn called the 'Ship and

Star,' at Sparrow Corner, near the Minories. In an address as President of the Midland Institute, Birmingham, on 28th October 1881, he related his first experiences in England, and how he secured his first success there.

Mr Siemens said: 'That form of energy known as the electric current was nothing more than the philosopher's delight forty years ago; its first application may be traced to this good town of Birmingham, where Mr George Richards Elkington, utilising the discoveries of Davy, Faraday, and Jacobi, had established a practical process of electroplating in 1842. . . . Although I was only a young student of Göttingen, under twenty years of age, who had just entered upon his practical career with a mechanical engineer, I joined my brother Werner Siemens, then a young lieutenant of artillery in the Prussian service, in his endeavour to accomplish electro-gilding. . . . I tore myself away from the narrow circumstances surrounding me, and landed at the East End of London, with only a few pounds in my pocket and without friends, but an ardent confidence of ultimate success within my breast.

'I expected to find some office in which inventions were examined into, and rewarded if found meritorious, but no one could direct me to such a place. In walking along Finsbury Pavement I saw written up in large letters, "So-and-So"—I forget the name—"undertaker," and the thought struck me that this must be the place I was in quest of; at any rate, I thought that a person advertising himself as an "undertaker" would not refuse to look into my invention, with the view of obtaining for me the sought for recognition or reward. On entering the place I soon convinced myself, however, that I came decidedly too soon for the kind of enterprise there contemplated.' By dint of perseverance, however, Siemens secured a letter from Messrs Poole and Carpmaell, of the Patent Office, to Mr Elkington of Birmingham. Elkington and his partner

Josiah Mason both met the young inventor in such a spirit of fairness that, as he says, he returned to his native country, and to his mechanical engineering, 'a comparative Crœsus.' After the lapse of forty years his heart still beat quick when thinking of this determining incident in his career.

The sum which Elkington paid him for his 'thermo-electrical battery' for depositing solutions of gold, silver, and copper was £1600, less £110 for the cost of the patent. Although quite successful at the time, other and cheaper processes speedily supplanted it; but the young German had gained a footing and the money he needed for future experiments. When he came back to Germany he was looked upon as quite a hero by his admiring family circle. It was indeed a creditable exploit for a youth of twenty. When he returned to England again in February 1844, he received so much encouragement from leading engineers and scientific men for his 'chronometric governor,' that he decided to settle permanently there, and he became a naturalised British subject in 1859. He joined with a civil engineer, named Joseph Woods, for the promotion and sale of his patents. 'Anastatic printing' was one of his early inventions, which, however, never became profitable. Then came schemes in paper-making, new methods of propelling ships, winged rockets, and locomotives on new principles, all of which were a continual drain on his own and his friends' resources without a corresponding return, so that in 1845 he took a situation and earned some money by railway work, which enabled him to pay another visit to Germany. In 1846, undaunted by previous failures, he threw himself heartily into the study of the action of heat as a power-giving agent, and invented an arrangement known as the 'regenerator' for saving certain portions of this waste. As afterwards applied to furnaces for iron, steel, zinc, glass, and other works, it was pronounced by Sir Henry Bessemer a beautiful invention, at once the most philosophic in principle, the most powerful in action, and the most economic of all the contrivances for producing heat by the combustion of coal. He now secured an appointment in 1849 with Fox & Henderson, Birmingham, at a fixed salary of £400 a year, and his interest in his patent. Here he profited largely by the experience gained, but the engagement terminated in 1851, when he afterwards settled as a civil engineer in 7 John Street, Adelphi, in March 1852.

His next great achievement was the production of steel direct from the raw ores by means of his regenerative furnace, which the President of the Board of Trade in 1883 mentioned in the House of Commons as one of the most valuable inventions ever produced under the protection of the English patent law, and he said further that it was then being used in almost every industry in the kingdom. Siemens had spent fourteen years in perfecting this regenerative furnace, and it took him other fourteen to utilise it, and perfect it in making steel direct from the raw ores. Martin of Sireil, who made one or two additions to the Siemens steel furnace, has been termed its inventor, but this claim has no foundation. What is known, however, as the 'Siemens-Martin process' is now competing very effectively with the Bessemer process. It consists essentially in first obtaining a bath of melted pig-iron of high quality, and then adding to this pieces of wrought-iron scrap or Bessemer scrap, such as crop ends of rails, shearings of plates, &c. These, though practically non-infusible in large quantities by themselves, become dissolved or fused in such a bath if added gradually. To the bath of molten metal thus obtained spiegeleisen or ferro-manganese is added to supply the required carbon and to otherwise act as in the Bessemer converter. The result is tested by small ladle samples, and when it is of the desired quality a portion is run off, leaving sufficient bath for the continuation of the process.

Siemens took out his patent for the 'open hearth' process of steel-making (the Forth Bridge is built of steel made in this way) in 1861, and four years later erected sample steel works at Birmingham. The engineer of the London and North-Western Railway adopted his system at Crewe in 1868, and the Great Western Railway works followed. In 1869 this process was being carried out on a large scale at the works of the Landore-Siemens Steel Company and elsewhere in England, as well as at various works on the Continent, including Krupp's, at Essen.

In 1862, Siemens was elected a Fellow of the Royal Society, and in 1874 was presented with the Royal Albert Medal, and in 1875 with the Bessemer Medal in recognition of his researches and inventions in heat and metallurgy. He filled the president's chair in the three principal engineering and telegraphic societies of Great Britain, and in 1882 was President of the British Association. As manager in England of the firm of Siemens Brothers, Sir William Siemens was actively engaged in the construction of overland and submarine telegraphs. The steamship *Faraday* was specially designed by him for cable-laying. In addition to his labours in connection with electric-lighting, Sir William Siemens also successfully applied, in the construction of the Portrush Electric Tramway, which was opened in 1883, electricity to the production of locomotion. In his regenerative furnace, as we have seen, he utilised in an ingenious way the heat which would otherwise have escaped with the products of combustion. The process was subsequently applied in many industrial processes, but notably by Siemens himself in the manufacture of steel.

The other inventions and researches of this wonderful man include a water-meter; a thermometer or pyrometer, which measures by the change produced in the electric conductivity of metals; the bathometer, for measuring ocean depths by variations in the attraction exerted on a delicately suspended body; and the hastening of vegetable growth by use of the electric light. He was knighted in April 1883, and died on November 19 of the same year. There is a memorial window to his memory in Westminster Abbey.

As the elder brother of Sir William Siemens was so closely connected with him in business life, and may be said to have encouraged and led him into the walk of life in which he excelled, he also deserves a notice here. WERNER VON SIEMENS, engineer and electrician, was born December 13, 1816, at Lenthe in Hanover. In 1834 he entered the Prussian Artillery; and in 1844 was put in charge of the artillery workshops at Berlin. He early showed scientific tastes, and in 1841 took out his first patent for galvanic silver and gold plating. By selling the right of using his process he made 40 louis d'or, which supplied him with the means for further experiments. During the Schleswig-Holstein war, he attracted considerable attention by using electricity for the firing of the mines which had been laid for the defence of Kiel harbour. He was of peculiar service in developing the telegraphic service in Prussia, and discovered in this connection the valuable insulating property of gutta-percha for underground and submarine cables. In 1849 he left the army, and shortly after the service of the state altogether, and devoted his energies to the construction of telegraphic and electrical apparatus of all kinds. The well-known firm of Siemens and Halske was established in 1847 in Berlin, and to them the Russian government entrusted the construction of the telegraph lines in that country. Subsequently branches were formed, chiefly under the management of the younger brothers of Werner Siemens, in St Petersburg (1857), in London (1858), in Vienna (1858), and in Tiflis (1863). In 1857, Siemens accomplished the remarkable feat of successfully laying a cable in deep water, at a depth of more than 1000 fathoms. This was between Sardinia and Bona. Shortly after he superintended the laying of cables in the Red Sea; and these successful experiments soon led to the greatest undertaking of all, the connection of America with Europe. Besides devising numerous useful forms of galvanometers and other electrical instruments of precision, Werner Siemens was one of the discoverers of the principle of the self-acting dynamo. He also made valuable determinations of the electrical resistance of different substances, the resistance of a column of mercury, one metre long, and one square millimetre cross section at 0° C., being known as the Siemens Unit. His numerous scientific and technical papers, written for the various journals, were republished in collected form in 1881. In 1886 he gave 500,000 marks for the founding of an imperial institute of technology and physics; and in 1888 he was ennobled. He died at Berlin, 6th December 1892. A translation of his *Personal Recollections* by Coupland appeared in 1893.

Space forbids us mentioning other worthy names in the steel and iron trade, although we cannot pass by Sir John Brown, founder of the Atlas Steel-works, Sheffield (1857), and one of the first to adopt the Bessemer process. He was also the pioneer of armour-plate making. The immense strides he made in business may be judged from the fact that when he started in 1857 his employees numbered 200, with a turnover of £3000 a year; in 1867 they numbered 4000, and the turnover was £1,000,000.

The weekly pay roll amounted to £7000 in 1883, and when he handed over the business to his successors, he was paid £200,000 for the goodwill.

KRUPP'S IRON AND STEEL WORKS AT ESSEN.

One of the largest iron and steel manufacturing establishments in the world is that founded by the late Alfred Krupp, the famous German cannon-founder, whose name is so well known in connection with modern improvements in artillery. His principal works are situated at Essen, in Prussia, in the midst of a district productive of both iron and coal. The town of Essen, which at the beginning of the present century contained less than four thousand inhabitants, has become an important industrial centre, with a population of nearly eighty thousand persons, this increase being chiefly due to the growth of the ironworks, and the consequent demand for labour. In the vicinity of the town, numerous coal and iron mines, many of which are owned by the Krupp firm, are in active working, and furnish employment to the large population of the surrounding district. Much of the output of iron ore and coal from these mines is destined for consumption in the vast Krupp works within the town. Those works had their origin in a small iron forge established at Essen in the year 1810 by Frederick Krupp, the father of Alfred Krupp. The elder Krupp was not prosperous; and a lawsuit in which he became involved, and which lasted for ten years, though finally decided in his favour, reduced him nearly to bankruptcy. He died in 1826, in impoverished circumstances, leaving a widow and three sons, the eldest of whom was Alfred, aged fourteen. The business was continued by the widow, who managed, though with difficulty, to procure a good education for her sons. When the eldest, Alfred, took control of the works in 1848, he found there, as he himself has described, 'three workmen, and more debts than fortune.'

Krupp's subsequent career affords a remarkable instance of success attained, despite adverse circumstances, by sheer force of ability and energy, in building up a colossal manufacturing business from a humble beginning. On his death in 1887 his only son succeeded him. At the present time, Krupp's works within the town of Essen occupy more than five hundred acres, half of which area is under cover. In 1895, the number of persons in his employ was 25,300, and including members of their families, over 50,000. Of the army of workers, about 17,000 were employed at the works in Essen, the remainder being occupied in the 550 iron and coal mines belonging to the firm, or at the branch works at Sayn Neuwied, Magdeburg, Duisburg, and Engers; or in the iron-mines at Bilbao, in Spain, which produce the best ores. In Krupp's Essen works there are one hundred and twelve steam-hammers, ranging in weight from fifty tons down to four hundred pounds. There are 15 Bessemer converters, 18 Martin-furnaces, 420 steam-engines—representing together 33,150 horse-power—and twenty-one rolling trains; the daily consumption of coal and coke being 3100 tons by 1648 furnaces. The average daily consumption of water, which is brought from the river Ruhr by an aqueduct, is 24,700 cubic metres. The electric light has been introduced, and the work ceases entirely only on Sunday and two or three holidays. Connected with the Essen works are fifty miles of railway, employing thirty-five locomotives and over 1000 wagons. There are two chemical laboratories; a photographic and lithographic studio; a printing-office, with steam and hand presses; and a bookbinding room, besides tile-works, coke-works, gas-works, &c.

Though, in the popular mind, the name of Krupp is

usually associated with the manufacture of instruments of destruction, yet two-thirds of the work done in his establishment is devoted to the production of articles intended for peaceful uses. The various parts of steam-engines, both stationary and locomotive; iron axles, bridges, rails, wheel-tires, switches, springs, shafts for steamers, mint-dies, rudders, and parts of all varieties of iron machinery, are prepared here for manufacturers. The production is, in Dominie Sampson's phrase, 'prodigious.' In one day the works can turn out 2700 rails, 350 wheel-tires, 150 axles, 180 railway wheels, 1000 railway wedges, 1500 bomb-shells. In a month they have produced 250 field-pieces, thirty 5.7-inch cannon, fifteen 9.33-inch cannon, eight 11-inch cannon, one 14-inch gun, the weight of the last named being over fifty tons, and its length twenty-eight feet seven inches. Till the end of 1894 the firm has produced 25,000 cannon for thirty-four different states.

Alfred Krupp devoted much attention to the production of steel of the finest quality, and was the first German manufacturer who succeeded in casting steel in large masses. In 1862 he exhibited in London an ingot of finest crucible steel weighing twenty-one tons. Its dimensions were nine feet high by forty-four inches diameter. The uniformity of quality of this mass of metal was proven by the fact that when broken across it showed no seam or flaw, even when examined with a lens. The firm can now make such homogeneous blocks of seventy-five tons weight if required. Such ingots are formed from the contents of a great number of small crucibles, each containing from fifty to one hundred pounds of the metal. The recent developments of the manufacture of steel by the open-hearth process have removed all difficulty in procuring the metal in masses large enough for all requirements, and of a tensile strength so high as thirty-three to thirty-seven tons to the square inch. Crucible steel, however, though more expensive, still holds its place as the best and most reliable that can be produced; and nothing else is ever used in the construction of a Krupp gun. By the perfected methods in use at the Essen works, such steel can be made of a tensile strength of nearly forty tons to the square inch, and of marvellous uniformity of quality. The ores used in the Krupp works for making the best steel are red hæmatite and spathic ore, with a certain proportion of ferro-manganese. The crucibles employed are formed of a mixture of plumbago and fire-clay, shaped by a mould into a cylindrical jar some eighteen inches in height, and baked in a kiln. When in use, they are filled with small bars of puddled metal, mixed with fragments of marble brought from Villmar, on the Lahn. They are then shovelled into large furnaces, whose floors are elevated three or four feet above the ground-level. In the earthen floor of the immense room containing the furnaces are two lines of pits, one set to receive the molten metal, the other intended for the red-hot crucibles when emptied of their contents. When the crucibles have undergone sufficient heating, the furnace doors are opened simultaneously at a given signal, and the attendant workmen draw out the crucibles with long tongs, and rapidly empty them into the pits prepared for the reception of the metal. The empty crucibles when cooled are examined, and if found unbroken, are used again; but if damaged, as is usually the case, are ground up, to be utilised in making new ones.

The production of steel by this method furnishes employment for eight or nine hundred men daily in the Krupp works. The Bessemer process for converting iron into steel is also largely used there for making steel for certain purposes. All material used in the different classes of manufactures is subjected at every stage to extreme and exact tests; the standards being fixed with reference to the purpose to which the metal is to be applied, and any material that proves faulty when suitably tested is rigorously rejected.

The guns originally manufactured by the Krupp firm were formed from solid ingots of steel, which were bored, turned, and fashioned as in the case of cast-iron smooth-bore cannon. With the development of the power of artillery, the greater strain caused by the increased powder-charges and by the adoption of rifling—involving enhanced friction between the projectile and the bore—had the result of demonstrating the weakness inherent in the construction of a gun thus made entirely from one solid forging, and that plan was eventually discarded. Artillerists have learnt that the strain produced by an explosive force operating in the interior of a cannon is not felt equally throughout the thickness of the metal from the bore to the exterior, but varies inversely as the square of the distance of each portion of the metal from the seat of effort. For example, in a gun cast solid, if two points be taken, one at the distance of one inch from the bore, and the other four inches from the bore, the metal at the former point will during the explosion be strained sixteen times as much as that at the distance of four inches. The greater the thickness of the material, the greater will be the inequality between the strains acting at the points respectively nearest to and farthest from the interior. The metal nearest the seat of explosion may thus be strained beyond its tensile strength, while that more remote is in imperfect accord with it. In such a case, disruption of the metal at the inner surface ensues, and extends successively through the whole thickness to the exterior, thus entailing the destruction of the gun.

This source of weakness is guarded against by the construction of what is termed the built-up gun, in which the several parts tend to mutual support. This gun consists of an inner tube, encircled and compressed by a long 'jacket' or cylinder, which is shrunk around the breech portion with the initial tension due to contraction in cooling. Over the jacket and along the chase, other hoops or cylinders are shrunk on successively, in layers, with sufficient tension to compress the parts enclosed. The number and strength of these hoops are proportionate to the known strain that the bore of the gun will have to sustain. The tension at which each part is shrunk on is the greater as the part is farther removed from the inner tube; the jacket, for example, being shrunk on at less tension than the outer hoops. The inner tube, on receiving the expansive force of the explosion, is prevented by the compression of the jacket from being forced up to its elastic limit; and the jacket in its turn is similarly supported by the outer hoops; and on the cessation of the internal pressure the several parts resume their normal position.

This system of construction originated in England, and is now in general use. The first steel guns on this principle were those designed by Captain Blakely and Mr J. Vavasseur, of the London Ordnance Works. At the Exhibition of 1862, a Blakely 8·5-inch gun, on the built-up system, composed wholly of steel, was a feature of interest in the Ordnance section. The plan devised by Sir W. Armstrong, and carried into effect for a series of years at Woolwich and at the Armstrong Works at Elswick, consisted in enclosing a tube of steel within a jacket of wrought iron, formed by coiling a red-hot bar round a mandrel. The jacket was shrunk on with initial tension, and was fortified in a similar manner by outer hoops of the same metal. The want of homogeneity in this gun was, however, a serious defect, and ultimately led to its abolition. The difference in the elastic properties of the two metals caused a separation, after repeated discharges, between the steel tube and its jacket, with the result that the tube cracked from want of support. Both at Woolwich and at Elswick (described on a later page), therefore, the wrought-iron gun has given place to the homogeneous steel built-up gun, which is also the form of construction adopted by the chief powers of Europe and by the United States of America.

The failure of some of his solid-cast guns led Krupp, about 1865, to the adoption of the built-up principle. With few exceptions, the inner tube of a Krupp gun is forged out of a single ingot, and in every case without any weld. The ingot destined to form the tube has first to undergo a prolonged forging under the steam-hammers, by which the utmost condensation of its particles is effected. It is then rough-bored and turned, and subsequently carefully tempered in oil, whereby its elasticity and tensile strength are much increased. It is afterwards fine-bored and rifled, and its powder-chamber hollowed out. The latter has a somewhat larger diameter than the rest of the bore, this having been found an improvement. The grooves of the rifling are generally shallow, and they widen towards the breech, so that the leaden coat of the projectile is compressed gradually and with the least friction. The jacket and hoops of steel are forged and rolled, without weld, and after being turned and tempered, are heated and shrunk around the tube in their several positions, the greatest strength and thickness being of course given to the breech end, where the force of explosion exerts the utmost strain. The completed gun is mounted on its appropriate carriage, and having been thoroughly proved and tested and fitted with the proper sights, is ready for service. The testing range is at Meppen, where a level plain several miles in extent affords a suitable site for the purpose.

For many years all guns of the Krupp manufacture have

been on the breech-loading system, and he has devoted much time and ingenuity to perfecting the breech arrangements. The subject of recoil has also largely occupied his attention. In the larger Krupp guns the force of recoil is absorbed by two cylinders, filled with glycerine and fitted with pistons perforated at the edges. The pistons are driven by the shock of the recoil against the glycerine, which is forced through the perforations. In England a similar arrangement of cylinders, containing water as the resisting medium, has been found effective; and in America, petroleum is employed for the same purpose. The advantages of the use of glycerine are that in case of a leak it would escape too slowly to lose its effect at once, and it is also more elastic than water, and is less liable to become frozen.

The resources of Krupp's establishment are equal to the production of guns of any size that can conceivably be required. He has made guns of one hundred and nineteen tons weight. The portentous development of the size and power of modern ordnance is exemplified by these guns and the Armstrong guns of one hundred and eleven tons made at Elswick. Amongst the class of modern cannon, one of the most powerful is Krupp's seventy-one-ton gun. This, like all others of his make, is a breech-loader. Its dimensions are—length, thirty-two feet nine inches; diameter at breech end, five feet six inches; length of bore, twenty-eight feet seven inches; diameter of bore, 15.75 inches; diameter of powder-chamber, 17.32 inches. The internal tube is of two parts, exactly joined; and over this are four cylinders, shrunk on, and a ring round the breech. Its rifling has a uniform twist of one in forty-five. It cannot possibly be fired until the breech is perfectly closed. Its maximum charge is four hundred and eighty-five pounds of powder, and a chilled iron shell of seventeen hundred and eight pounds.

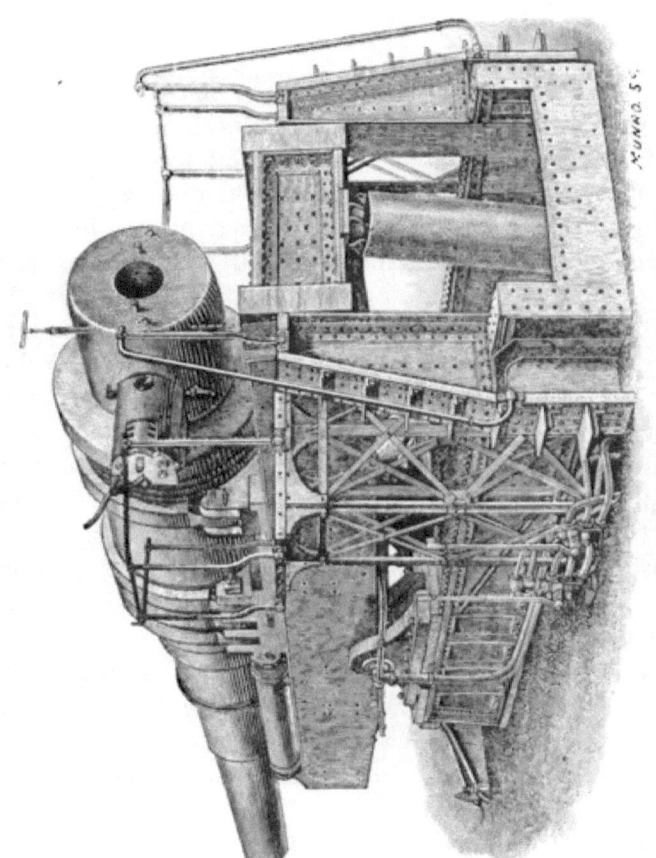

Krupp's 15·6 Breech-loading Gun (breech open).

Krupp did much to promote the welfare and comfort of his workpeople. For their accommodation, he erected around Essen nearly four thousand family dwellings, in which more than sixteen thousand persons reside. The dwellings are in suites of three or four comfortable rooms, with good water-arrangements; and attached to each building is a garden, large enough for the children to play in. There are one hundred and fifty dwellings of a better kind for officials in the service of the firm. Boarding-houses have also been built for the use of unmarried labourers, of whom two thousand are thus accommodated. Several churches, Protestant and Catholic, have also been erected, for the use of his workmen and their families. There have likewise been provided two hospitals, bathing establishments, a gymnasium, an unsectarian free school, and six industrial schools—one for adults, two for females. In the case of the industrial schools, the fees are about two shillings monthly, but the poorest are admitted free. A Sick Relief and Pensions Fund has been instituted, and every foreman and workman is obliged to be a member. The entrance fee is half a day's pay, the annual payment being proportioned to the wages of the individual member; but half of each person's contribution is paid by the firm. There are three large surgeries; and skilful physicians and surgeons, one of whom is an oculist, are employed at fixed salaries. For a small additional fee each member can also secure free medical aid for his wife and children. The advantages to members are free medical or surgical treatment in case of need, payment from the fund of funeral expenses at death, pensions to men who have been permanently disabled by injuries while engaged in the works, pensions to widows of members, and temporary support to men who are certified by two of the physicians as unable to work. The highest pension to men is five pounds monthly, the average being about two pounds sixteen shillings monthly. The average pension to widows is about one pound fourteen shillings monthly.

The firm have made special arrangements with a number of life insurance companies whereby the workmen can, if they choose, insure their lives at low rates. They have formed a Life Insurance Union, and endowed it with a reserve fund of three thousand pounds, from which aid is given to members needing assistance to pay their premiums. An important institution in Essen is the great Central Supply Store, established and owned by the firm, where articles of every description—bread, meat, and other provisions, clothing, furniture, &c.—are sold on a rigidly cash system at cost price. Connected with the Central Store are twenty-seven branch shops, in positions convenient for the workpeople, placing the advantages of the system within the easy reach of all.

The original name, 'Frederick Krupp,' has been retained through all vicissitudes of fortune as the business title of the firm. The small dwelling in which Alfred Krupp was born is still standing, in the midst of the huge workshops that have grown up around it, and is preserved with the greatest care. At his expense, photographs of it were distributed among his workmen, each copy bearing the following inscription, dated Essen, February 1873: 'Fifty years ago, this primitive dwelling was the abode of my parents. I hope that no one of our labourers may ever know such struggles as have been required for the establishment of these works. Twenty-five years ago that success was still doubtful which has at length—gradually, yet wonderfully — rewarded the exertions, fidelity, and perseverance of the past. May this example encourage others who are in difficulties! May it increase respect for small houses, and sympathy for the larger sorrows they too often contain. The object of labour should be the common weal. If work bring blessing, then is labour prayer. May every one in our community, from the highest to the lowest, thoughtfully and wisely strive to secure and build his prosperity on this principle! When this is done, then will my greatest desire be realised.'

Germany has become a formidable competitor to Great Britain in the iron and steel trade, and German steel rails, girders, and wire come in freely to this country. From reports we learn that Great Britain produced in 1882 $8\frac{1}{2}$ million tons of iron and 5 million tons of finished iron and steel, while the production of Germany was then less than $3\frac{1}{2}$ and $2\frac{1}{3}$ million tons respectively. English production had fallen to $7\frac{1}{2}$ million tons of iron and 4 million tons of finished iron and steel in 1895, while Germany had risen to 5 million tons and 6 million tons respectively.

Contrary to what has been commonly believed, it appears that the difference all round in wages amongst ironworkers, as between England and Germany, is not great.

Chicago, Pittsburg, Buffalo, and New York are the chief centres of the American iron and steel trade, the production of pig-iron in 1895 being about $9\frac{1}{4}$ million tons, whereas in 1880 it was well under 4 million. At present over 4 millions of tons are produced of Bessemer pig-iron.

CHAPTER II.

POTTERY AND PORCELAIN.

Josiah Wedgwood and the Wedgwood Ware—Worcester Porcelain.

HEN Mr Godfrey Wedgwood, a member of the famous firm of potters at Etruria, near Burslem, Staffordshire, went to work about forty years ago, his famous ancestor and founder of the world-famed Wedgwood ware was still named amongst the workmen as 'Owd Wooden Leg.' A son of Mr Godfrey Wedgwood, now in the firm, is the fifth generation in descent, and the manufactory is still carried on in the same buildings erected by Josiah Wedgwood one hundred and twenty years ago.

One hundred years ago Josiah Wedgwood, the creator of British artistic pottery, passed away at Etruria, near Burslem, surrounded by the creations of his own well-directed genius and industry, having 'converted a rude and inconsiderable manufacture into an elegant art and an important part of national commerce.' His death took place on 3d January 1795, the same year in which Thomas Carlyle saw the light at Ecclefechan, and one year and a half before the death of Burns at Dumfries. During fifty years of his working life, largely owing to his own successful efforts, he had witnessed the output of the Staffordshire potteries increased fivefold, and his wares

JOSIAH WEDGWOOD.

were known and sold over Europe and the civilised world. In the words of Mr Gladstone, his characteristic merit lay ' in the firmness and fullness with which he perceived the true law of what we may call Industrial Art, or, in other words, of the application of the higher art to Industry.' Novalis once compared the works of Goethe and Wedgwood in these words: 'Goethe is truly a practical poet. He is in his works what the Englishman is in his wares, perfectly simple, neat, fit, and durable. He has played in the German world of literature the same part that Wedgwood has played in the English world of art.'

Long ago, in his sketch of Brindley and the early engineers, Dr Smiles had occasion to record the important service rendered by Wedgwood in the making of the Grand Trunk Canal—towards the preliminary expense of which he subscribed one thousand pounds—and in the development of the industrial life of the Midlands. Since that time Smiles has himself published a biography of Wedgwood, to which we are here indebted.

More than once it has happened that the youngest of thirteen children has turned out a genius. It was so in the case of Sir Richard Arkwright, and it turned out to be so in the case of Josiah Wedgwood, the youngest of the thirteen children of Thomas Wedgwood, a Burslem potter, and of Mary Stringer, a kind-hearted but delicate, sensitive woman, the daughter of a nonconformist clergyman. The town of Burslem, in Staffordshire, where Wedgwood saw the light in 1730, was then anything but an attractive place. Drinking and cock-fighting were the common recreations; roads had scarcely any existence; the thatched hovels had dunghills before the doors, while the hollows from which the potter's clay was excavated were filled with stagnant water, and the atmosphere of the whole place was coarse and unwholesome, and a most unlikely nursery of genius.

It is probable that the first Wedgwoods take their name from the hamlet of Weggewood in Staffordshire. There had been Wedgwoods in Burslem from a very early period, and this name occupies a large space in the parish registers during the seventeenth and eighteenth centuries; of the fifty small potters settled there, many bore this honoured name. The ware consisted of articles in common use, such as butter-pots, basins, jugs, and porringers. The black glazed and ruddy pottery then in use was much improved after an immigration of Dutchmen and Germans. The Elers, who followed the Prince of Orange, introduced the Delft ware and the salt glaze. They produced a kind of red ware, and Egyptian black; but disgusted at the discovery of their secret methods by Astbury and Twyford, they removed to Chelsea in 1710. An important improvement was made by Astbury, that of making ware white by means of burnt flint. Samuel Astbury, a son of this famous potter, married an aunt of Josiah Wedgwood. But the art was then in its infancy, not more than one hundred people being employed in this way in the district of Burslem, as compared with about ten thousand now, with an annual export of goods amounting to about two hundred thousand pounds, besides what are utilised in home-trade. John Wesley, after visiting Burslem in 1760, and twenty years later in 1781, remarked how the whole face of the country had been improved in that period. Inhabitants had flowed in, the wilderness had become a fruitful field, and the country was not more improved than the people.

All the school education young Josiah received was over in his ninth year, and it amounted to only a slight grounding in reading, writing, and arithmetic. But his practical or technical education went on continually, while he afterwards supplemented many of the deficiencies of early years by a wide course of study. After the death of his father, he began the practical business of life as a potter in his ninth year, by learning the throwing branch of the trade. The thrower moulds the vessel out of the moist clay from the potter's wheel into the required shape, and hands it on to be dealt with by the stouker, who adds the handle. Josiah at eleven proved a clever thrower of the black and mottled ware then in vogue, such as baking-dishes, pitchers, and milk-cans. But a severe attack of virulent smallpox almost terminated his career, and left a weakness in his right knee, which developed, so that this limb had to be amputated at a later date. He was bound apprentice to his brother Thomas in 1744, when in his fourteenth year; but this weak knee, which hampered him so much, proved a blessing in disguise, for it sent him from the thrower's place to the moulder's board, where he improved the ware, his first effort being an ornamental teapot made of the ochreous clay of the district. Other work of this period comprised plates, pickle-leaves, knife-hafts, and snuff-boxes. At the same time he made experiments in the chemistry of the material he was using. Wedgwood's great study was that of different kinds of colouring matter for clays, but at the same time he mastered every branch of the art. That he was a well-behaved young man is evident from the fact that he was held up in the neighbourhood as a pattern for emulation.

But his brother Thomas, who moved along in the old rut, had small sympathy with all this experimenting, and thought Josiah flighty and full of fancies. After remaining for a time with his brother, at the completion of his apprenticeship Wedgwood became partner in 1752, in a small pottery near Stoke-upon-Trent: soon after, Mr Whieldon, one of the most eminent potters of the day, joined the firm. Here Wedgwood took pains to discover new methods and striking designs, as trade was then

Wedgwood at Work.

depressed. New green earthenware was produced, as smooth as glass, for dessert service, moulded in the form of leaves; also toilet ware, snuff-boxes, and articles coloured in imitation of precious stones, which the jewellers of that time sold largely. Other articles of manufacture were blue-flowered cups and saucers, and varicoloured teapots. Wedgwood, on the expiry of his partnership with Whieldon, started on his own account in his native Burslem in 1760. His capital must have been small, as the sum of twenty pounds was all he had received from his father's estate. He rented Ivy House and Works at ten pounds a year, and engaged his second-cousin, Thomas, as workman at eight shillings and sixpence a week. He gradually acquired a reputation for the taste and excellence of design of his green glazed ware, his tortoiseshell and tinted snuff-boxes, and white medallions. A specially designed tea-service, representing different fruits and vegetables, sold well, and, as might be expected, was at once widely imitated. He hired new works on the site now partly occupied by the Wedgwood Institute, and introduced various new tools and appliances. His kilns for firing his fine ware gave him the greatest trouble, and had to be often renewed. James Brindley, when puzzled in thinking out some engineering problem, used to retire to bed and work it out in his head before he got up. Sir Josiah Mason, the Birmingham pen-maker, used to simmer over in his mind on the previous night the work for the next day. Wedgwood had a similar habit, which kept him often awake during the early part of the night. Probably owing to the fortunate execution of an order through Miss Chetwynd, maid of honour to Queen Charlotte, of a complete cream service in green and gold, Wedgwood secured the patronage of royalty, and was appointed Queen's Potter in 1763. His Queen's ware became popular, and secured him much additional business.

An engine lathe which he introduced greatly forwarded his designs; and the wareroom opened in London for the exhibition of his now famous Queen's ware, Etruscan vases, and other works, drew attention to the excellence of his work. He started works besides at Chelsea, supervised by his partner Bentley, where modellers, enamellers, and artists were employed, so that the cares of his business, 'pot-making and navigating'—the latter the carrying through of the Grand Trunk Canal—entirely filled his mind and time at this period. So busy was he, that he sometimes wondered whether he was an engineer, a landowner, or a potter. Meanwhile, a step he had no cause to regret was his marriage in 1764 to Sarah Wedgwood, no relation of his own, a handsome lady of good education and of some fortune.

Wedgwood had begun to imitate the classic works of the Greeks found in public and private collections, and produced his unglazed black porcelain, which he named Basaltes, in 1766. The demand for his vases at this time was so great that he could have sold fifty or one hundred pounds' worth a day, if he had been able to produce them fast enough. He was now patronised by royalty, by the Empress of Russia, and the nobility generally. A large service for Queen Charlotte took three years to execute, as part of the commission consisted in painting on the ware, in black enamel, about twelve hundred views of palaces, seats of the nobility, and remarkable places. A service for the Empress of Russia took eight years to complete. It consisted of nine hundred and fifty-two pieces, of which the cost was believed to have been three thousand pounds, although this scarcely paid Wedgwood's working expenses.

Prosperity elbowed Wedgwood out of his old buildings in Burslem, and led him to purchase land two miles away, on the line of the proposed Grand Trunk Canal, where his flourishing manufactories and model workmen's houses sprang up gradually, and were named *Etruria*, after the Italian home of the famous Etruscans, whose work he admired and imitated. His works were partly removed thither in 1769, and wholly in 1771. At this time he showed great public spirit, and aided in getting an Act of Parliament for better roads in the neighbourhood, and backed Brindley and Earl Gower in their Grand Trunk Canal scheme, which was destined, when completed, to cheapen and quicken the carriage of goods to Liverpool, Bristol, and Hull. The opposition was keen: and Wedgwood issued a pamphlet showing the benefits which would accrue to trade in the Midlands by the proposed waterway. When victory was secured, after the passing of the Act there was a holiday and great rejoicing in Burslem and the neighbourhood, and the first sod of the canal was cut by Wedgwood, July 26, 1766. He was also appointed treasurer of the new undertaking, which was eleven years in progress. Brindley, the greatest engineer then in England, doubtless sacrificed his life to its success, as he died of continual harassment and diabetes at the early age of fifty-six. Wedgwood had an immense admiration for Brindley's work and character. In the prospect of spending a day with him, he said: 'As I always edify full as much in that man's company as at church, I promise myself to be much wiser the day following.' Like Carlyle, who whimsically put the builder of a bridge before the writer of a book, Wedgwood placed the man who designed the outline of a jug or the turn of a teapot far below the creator of a canal or the builder of a city.

In the career of a man of genius and original powers, the period of early struggle is often the most interesting. When prosperity comes, after difficulties have been surmounted, there is generally less to challenge attention. But Wedgwood's career was still one of continual progress up to the very close. His Queen's ware, made of the whitest clay from Devon and Dorset, was greatly in demand, and much improved. The fine earthenwares and porcelains which became the basis of such manufactures were originated here. Young men of artistic taste were employed and encouraged to supply designs, and a school of instruction for drawing, painting, and modelling was started. Artists such as Coward and Hoskins modelled the 'Sleeping Boy,' one of the finest and largest of his works. John Bacon, afterwards known as a sculptor, was one of his artists, as also James Tassie of Glasgow. Wedgwood engaged capable men wherever they could be found. For his Etruscan models he was greatly indebted to Sir W. Hamilton. Specimens of his famous portrait cameos, medallions, and plaques will be found in most of our public museums.

The general health of Wedgwood suffered so much between 1767 and 1768 that he decided to have the limb which had troubled him since his boyhood amputated. He sat, and without wincing, witnessed the surgeons cut off his right leg, for there were then no anæsthetics. 'Mr Wedgwood has this day had his leg taken off,' wrote one of the Burslem clerks at the foot of a London invoice, 'and is as well as can be expected after such an execution.' His wife was his good angel when recovering, and acted as hands and feet and secretary to him; while his partner Bentley (formerly a Liverpool merchant) and Dr Darwin were also kind; and he was almost oppressed with the inquiries of many noble and distinguished persons during convalescence. He had to be content with a wooden leg now. 'Send me,' he wrote to his brother in London, 'by the next wagon a spare leg, which you will find, I believe, in the closet.' He lived to wear out a succession of wooden legs.

Indifference and idleness he could not tolerate, and his fine artistic sense was offended by any bit of imperfect work. In going through his works, he would lift the stick upon which he leaned and smash the offending article, saying, 'This won't do for Josiah Wedgwood.' All the while he had a keen insight into the character of his workmen, although he used to say that he had everything to teach them, even to the making of a table plate.

He was no monopolist, and the only patent he ever took out was for the discovery of the lost art of burning in colours, as in the Etruscan vases. 'Let us make all the good, fine, and new things we can,' he said to Bentley once; 'and so far from being afraid of other people getting our patterns, we should glory in it, and throw out all the hints we can, and if possible, have all the artists in Europe working after our models.' By this means he hoped to secure the goodwill of his best customers and of the public. At the same time he never sacrificed excellence to cheapness. As the sale of painted Etruscan ware declined, his Jasper porcelain— so called from its resemblance to the stone of that name— became popular. The secret of its manufacture was kept for many years. It was composed of flint, potter's clay, carbonate of barytes, and *terra ponderosa*. This and the Jasper-dip are in several tones and hues of blue; also yellow, lilac, and green. He called in the good genius of Flaxman in 1775; and, for the following twelve years, the afterwards famous sculptor did an immense amount of work and enhanced his own and his patron's reputation. Flaxman did some of his finest work in this Jasper porcelain. Some of Flaxman's designs Wedgwood could scarcely be prevailed upon to part with. A bas-relief of the 'Apotheosis of Homer' went for seven hundred and thirty-five pounds at the sale of his partner Bentley;

and the 'Sacrifice to Hymen,' a tablet in blue and white Jasper (1787), brought four hundred and fifteen pounds. The first named is now in the collection of Lord Tweedmouth. Wedgwood's copy of the Barberini or Portland Vase was a great triumph of his art. This vase, which had contained the ashes of the Roman Emperor Alexander Severus and his mother, was of dark-blue glass, with white enamel figures. It now stands in the medal room of the British Museum alongside a model by Wedgwood.

Portland Vase.

It stands 10 inches high, and is the finest specimen of an ancient cameo cut-glass vase known. It was smashed by a madman in 1845, but was afterwards skilfully repaired. Wedgwood made fifty copies in fine earthenware, which were originally sold at 25 guineas each. One of these now fetches £200. The vase itself once changed hands for eighteen hundred guineas, and a copy fetched two hundred and fifteen guineas in 1892.

Josiah Wedgwood now stood at the head of the potters of Staffordshire, and the manufactory at Etruria drew visitors from all parts of Europe. The motto of its founder was still 'Forward;' and, as Dr Smiles expresses it, there was with him no finality in the development of his profession. He studied chemistry, botany, drawing, designing, and conchology. His inquiring mind wanted to get to the bottom of everything. He journeyed to Cornwall, and was successful in getting kaolin for chinaware. Queen Charlotte patronised a new pearl-white teaware; and he succeeded in perfecting the pestle and mortar for the apothecary. He invented a pyrometer for measuring temperatures; and was elected Fellow of the Royal Society. Amongst his intimate friends were Dr Erasmus Darwin, poet and physician (the famous Charles Robert Darwin was a grandson, his mother having been a daughter of Wedgwood's), Boulton of Soho Works, James Watt, Thomas Clarkson, Sir Joseph Banks, and Thomas Day.

We have an example of the generosity of Wedgwood's disposition in his treatment of John Leslie, afterwards Professor Sir John Leslie of Edinburgh University. He was so well pleased with his tutoring of his sons that he settled an annuity of one hundred and fifty pounds upon him; and it may be that the influence of this able tutor led Thomas Wedgwood to take up the study of heliotype, and become a pioneer of photographic science, even before Daguerre. How industrious Wedgwood had been in his profession is evident from the seven thousand specimens of clay from all parts of the world which he had tested and analysed. The six entirely new pieces of earthenware and porcelain which, along with his Queen's ware, he had introduced early in his career, as painted and embellished, became the foundation of nearly all the fine earthenware and porcelains since produced. He had his reward, for besides a flourishing business, he left more than half a million of money.

WORCESTER PORCELAIN.

One of the most artistic and interesting industries in this country is the manufacture of porcelain in the ancient city of Worcester. There is no special local reason for the establishment of such works there, but Worcester has been noted as the home of the famous porcelain for more than

The Worcester Royal Porcelain Works.

a century. It was in 1751 that Dr Wall, a chemist and artist, completed his experiment in the combination of various elements, and produced a porcelain which was more like the true or natural Chinese porcelain than any ever devised. This was the more remarkable because kaolin had not then been discovered in this country. The inventor set up his factory in Worcester, close to the cathedral, and for a long time he produced his egg-shell and Tonquin porcelain in various forms, chiefly, however, those of table services. Transfer-printing was introduced later on, and was executed with much of the artist's spirit by experts who attached themselves to the Worcester works after the closing of the enamel works at Battersea. It was a remarkable century in its devotion to ceramic art; and it was characteristic of the ruling princes of the Continent that they should patronise lavishly various potteries of more or less repute. Towards the end of the century the first sign of this royal favour was vouchsafed to Worcester. George III. visited the factories, and under the impetus given by his patronage, the wares of the city advanced so much in popularity that, in the early part of this century, it is said, there were few noble families which had not in their china closets an elaborate service of Worcester, bearing the family arms and motto in appropriate emblazonment. In 1811, George IV. being then Prince Regent, several splendid services of Worcester porcelain were ordered to equip his table for the new social duties entailed by his regency, and one of these alone cost £4000. In the museums at the Worcester works there are specimens of many beautiful services, designed in accordance with the contemporary ideas of pomp and stateliness. The porcelain artists in those days must have been well versed in heraldry; for their chief duties seem to have been the reproduction of crests and coats-of-arms. Some of the services have interesting stories. There is one of deep royal blue, beautifully decorated, and bearing in the centre an emblematical figure of Hope. The story ran that it was ordered by Nelson for presentation to the Duke of Cumberland, and that the figure of Hope was really a portrait of Lady Hamilton. This, however, was an error: the service was ordered by the Duke himself in the ordinary way, and though Lord Nelson did order a service of Worcester porcelain, he died before it could be completed, and it was afterwards dispersed. Another story attaches to a plate adorned with a picture of a ship in full sail approaching harbour. The Imaum of Muscat sent many presents to the Prince Regent, and hinted that he would like a ship of war in return. The English authorities, however, did not see fit to give attention to this request, and sent him instead many beautiful things, including a service of Worcester ware, bearing on each piece a scene showing the royal yacht which bore the gifts entering the cove of Muscat. When the potentate heard, however, that his dearest wish had been thwarted in this way, he refused to allow the vessel to enter the harbour, and all the presents had to be brought back again. The picture on the plate, therefore, is more imaginative than accurate.

The Worcester porcelain began to develop in fresh directions soon after the Great Exhibition of 1851, which gave an impulse to the efforts of the artists, and the decorative side of the work was brought into a much more prominent position. For instance, the 'Worcester enamels,' in the style of those of Limoges, were introduced, and an illustration of this work is to be seen in a pair of remarkable vases, bearing enamel reproductions of Maclise's drawings, founded on the Bayeux tapestries. About this time, too, after several years of experiment, the ivory ware—an idea inspired by the lovely ivory sculptures in the Exhibition—was brought to perfection. It is a beautiful, creamy, translucent porcelain, singularly fitted for artistic treatment, and it is now the most characteristic of the later developments of the Worcester work. In fact, the art directors of the enterprise will not issue now any new wares in the style of those which found favour at an earlier period, for they know that they would instantly be palmed off on the unwary as the genuine products of the bygone times.

To trace the process of the manufacture, from the mixing of the ingredients to the burning of the last wash in the decorated piece, is very interesting. It is a process freely shown to visitors, and forms one of the principal lions in the sober old town which has lain for so many centuries on the banks of the Severn. The materials are brought from all parts of the world. Kaolin, or china clay, which is the felspar of decomposed granite washed from the rocks, is brought from Cornwall, so is the Cornish or china stone; felspar is brought from Sweden, and though of a rich red, it turns white when burnt; marl and fire-clay come from Broseley, in Shropshire, and Stourbridge; flints are brought from Dieppe; and bones— those of the ox only—come all the way from South America to be calcined and ground down. The grinding is a slow matter; each ingredient is ground separately in a vat, the bottom of which is a hard stone, whereon other hard stones of great weight revolve slowly. From twelve hours' to ten days' constant treatment by these remorseless mills is required by the various materials, some needing to be ground much longer than others before the requisite fineness is attained. It is essential that all the ingredients should be reduced to a certain standard of grain; and the contents of each vat must pass through a lawn sieve with four thousand meshes to the square inch. When the materials are sufficiently ground to meet this test, they are taken to the 'slip-house,' and mixed together with the clays, which do not need grinding. A magnet of great strength is in each mixing trough, and draws to itself every particle of iron, which, if allowed to remain in the mixture, would injure the ware very much. When properly mixed, the water is pressed out, and the paste or clay is beaten so that it may obtain consistency. Then it is ready to be made into the many shapes which find popular favour.

The process of manufacture depends on the shape to be obtained. A plain circular teacup may be cast on a potter's wheel of the ancient kind. When it is partly dried in a mould, it is turned on a lathe and trimmed; then the handle, which has been moulded, is affixed with a touch of the 'slip'—the porcelain paste in a state of dilution is the cement used in all such situations—and the piece is ready for the fire. A plate or saucer, however, is made by flat pressing; a piece of clay like a pancake is laid on the mould, which is set revolving on a wheel; the deft fingers of the workmen press the clay to the proper shape, and it is then dried. But the elaborate ornamental pieces of graceful design are made in moulds, and for this process the clay is used in the thin or 'slip' state. The moulds are pressed together, the slip is poured into them through a hole in one side, and when the moisture has been absorbed by the plaster moulds sufficiently, the piece is taken out. It is often necessary, in making a large or complicated piece, to have as many as twenty or thirty castings. In moulding a figure, for instance, the legs and arms and hands, even the thumbs in many cases, are cast separately, and with many other parts of the design are laid before a workman, who carefully builds up the complete figure out of the apparent chaos of parts, affixing each piece to the body with a touch of slip. When these wares are complete, they have to be fired for the first time; and they are taken to a kiln, and placed with great care and many precautions in the grim interior. The contraction of the clay under fire is a matter to which the designers must give much study; and the change which takes place during forty hours' fierce firing in the kiln is shown by contrasting an unburnt piece and a piece of 'biscuit' or burnt ware, and marking the shrinkage. Your ware must be calculated to shrink only so much; if it shrink a shade further, the whole process may be spoiled. There is a loss of twenty-five per cent. sometimes in these kilns, in spite of the assiduous care of the workmen. When the biscuit ware has cooled, it is dipped in the glaze, which is a compound of lead and borax and other materials—virtually a sort of glass—and then it is fired for sixteen hours in the 'glost oven.' There is no contraction in this ordeal; but there is a risk none the less from other causes. In fact, there is the danger of injury every time the ware goes to the fire, and as the highly decorated pieces have to go to the kiln many times, it may be inferred that the labour of weeks and even months is sometimes nullified by an untoward accident in the burning.

It is during the process of decoration that the ornate vases and figures make so many trips to the fire. The artist department is a very large and important one. The designers, however, are a class of themselves. They project the idea; it is the business of the artist, in these circumstances, to execute it. The painters are taken into the works as lads and trained for the special service. What you remark chiefly in going through the decorating rooms is the great facility of the artists. You see a man with a plate or vase on which he is outlining a landscape, and you marvel at the rapid, accurate touches with which he does the work. Flowers, birds, and figures they can reproduce with great skill, and many of them are artists not merely in facility but in instinct. They work with metallic colours only. They rely on copper, for instance, to give black and green, on iron to yield red hues, and so on; and the gold work is done with what seems to be a dirty brown paste, but is really pure gold mixed with flux and quicksilver. When the first wash is put on, the piece must be fired, so that the colours shall be burnt into the glaze. Then it returns to the painter, who adds the next touches so far as he can; the firing again follows; the piece is returned to him once more; and so on it goes till the work is complete.

It is therefore a highly technical business, especially as the colours change very much in the fire, and the painter has to work with full knowledge of the chemical processes in every firing. There is one form of the decorative process which is very singular—that is, the piercing work. The artist has the vase in the dried state before the firing, and with a tiny, sharp-pointed knife he cuts out little pieces according to the design in his mind, and produces an extremely beautiful perforated ware, the elaborate pattern and the lace-like delicacy of which almost repel the idea that the work is done by the unaided hand of man. In the colour processes, the work is virtually complete when the dull gold has been burnished; and the porcelain is then ready to be transferred to the showrooms, or exported to America, which is the greatest patron, at present, of Worcester art. America, however, failed to retain one lovely vase no less than four feet high, the largest ever made in the works; it was taken to the Chicago Exhibition and back without accident, and was then sold in England for one thousand pounds.

It is important to remember the distinction between 'pottery' and 'porcelain:' the porcelain is clay purified by the fire, whereas pottery leaves the oven as it entered it—clay. The purification of the ware is really an illustration of the process which sustains the artistic inspiration of the work. The gross, the vulgar, the mean are eliminated; a standard of beauty is set up, and to it every article must conform. It is to this ideal, sustained by a long succession of artists through a century and a half, that Worcester owes its world-wide reputation as the birthplace of some of the loveliest porcelain ever burnt in a kiln.

Chinese Porcelain Vase.

CHAPTER III.

THE SEWING-MACHINE.

Thomas Saint—Thimonnier—Hunt—Elias Howe—Wilson—Morey—Singer.

LTHOUGH the sewing-machine has not put an end to the slavery of the needle, and although 'The Song of the Shirt' may be heard to the accompaniment of its click and whirr, just as it was to the 'stitch, stitch' of Tom Hood's time, yet has it unquestionably come as a boon and a blessing to man—and woman. Its name now is legion, and it has had so many inventors and improvers that the present generation is fast losing sight of its original benefactors. Indeed, we take the sewing-machine to-day as an accomplished fact so familiar as to be commonplace. And yet that fact is a product of as moving a history as any in the story of human invention.

It is the growth of the last half-century, prior to which the real sewing-machine was the heavy-eyed, if not tireless, needlewoman, whose flying fingers seemed ever in vain pursuit of the flying hours. Needlework is as old as human history, for we may see the beginnings of it in the aprons of fig-leaves which Mother Eve sewed. What instrument she used we know not, but we do know from Moses that needles were in use when the tabernacle was built. Yet, strange to say, it was not until the middle of last century that any one tried to supersede manual labour in the matter of stitching. It is said that a German tailor, named Charles Frederick Weisenthal, was the first to attempt it, but for hand-embroidery only—with a double-pointed needle, eyed in the middle. This was in 1755, and fifty years later, one John Duncan, a Glasgow machinist, worked out Weisenthal's idea into a genuine embroidering machine, which really held the germ of the idea of the 'loop-stitch.' But neither of these was a sewing-machine, and before Duncan's invention some one else had been seized with another idea.

This was a London cabinetmaker called Thomas Saint, who in or about 1790 took out a patent for a machine for sewing leather, or rather for 'quilting, stitching, and making shoes, boots, spatterdashes, clogs, and other articles.' This patent, unfortunately, was taken out along with other inventions in connection with leather, and it was quite by accident that, some eighty years later, the specification of it was discovered by one who had made for himself a name in connection with sewing-machines. Even the Patent Office did not seem to have known of its existence, yet now it is clear enough that Thomas Saint's leather-sewing-machine of 1790 was the first genuine sewing-machine ever constructed, and that it was on what is now known as the 'chain-stitch' principle. Rude as it was, it is declared by experts to have anticipated most of the ingenious ideas of half a century of successive inventors, not one of whom, however, could in all human probability have as much as heard of Saint's machine. This is not the least curious incident in the history of the sewing-machine.

In Saint's machine the features are—the overhanging arm, which is the characteristic of many modern machines; the perpendicular action of the Singer machine; the eye-pointed needle of the Howe machine; the pressure surfaces peculiar to the Howe machine; and a 'feed' system equal to that of the most modern inventions. Whether Saint's machine was ever worked in a practical workshop or not, it was unquestionably a practicable machine, constructed by one who knew pretty well what he was about, and what he wanted to achieve.

Now note the date of Thomas Saint's patent (1790), and next note the date of the invention of Barthelmy Thimonnier, of St Etienne, who is claimed in France as the inventor of the sewing-machine. In 1830, Thimonnier constructed a machine, principally of wood, with an arrangement of barbed needles, for stitching gloves, and in the following year he began business in Paris, with a partner, as an army clothier. The firm of Thimonnier, Petit, & Co., however, did not thrive, because the workpeople thought they saw in the principal's machine an instrument destined to ruin them; much as the Luddites viewed steam-machinery in the cotton districts of England. An idea of that sort rapidly germinates heat, and Thimonnier's workshop was one day invaded by an angry mob, who smashed all the machines, and compelled the inventor to seek safety in flight. Poor Thimonnier was absent from Paris for three years, but in 1834 returned with another and more perfect machine. This was so coldly received, both by employers and workmen in the tailoring trade, that he left the capital, and, journeying through France with his machine, paid his way by exhibiting it in the towns and villages as a curiosity. After a few years, however, Thimonnier fell in with a capitalist who believed in him and his machine, and was willing to stake money on both. A partnership was entered into for the manufacture and sale of the machine, and all promised well for the new firm, when the Revolution of 1848 broke out, stopped the business, and ruined both the inventor and the capitalist.

Thimonnier died in 1857, in a poorhouse, of a broken heart.

This French machine was also on the chain-stitch principle, but it was forty years later than Saint's. In between the two came, about 1832, one Walter Hunt, of New York, who is said to have constructed a sewing-machine with the lock-stitch movement. Some uncertainty surrounds this claim, and Elias Howe is the person usually credited with this important, indeed invaluable invention. Whether Howe had ever seen Hunt's machine, we know not; but Hunt's machine was never patented, seems never to have come into practical working, and is, indeed, said to have been unworkable. There is, besides, in the Polytechnic at Vienna, the model of a machine, dated 1814, constructed by one Joseph Madersberg, a tailor of the Tyrol, which embodies the lock-stitch idea—working with two threads. But this also was unworkable, and Elias Howe has the credit of having produced the first really practical lock-stitch sewing-machine.

His was a life of vicissitude and of ultimate triumph, both in fame and fortune. He was born at a small place in Massachusetts in 1819, and as a youth went to Boston, there to work as a mechanic. While there, and when about twenty-two years old, the idea occurred to him at his work of passing a thread through cloth and securing it on the other side by another thread. Here we perceive the germ of the lock-stitch—the two threads. Howe began to experiment with a number of bent wires in lieu of needles, but he lacked the means to put his great idea to a thorough practical test. Thus it slumbered for three years, when he went to board and lodge with an old schoolfellow named Fisher, who, after a while, agreed to advance Howe one hundred pounds in return for a half share in the invention should it prove a success. Thus aided, in 1845 Howe completed his first machine, and actually made himself a suit of clothes with it; and this would be just about the time of Thimonnier's temporary prosperity in alliance with the capitalist, Mogrini.

Feeling sure of his ground, Howe took bold steps to 'boom' his invention. He challenged five of the most expert sewers in a great Boston clothing factory to a sewing match. Each of them was to sew a certain strip of cloth, and Howe undertook to sew five strips, torn in halves, before each man had completed his one strip. The arrangements completed, the match began, and to the wonder of everybody, Howe finished his five seams before the others were half done with one seam. But murmurs instead of cheers succeeded the victory. He was angrily reproached for trying to take the bread out of the mouth of the honest working-man, and a cry was raised among the workers (as it has been heard time and again in the history of industrial development) to smash the machine. Howe, indeed, had much difficulty in escaping from the angry mob, with his precious machine under his arm.

In Howe's experience we thus see one parallel with Thimonnier's; but there was another. The American was quite as poor and resourceless as the Frenchman, and the next step in Howe's career was that he went on tour to the country fairs to exhibit his machine for a trifling fee, in order to keep body and soul together. People went in flocks to see the thing as a clever toy, but no one would 'take hold' of it as a practical machine. And so, in despair of doing any good with it in America, Elias Howe, in 1846, sent his brother to England to see if a market could not be found for the invention there. The brother succeeded in making terms with one William Thomas, staymaker, in Cheapside, London, and he sent for Elias to come over.

The price to be paid by Thomas for the patent was two hundred and fifty pounds, but Howe was to make certain alterations in it so as to adapt it to the special requirements of the purchaser. While engaged in perfecting the machine, he was to receive wages at the rate of three pounds per week, and this wage he seems to have received for nearly two years. But he failed to achieve what Thomas wanted, and Thomas, after spending a good deal of money over the experiments, abandoned the thing altogether. Howe was thus astrand again, and he returned to America as poor as ever, leaving his machine behind him in pawn for advances to pay his passage home. And yet there were 'millions in it.'

This was in the year 1849, and just about the time when Howe was returning to America, another American, named Bostwich, was sending over to England a machine which he had invented for imitating hand-stitching, by means of cog-wheels and a bent needle. And a year or two after Howe's return, one Charles Morey, of Manchester, attempted to carry out the same stitch on a somewhat different plan, but failed to find sufficient pecuniary support. Indeed, poor Morey had a tragic end, for, taking his machine to Paris in the hope of finding a purchaser there, he incurred some debt which he could not pay, and was clapped into the Mazas prison. While there, he inadvertently broke the rules, and was shot by the guard for failing to reply to a challenge which he did not understand.

When Howe got back to the United States, he found a number of ingenious persons engaged in producing or experimenting in sewing-machines, and some of them were trenching on his own patent rights. He raised enough money, somehow, to redeem his pawned machine in England, and then raised actions against all who were infringing it. The litigation was tremendous both in duration and expense, but it ended in the victory of Elias Howe, to whom, by the finding of the court, the other patentees were found liable for royalty. It is said that Howe, who as we have seen left London in debt, received, before his patent expired in 1867, upwards of two million dollars in royalties alone.

But ingenious men were now busy in both hemispheres in perfecting what, up till about fifty years ago, was regarded as nothing better than a clever toy. Besides Morey, the Manchester man we have mentioned, a Huddersfield machinist, named Drake, brought out a machine to work with a shuttle. About the same time, or a little later, a young Nottingham man, named John Fisher, constructed a machine with a sort of lock-stitch movement, which he afterwards adapted to a double loop-stitch. But Fisher's machine was intended rather for embroidering than for plain sewing.

Passing over some minor attempts, the next great development was that of Allen Wilson, who, without having heard either of Howe's or of any other machine, constructed one in 1849, the design of which, he said, he had been meditating for two years. His first machine had original features, however much it may have been anticipated in principle by Howe's patent. In Wilson's second design, a rotary hook was substituted for a two-pointed shuttle, and by other improvements he achieved a greater speed than had been attained by other inventors. Later still, he added the 'four-motion feed,' which is adopted on most of the machines now in general use.

This idea was an elaboration of a principle which seems to have first occurred to the unfortunate Morey. In Morey's machine there was a horizontal bar with short teeth, which caught the fabric and dragged it forward as the stitches were completed. It took nearly thirty years, however, to evolve the perfect 'feed' motion out of Morey's first crude germ.

While Wilson was working away, perfecting his now

famous machine, an observing and thoughtful young millwright was employed in a New York factory. One day a sewing-machine was sent in for repairs, and after examining its mechanism, this young man, whose name was Isaac Singer, confidently expressed his belief that he could make a better one. He did not propose either to appropriate or abandon the principle, but to improve upon it. Instead of a curved needle, as in Howe's and Wilson's machines, he adopted a straight one, and gave it a perpendicular instead of a curvular motion. And for propelling the fabric he introduced a wheel, instead of the toothed bar of the Morey design.

It need hardly be said that the Singer machine is now one of the most widely known, and is turned out in countless numbers in enormous factories on both sides of the Atlantic. It is not so well known, perhaps, that Singer, who was a humble millwright in 1850, and who died in 1875, left an estate valued at three millions sterling—all amassed in less than twenty-five years!

The machines of Howe, Wilson, and Singer were on the lock-stitch principle, and the next novelty was the invention of Grover and Baker, who brought out a machine working with two needles and two continuous threads. After this came the Gibbs machine, the story of which may be briefly told.

About the year 1855, James G. Gibbs heard of the Grover and Baker machine, and having a turn for mechanics, began to ponder over how the action described was produced. He got an illustration, but could make nothing of it, and not for a year did he obtain sight of a Singer machine at work. As in the case of Singer with Wilson's machine, so Gibbs thought he could improve on Singer's, and turn out one less ponderous and complicated. He set to work, and in a very short time took out a patent for a new lock-stitch machine. But he was not satisfied with this, and experimented away, with an idea of making a chain-stitch by means of a revolving looper. This idea he eventually put into practical form, and took out a patent for the first chain-stitch sewing-machine.

Since the days of Elias Howe, the number of patents taken out for sewing-machines has been legion—certainly not less than one thousand—and probably no labour-saving appliance has received more attention at the hands both of inventors and of the general public. There is scarcely a household in the land now, however humble, without a sewing-machine of some sort, and in factories and warehouses they are to be numbered by the thousand. Some machinists have directed their ingenuity to the reduction of wear and tear, others to the reduction of noise, others to acceleration of speed, others to appliances for supplying the machine in a variety of ways, others for adapting it to various complicated processes of stitching and embroidering. Some users prefer the lock-stitch, and some the chain-stitch principle, and each system has its peculiar advantages according to the character of the work to be sewn.

A recent development is a combination of both principles in one machine. Mr Edward Kohler patented a machine which will produce either a lock-stitch or a chain-stitch, as may be desired, and an embroidery stitch as well. By a very ingenious contrivance the machinery is altered by the simple movement of a button, and (when the chain-stitch is required) the taking out of the bobbin from the shuttle. If the embroidery stitch is wanted, the button is turned without removing the bobbin, and the lock-stitch and chain-stitch are combined in one new stitch, with which very elaborate effects can be produced. It is said that the Kohler principle can be easily adapted to all, or most, existing machines.

CHAPTER IV.

WOOL AND COTTON.

WOOL.—What is Wool?—Chemical Composition—Fibre—Antiquity of Shepherd Life—Varieties of Sheep—Introduction into Australia—Spanish Merino—Wool Wealth of Australia—Imports and Exports of Wool and Woollen Produce—Woollen Manufacture.

COTTON.—Cotton Plant in the East—Mandeville's Fables about Cotton—Cotton in Persia, Arabia, and Egypt—Columbus finds Cotton-yarn and Thread in 1492—In Africa—Manufacture of Cloth in England—The American Cotton Plant.

WOOL.

WHAT is wool? 'The covering of the sheep, of course,' replies somebody. Yes; but what *is* it? Let us ask Professor Owen. 'Wool,' he says, 'is a peculiar modification of hair, characterised by fine transverse or oblique lines from two to four thousand in the extent of an inch, indicative of a minutely imbricated scaly surface, when viewed under the microscope, on which and on its curved or twisted form depends its remarkable felting property.' At first sight this definition seems bewildering, but it will bear examination, and is really more tangible than, for instance, Noah Webster's definition of wool: 'That soft curled or crisped species of hair which grows on sheep and some other animals, and which in fineness sometimes approaches to fur.' It is usually that which grows on

Wool-sorters at Work.

sheep, however, that we know as wool, and the number of imbrications, serratures, or notches indicates the quality of the fibre. Thus, in the wool of the Leicester sheep there are 1850 — in Spanish merino, 2400 — in Saxon merino, 2700, to an inch, and the fewer there are the nearer does wool approach to hair.

Here is a still more minute description by Youatt, a great authority on wool: 'It consists of a central stem or stalk, probably hollow, or at least porous, and possessing a semi-transparency, found in the fibre of the hair. From this central stalk there springs, at different distances in different breeds of sheep, a circlet of leaf-shaped projections. In the finer species of wool these circles seemed at first to be composed of one indicated or serrated ring; but when the eye was accustomed to them, this ring was resolvable into leaves or scales. In the larger kinds, the ring was at once resolvable into these scales or leaves, varying in number, shape, and size, and projecting at different angles from the stalk, and in the direction of the leaves of vegetables—that is, from the root to the point. They give to the wool the power of felting.'

This is the estimate of the chemical composition of good wool: Carbon, 50·65; hydrogen, 7·03; nitrogen, 17·71; oxygen and sulphur, 24·61. Out of a hundred parts, ninety-eight would be organic, and two would be ash, consisting of oxide of iron, sulphate of lime, phosphate of lime, and magnesia. What is called the 'yolk' of wool is a compound of oil, lime, and potash. It makes the pile soft and pliable, and is less apparent on English sheep than on those of warmer countries, the merino sheep having the most 'yolk.'

The fibre of wool varies in diameter, the Saxon merino measuring $\frac{1}{1370}$ of an inch, and the Southdown, $\frac{1}{1100}$. Lustrous wool, it is said, should be long and strong; but if it is very fine it is not long. Strong wool may be as much as twenty inches in length. The wool of the best sheep adheres closely, and can only be removed by shearing; but there are varieties of sheep which shed their wool, as, for instance, the Persian, which drop the whole of their fleeces between January and May, when feeding on the new grass.

This, then, is wool, the first use of which for cloth-making is lost in antiquity. There is no doubt that the pastoral industry is the oldest industry in the world; for even when the fruits of the earth could be eaten without tillage and without labour, the flocks and herds required care and attention. The shepherd may be regarded as the earliest pioneer of industry, as he has been for centuries the centre of fanciful romance, and the personification of far from romantic fact. The old legend of Jason and the Golden Fleece is in itself evidence of the antiquity of the knowledge of the value of wool; and much as the mythologists make out of the legend, there are some who hold that it merely is meant to record how the Greeks imported a superior kind of sheep from the Caucasus and made money thereby.

Australia is now the land of the Golden Fleece, and millions of money have been made there out of the docile sheep. It is not indigenous, of course, to the land of the Southern Cross, where the only mammal known when Europeans discovered it was the kangaroo. Mr James Bonwick, a gentleman well known in Australian literature, gathered together many records of the introduction of the sheep into Australia, and of the marvellous development of the pastoral industry there in his very interesting book, *The Romance of the Wool-trade.*

But, first, as to the different kinds of sheep. The Bighorn is the wild-sheep of Kamchatka, and it may be taken for granted that all species of the domestic sheep were at one time wild, or are descended from wild tribes.

When the Aryan Hindus invaded India, it is recorded that they took their flocks with them; but whether the wild-sheep still to be found on the hills of Northern India are the descendants of wanderers from these flocks, or descendants of the progenitors of them, we do not pretend to say.

Chief among the domesticated sheep of the British Isles is the Southdown, whose characteristics used to be—although we are told they are changed somewhat now—thin chine, low fore-end, and rising backbone, a small hornless head, speckled face, thin lips, woolled ears, and bright eyes. The wool should 'be short, close, curled, fine, and free from spiry projecting fibres.' Then there are the Romney Marsh, the Cotswold, the Lincoln, the Leicester, and the Hardwick sheep, each with its distinctive marks and value. The Welsh sheep have long necks, high shoulders, narrow breasts, long bushy tails, and small bones; the wool is not first class, but the mutton is excellent. The Irish native sheep are of two kinds, the short-woolled and long-woolled; but South-downs and Leicesters have been so long crossed with them that their idiosyncrasies are no longer marked. The Shetland sheep are supposed to have come from Denmark, but have also been crossed with English and Scotch varieties. In Scotland, the Cheviot and the Blackfaced are the two ruling types. The Cheviot is a very handsome animal, with long body, white face, small projecting eyes, and well-formed legs. The wool is excellent, as the 'tweed'-makers of the Border know, but is not so soft as that of the English Southdowns. The Blackfaced is the familiar form we see in the Highlands, supposed to have come originally 'from abroad,' but now regarded as the native sheep of Scotland. It is a hardy animal, accustomed to rough food and rough weather, with a fine deep chest, broad back, slender legs, attractive face, and picturesque horns. The wool is not so good as that of the Cheviot variety, but the mutton is better. Of course, English varieties have been largely crossed with the two native Scotch kinds; yet these still remain distinct, and are easily recognisable.

As long ago as the time of the Emperor Constantine, the wool of English sheep had a high reputation, and had even then found its way to Rome. Of English monarchs, Edward III. seems to have been the first to endeavour to stimulate the pastoral industry by the manufacture of woollen cloths and the export of raw wool. But Henry VIII. thought that sheep-breeding had been carried too far, and the farmers were making too much money out of it; so he decreed that no one should keep more than two thousand four hundred sheep at one time, and that no man should be allowed to occupy more than two farms. In the time of Charles II. the export of both sheep and wool was strictly prohibited. As late as 1788, there were curious prohibitory enactments with reference to sheep; and the date is interesting, because it was the date of the settlement of New South Wales. There was a fine of three pounds upon the carrying off of any sheep from the British Isles, except for use on board ship; and even between the islands and the mainland of Scotland, or across a tidal river, sheep could not be transported without a special permit and the execution of a bond that the animals were not for exportation. Indeed, no sheep could be shorn within five miles of the sea-coast without the presence of a revenue officer, to see that the law was not evaded.

It is not surprising, then, that the first sheep settled in Australia—the only great pastoral country that has never had a native variety—did not go from England. It is very curious that in Australia, New Zealand, and Tasmania, where now lies a great portion of the pastoral wealth of the world, there never was any animal in the smallest degree resembling a sheep until some enterprising Britons took it there.

The first sheep introduced into Australia were from the Cape and from India. The ships which went out with the convicts of 1788 had a few sheep on board for the officers' mess, which were presumably consumed before the Cape of Good Hope was reached. There, some animals were procured for the new settlement. The Cape at the time was in the hands of the Dutch, who had large flocks of sheep and immense herds of cattle. The sheep they had were not imported from Europe, but were the native breed they had found in the hands of the aborigines when the Dutch colony was founded one hundred and thirty years previously.

The native African sheep is of the fat-tail kind. Wool was not then an item of wealth in the Dutch colony; but the fat tails were appreciated as an excellent substitute for butter. All over Africa and over a large part of Asia, varieties of the fat-tail species are still to be found. In Tibet they abound; and the Turcomans have vast flocks of them. But Tibet has also other varieties, and notably one very like the llama of Peru, with a very soft and most useful fleece, providing the famous Tibetan wool. In Palestine and Syria the fat-tail sheep is abundant; and of the Palestine breed it is recorded that they 'have a monstrous round of fat, like a cushion, in place of the tail, which sometimes weighs thirty or forty pounds. The wool of this sheep is coarse, much tangled, and felted, and mixed with coarse dark-coloured hair.'

Although the first sheep taken to Australia were from the Cape, the most important of the earlier consignments were from India, the nearest British possession to the new colony. Indeed, for over thirty years Australia was ecclesiastically within the see of the Bishop of Calcutta, and letters to England usually went by way of the Indian capital.

The Bengalee sheep are described as 'small, lank, and thin, and the colour of three-fourths of each flock is black or dark gray. The quality of the fleece is worse than the colour; it is harsh, thin, and wiry to a very remarkable degree, and ordinarily weighs but half a pound.' Not a very promising subject, one would think, for the Australian pastures, but the flesh was excellent; and climate and crossing of breeds work wonders.

That which gave value to the Australian breed of sheep, however, was the introduction of the Spanish merino, which in time found its way to the Cape, and thence to Australia. There is an old tradition that the famous merino sheep of Spain came originally from England; but it appears from Pliny and others that Spain had a reputation for fine wool long before the Roman occupation. The Spanish word merino originally meant an inspector of sheepwalks, and is derived from the Low Latin *majorinus*, a steward of the household. Some writers believe that the merino came originally from Barbary, probably among the flocks of the Moors when they captured Southern Spain. The merinos are considered very voracious, and not very prolific; they yield but little milk, and are very subject to cutaneous diseases. Youatt describes two varieties of them in Spain, and the wool is of remarkable fineness.

About the year 1790, the Spanish merino began to be imported into the Cape, and a few years later a certain Captain Waterhouse was sent from Sydney to Capetown to buy stock for the colonial establishment. He thought the service in which he was engaged 'almost a disgrace to an officer;' but when he left the Cape again, he brought with him 'forty-nine head of black-cattle, three mares, and one hundred and seven sheep'—arriving at Port Jackson with the loss of nine of the cattle and about one-third of the sheep. Three cows, two mares, and twenty-four of the sheep belonged to that officer, and with this voyage he founded not only his own fortune, but also the prosperity of the great Australian colony. Further importations followed; and a Captain Macarthur, early in the present century, went home to London to endeavour to form a company to carry on sheep-rearing on an extensive scale. He did not succeed, and returned to Port Jackson to pursue his enterprise himself. Eventually he obtained the concession of a few square miles of land, and thus became the father of Australian 'squatting.' He located himself on the Nepean River, to the south-west of Sydney; and to his industry and sagacity is attributed in great part the origin of the immense wool-trade which has developed between the colony and the mother-country.

And what is now the wool wealth of Australasia? In 1820 there were not more than ten thousand sheep of 'a good sort' in New South Wales; and in the same year, wool from the colony was sold in London at an average of three shillings and sevenpence the pound. This led to the circulation of fabulous reports of the profits to be made out of sheep; and there was quite a run for some years on the squatting lots. In 1848 some Australians started sheep-running in New Zealand; and by 1860 the sheep in these islands had increased to 2,400,000. In 1865 the number there had grown to 5,700,000; in 1870, to 9,500,000; and in 1894, to 19,000,000.

In 1886 the pastoral wealth of the whole of the Australian colonies consisted of 84,222,272 sheep. At only ten shillings per head, this represents a capital of over forty-two millions sterling, without counting the value of the land. The number of sheep in 1894 was over 99,000,000.

But now as to the yield of the flocks. The value of the wool for 1884 was £20,532,429.

The total importations of wool into England in 1885-86 were 1,819,182 bales, of which no fewer than 1,139,842 bales, or nearly three-fourths of the whole, came from Australasia. The rest came from the Cape and Natal, India, the Mediterranean, Russia, other European countries, China, and the Falkland Islands. The imports in 1894, from all quarters, consisted of 705 million pounds, of a value of £25,000,000.

It would transcend the limits of our space to attempt to sketch the history and growth of the woollen industry in the manufacture of cloths. It is an industry, if not as old as the hills, at least very nearly as old as the fig-leaves of Eden; for we may assume as a certainty that the next garments worn by our forefathers were constructed in some way from the fleecy coats of these bleating followers. We exported woollen and worsted yarns of a value of over four million pounds sterling in 1894, and of woollen and worsted manufactures, a value of 14 millions sterling.

In the middle ages all the best wool was produced in England, and the woollen manufacture centred in Norfolk, although both the west of England and Ireland had also factories. There are in existence specimens of cloth made in these medieval days which show that the quality of the wool employed was not equal to that which we now use. The art of weaving is supposed to have been brought from the Netherlands; at any rate there were strong political alliances between the English sovereigns and the weavers of Bruges and of Ghent. In these old days, when Norwich, Aylsham, and Lynn had the lion's share of the woollen trade, the great mart for English and foreign cloths was at Stourbridge, near Cambridge, where a fair was held which lasted a month every year.

There were 2546 woollen and worsted mills in the United Kingdom in 1890. The chief seats of the wool manufacture in England in the 14th century were Bristol, London, and Norwich. Now Wiltshire and Gloucestershire are famous for broadcloths, while the towns of Leeds and Huddersfield in Yorkshire are important centres. Galashiels and Hawick are noted for their tweeds.

COTTON.

The Father of History, in writing about India—'the last inhabited country towards the East'—where every species of birds and quadrupeds, horses excepted, are 'much larger than in any other part of the world,' and where they have also 'a great abundance of gold,' made the following remarkable statement. 'They possess likewise,' he said, 'a kind of plant, which, instead of fruit, produces wool of a finer and better quality than that of the sheep, and of this the natives make their clothes.' This was the vegetable wool of the ancients, which many learned authorities have identified with the byssus, in bandages of cloth made from which the old Egyptians wrapped their mummies. But did Egypt receive the cotton plant from India — or India from Egypt — and when? However that may be, there is good reason to believe that cotton is the basis of one of the oldest industries in the world, although we are accustomed to think of it as quite modern, and at any rate as practically unknown in Europe before the last century. As a matter of fact, nevertheless, cotton was being cultivated in the south of Europe in the 13th century, although whether the fibre was then used for the making of cloth is not so certain. Its chief use then seems to have been in the manufacture of paper.

The beginning of the Oriental fable of the Vegetable Lamb is lost in the dateless night of the centuries. When and how it originated we know not; but the story of a Plant-Animal in Western Asia descended through the ages, and passed from traveller to traveller, from historian to historian, until in our time the fable has received a practical verification. Many strange things were gravely recorded of this Plant-Animal: as, that it was a tree bearing seed-pods, which, bursting when ripe, disclosed within little lambs with soft white fleeces, which Scythians used for weaving into clothing. Or, that it was a real flesh-and-blood lamb, growing upon a short stem flexible enough to allow the lamb to feed upon the surrounding grass.

There were many versions of the marvellous tale as it reached Europe; and the compiler and concocter of the so-called Sir John Mandeville's travels, as usual, improved upon it. He vouched for the flesh-and-blood lamb growing out of a plant, and declared that he had both seen and *eaten it*—whereby the writer proved himself a somewhat greater romancer than usual. Nevertheless, he has a germ of truth amid his lies, for he relates of 'Bucharia' that in the land are 'trees that bear wool, as though it were of sheep, whereof men make clothes and all things that are made of wool.' And again, of Abyssinia, that mysterious kingdom of the renowned Prester John, he related: 'In that country, and in many others beyond, and also in many on this side, men sow the seeds of cotton, and they sow it every year; and then it grows into small trees which bear cotton. And so do men every year, so that there is plenty of cotton at all times.' This statement, whencesoever it was borrowed, may be true enough, and if so, is evidence that, eighteen centuries after Herodotus, cotton was still being cultivated, as the basis of a textile industry, both in Western Asia and in Africa. It is said that in the Sacred Books of India there is evidence that cotton was in use for clothing purposes eight centuries before Christ.

The expedition of Alexander the Great from Persia into the Punjab was a good deal later, say, three hundred and thirty years before Christ. On the retreat down the Indus, Admiral Nearchus remarked 'trees bearing as it were flocks or bunches of wool,' of which the natives made 'garments of surpassing whiteness, or else their black complexions make the material whiter than any other.' The Alexandrine general, Aristobulus, is more precise: he tells of a wool-bearing tree yielding a capsule that contains 'seeds which were taken out, and that which remained was carded like wool.' And long before Pliny referred to cotton in Egypt—'a shrub which men call "gossypium," and others "xylon," from which stuffs are made which we call xylina'—Strabo had noted the cultivation of the plant on the Persian Gulf.

At the beginning of the Christian era we find cotton in cultivation and in use in Persia, Arabia, and Egypt—but whether indigenous to these countries, or conveyed westward during the centuries from India, we know not. Thereafter, the westward spread was slow; but the plant is to be traced along the north coast of Africa to Morocco, which country it seems to have reached in the 9th century. The Moors took the plant, or seeds, to Spain, and it was being grown on the plains of Valencia in the 10th century; and by the 13th century it was, as we have said, growing in various parts of Southern Europe.

Yet, although the Indian cloths were known to the Greeks and Romans a century or two before the Christian era, and although in the early centuries Arab traders brought to the Red Sea ports Indian calicoes, which were distributed in Europe, we find cotton known in England only as material for candle-wicks down to the 17th century. At any rate, M'Culloch is our authority for believing that the first mention of cotton being manufactured in England is in 1641; and that the 'English cottons,' of which earlier mention may be found, were really *woollens*.

And now we come to a very curious thing in the Romance of Cotton. Columbus discovered—or, as some say, rediscovered—America in 1492; and when he reached the islands of the Caribbean Sea, the natives who came off to barter with him brought, among other things, cotton yarn and thread. Vasco da Gama, a few years later than Bartholomew Diaz, in 1497 rounded the Cape of Good Hope and reached the Zanzibar coast. There the natives were found to be clothed in cotton, just as Columbus found the natives of Cuba to be, as Pizarro found the Peruvians, and as Cortes found the Mexicans. These Europeans, proceeding from the Iberian Peninsula east and west, found the peoples of the new worlds clothed with a material of which they knew nothing. Cotton was king in America, as in Asia, before it began even to be known in Western Europe.

Not only that, but cotton must have been cultivated in Africa at the time when the mariners of Prince Henry the Navigator first made their way cautiously down the west coast. It is, at any rate, upwards of four hundred years since cotton cloth was brought from the coast of Guinea and sold in London as a strange barbaric product. Whether the plant travelled to the Bight of Benin from the land of Prester John, or from the land of the Pharaohs, or across from the Mozambique coast, where the Arabians are supposed to have had settlements and trading stations in prehistoric days, who can now say? But it is curious enough that when Africa was discovered by Europeans, the Dark Continent was actually producing both the fibre and the cloth for which African labour and English skill were afterwards to be needed. The cotton plantations of Southern America were worked by the negroes of Africa in order that the cotton-mills of Lancashire might be kept running. And yet both Africa and America made cotton cloth from the vegetable wool long before we knew of it otherwise than as a traveller's wonder.

Even in Asia, the natural habitat of the cotton plant, the story has been curious. Thus, according to the records above named, cotton has been in use for clothing for three thousand years in India, and India borders upon the ancient and extensive Empire of China. Yet cotton was not used in China for cloth-making until the coming of the Tartars, and has been cultivated and manufactured there for only about five hundred years. This was because of the 'vested interests' in wool and silk, which combined to keep out the vegetable wool from general use.

To understand aright the romance of cotton we must understand the nature of the plant in its relation to climate. It has been called a child of the tropics, and yet it grows well in other than tropical climes. As Mr Richard Marsden — an authority on cotton-spinning — says: 'Cotton is or can be grown (along) a broad zone extending forty-five degrees north to thirty-five degrees south of the equator. Reference to a map will show that this includes a space extending from the European shores of the Mediterranean to the Cape of Good Hope, from Japan to Melbourne in Australia, and from Washington in the United States to Buenos Ayres in South America, with all the lands intermediate between these several points. These include the Southern States of the American Union, from Washington to the Gulf of Mexico, and three-fourths of South America, the whole of the African Continent, and Southern Asia from the Bosphorus to Pekin in China. The vast area of Australia is also within the cotton zone, and the islands lying between that country and Asia.'

The exact period at which the manufacture of cotton was begun in England is not known with absolute certainty. But as we have said, the first authentic mention of it occurs in 1641; and it is in a book called *Treasure of Traffic*, by Lewis Roberts. The passage runs thus: 'The town of Manchester, in Lancashire, must be also herein remembered, and worthily for their encouragement commended, who buy the yarne of the Irish in great quantity, and weaving it, returne the same again into Ireland to sell. Neither doth their industry rest here; for they buy *cotton-wool* in London that comes first from Cyprus and Smyrna, and at home worke the same, and perfect it into fustians, vermilions, dimities, and other such stuffs; and then return it to London, where the same is vended and sold, and not seldom sent into foreign parts, who have means, at far easier terms, to provide themselves of the said first materials.'

But here it should be explained that from the first introduction of the cotton fibre into this country, and until about the year 1773, in the manufacture of cloth it was only the weft that was of cotton. Down to about 1773, the warp was invariably of linen yarn, brought from Ireland and Germany. The Manchester merchants began in 1760 to employ the hand-loom weavers in the surrounding villages to make cloth according to prescribed patterns, and with the yarns supplied by the buyers. Thus they sent linen yarn for warp, and raw cotton—which the weaver had first to card and spin on a common distaff—for weft. Such was the practice when, in 1767, James Hargreaves of Blackburn inaugurated the textile revolution by inventing the spinning-jenny, which, from small beginnings, was soon made to spin thirty threads as easily as one. The thread thus spun, however, was still only available for weft, as the jenny could not turn out the yarn hard and firm enough for warp. The next stage, therefore, was the invention of a machine to give the requisite quality and tenuity to the threads spun from the raw cotton. This was the spinning-frame of Richard Arkwright, the story of which every schoolboy is supposed to know.

Here, then, we reach another point in our romance. The manufacture of cotton cloths in England from raw cotton is older than the cotton culture of North America. It is, in fact, only about one hundred years since we began to draw supplies of raw cotton from the Southern States, which, previous to 1784, did not export a single pound, and produced only a small quantity for domestic consumption. The story of the development of cotton-growing in America is quite as marvellous as the story of the expansion of cotton-manufacturing in England. In both cases the most stupendous extension ever reached by any single industry in the history of the world has been reached in less than a hundred years.

And yet Columbus found the Cubans, as Pizarro found the Peruvians, and Cortes found the Mexicans, clothed in cotton. Was it from the same plant as now supplies 'half the calico used by the entire human race' (as an American writer has computed)? This estimate, by the way, was arrived at thus: In 1889–90 the cotton crop of the world was 6094 millions of pounds, and the population of the world was computed at 1500 millions. This gave four pounds of raw cotton, equal to twenty yards of calico, per head; and the proportion of raw cotton provided by the Southern States was equal to eleven and a half yards per head. The raw cotton imported by Great Britain in 1894 had a value of nearly 33 million pounds sterling; the exports of cotton yarn and manufactured goods amounted to about 66 millions sterling.

There are several species of the cotton plant; but those of commercial importance are four in number. Herbaceous Cotton ('Gossypium herbaceum') is the plant which yields the East Indian 'Surat' and some varieties of the Egyptian cotton. Its habitats are India, China, Arabia, Egypt, and Asia Minor. It is an annual: it grows to a height of five or six feet, it has a yellow flower, and it yields a short staple. Tree Cotton ('Gossypium arboreum'), on the other hand, grows to a height of fifteen or twenty feet, has a red flower, and yields a fine silky wool. Its habitats are Egypt, Arabia, India, and China. Hairy Cotton ('Gossypium hirsutum') is a shrub of some six or seven feet high, with a white or straw-coloured flower, and hairy pods, which yield the staple known as American 'Upland' and 'Orleans' cotton. Another variety, called 'Gossypium Barbadense,' because it was first found in Barbadoes, grows to a height of about fifteen feet, and has a yellow flower, yielding a long staple, and fine silky wool known as 'Sea Island' cotton. This now grows most extensively on the coasts of Georgia and Florida; but has been experimented with in various parts of the world, notably in Egypt, where it has succeeded; and in the Polynesian islands, where, for some reason or another, it has failed.

The cotton plant of the American cotton plantations is an annual, which shoots above ground in about a fortnight after sowing, and which, as it grows, throws out flowerstalks, at the end of each of which develops a pod with fringed calyces. From this pod emerges a flower which, in some of the American varieties of the general species, will change its colour from day to day. The complete bloom flourishes for only twenty-four hours, at the end of which time the flower twists itself off, leaving a pod or boll, which grows to the size of a large filbert, browns and hardens like a nut, and then bursts, revealing the fibre or wool encased in three or four (according to the variety) cells within. This fibre or wool is the covering of the seeds, and in each cell will be as many separate fleeces as seeds, yet apparently forming one fleece.

Upon the characteristics of this fleece depends the commercial value of the fibre. The essential qualities of good and mature cotton are thus enumerated by an expert: 'Length of fibre; smallness or fineness in diameter; evenness and smoothness; elasticity; tensile strength and colour; hollowness or tube-like construction; natural twist; corrugated edges; and moisture.' The fibre of Indian cotton is only about five-eighths of an inch long; that of Sea Island about two inches. Then Sea Island cotton is a sort of creamy-white colour; and some kinds of American and Egyptian cotton are not white at all, but golden in hue; while other kinds, again, are snow-white.

Although the term 'American Cotton' is applied to all the cotton produced in the United States of America, it really applies to a number of different varieties—such as Texas, Mobile, Upland, Orleans, &c.—each one known by its distinctive name. The differences are too technical for explanation here; but, generally speaking, the members of the 'hirsutum' species of the 'Gossypium' tribe now rule the world of cotton.

They are the product of what is called the 'Cotton-belt' of the United States, an area stretching for about two thousand miles between its extreme points in the Southern States, which are North and South Carolina, Georgia, Alabama, Mississippi, Florida, Louisiana, Arkansas, and Texas. Over this area, soil and climate vary considerably. The 'Cotton-belt' lies, roughly speaking, between the thirtieth and fortieth parallels of north latitude. As an American expert says: 'Cotton can be produced with various degrees of profit throughout the region bounded on the north by a line passing through Philadelphia; on the south by a line passing a little south of New Orleans; and on the west by a line passing through San Antonio. This is the limit of the possibilities.'

The cotton plant likes a light sandy soil, or a black alluvial soil like that of the Mississippi margins. It requires both heat and moisture in due proportions, and is sensitive to cold, to drought, and to excessive moisture. The American cotton-fields are still worked by negroes, but no longer slaves, as before the war; and, in fact, the negroes are now not only free, but some of them are considerable cotton-growers on their own account. On the other hand, one finds nowadays little of the old system of spacious plantations under one ownership. Instead, the cultivation is carried on on small farms and allotments, not owned but rented by the cultivators. Large numbers of these cotton farmers are 'financed' by dealers, by landowners, or even by local storekeepers.

The cotton factor is the go-between of the grower and the exporting agent in Galveston or New Orleans, or other centre of business. After the crop is picked by the negroes—men, women, and children—and the harvest is a long process—the seeds are separated from the fibre by means of a 'gin;' and then the cotton-wool is packed into loose bales for the factor, while the seeds are sent to a mill to be crushed for cotton-seed oil and oil-cake for cattle-feeding. The loose cotton bales are collected by the factors into some such central town as Memphis, where they are sorted, sampled, graded, and then compressed by machinery into bales of about four hundred and forty pounds each, for export. In calculating crops, &c., a bale is taken as four hundred pounds net.

The cotton then passes into the hands of the shipping agent, who brands it, and forwards it by river-steamer to one of the Southern ports, or by rail to New York or Boston, where it is put on board an ocean steamer for

Europe. The beautiful American clippers with which some of us were familiar in the days of our youth are no longer to be seen; they have been run off the face of the waters by the 'ocean liner' and the 'tramp.' Arrived in Liverpool, cotton enters upon a new course of adventures altogether, and engages the thoughts and energies of a wholly new set of people.

Cotton Plant.

CHAPTER V.

GOLD AND DIAMONDS.

GOLD.—How widely distributed—Alluvial Gold-mining—Vein Gold-mining—Nuggets—Treatment of Ore and Gold in the Transvaal—Story of South African Gold-fields—Gold-production of the World—Johannesburg the Golden City—Coolgardie Gold-fields—Bayley's discovery of Gold there.
DIAMONDS.—Composition—Diamond-cutting—Diamond-mining—Famous Diamonds—Cecil J. Rhodes and the Kimberley Mines.

IN the getting of gold—the metal—for the purpose of possessing gold—as money—there has always been an element of excitement and romance.

'How quickly nature falls into revolt when gold becomes her object!' as Shakespeare says:

> For gold the merchant ploughs the main,
> The farmer ploughs the manor.

There is a vast difference between the way in which the precious metal is now extracted and the primitive methods which were considered perfect in the earlier part of the century. The miner of fifty years ago never dreamt of machinery, costly and magnificent, capable of crushing thousands of tons of quartz per week. He 'dollied,' or ground, his little bits of rock by means of a contrivance resembling a pestle and mortar, and it was only the very richest stone that repaid him for his labour. In fact, there was very little crushing in those days, quartz not being easily found sufficiently rich to make such work a paying concern, and it was therefore alluvial gold which was chiefly sought for. The gold-seeker having decided on the place where he was to make his first venture, provided

The Hand-cradle Method of extracting Gold.

himself with a shovel and pick and started for the 'diggings.' Gold-mining was then carried on all over California, and he had his choice of many camps.

But what a wild and lawless place was California in those days! Here in these gold-fields were gathered together thousands of the greatest desperadoes that the earth could boast of, and thousands of needy, if harmless, adventurers from every country in the world. Fortunately with them were mixed thousands of honest hard-working men, of every condition in life, from the peer to the peasant, men who had been doing well, or fairly well, at their professions, or in their business offices at home, but for whom the attractions of this El Dorado had proved too powerful.

Gold is perhaps the most widely and universally sought product of the earth's crust. In the very earliest writings which have come down to us gold is mentioned as an object of men's search, and as a commodity of extreme value for purposes of adornment and as a medium of exchange. The importance which it possessed in ancient times has certainly not lessened in our day. Without the enormous supplies of gold produced at about the time when the steam-engine was being brought into practical use it is difficult to imagine how our commerce could have attained its present proportions; and but for the rush of immigrants to the gold-fields in the beginning of the second half of this century Australia might have remained a mere convict settlement, California have become but a granary and vineyard, and the Transvaal an asylum of the Boers who were discontented with the Cape government.

On the score of geographical distribution, gold must be deemed a common metal, as common as copper, lead, or silver, and far more common than nickel, cobalt, platinum, and many others. Theorists have propounded curious rules for the occurrence of gold on certain lines and belts, which have no existence but in their own fancy. Scarcely a country but has rewarded a systematic search for gold, though some are more richly endowed than others, and discoveries are not always made with the same facility. The old prejudices, which made men associate gold only with certain localities hindered the development of a most promising industry even within the British shores. Despite the abundant traces of ancient Roman and other workings, the gold-mines of Wales were long regarded as mythical; but recent extended exploitation has proved them to be rich. This is notably the case in the Dolgelly district, where considerable gold occurs, both in alluvial gravels and in well-formed quartz veins traversing the Lower Silurian Lingula beds and the intruded diabasic rocks called 'greenstone' in the Geological Survey. A peculiarity of the veins is the common association of magnesian minerals. The gold is about 20 or 21 carats fine, and often shows traces of iron sesquioxide. So long ago as 1861 some £10,000 worth of gold per annum was taken out of the Clogan mine by imperfect methods. Some samples have afforded 40 to 60 ounces per ton—a most remarkable yield. There are probably many veins still waiting discovery.

A calculation was made in 1881 that the total gold extracted from all sources up to that date from the creation had been over 10,000 tons, with a value of about 1500 millions sterling. California, to the end of 1888, was reckoned to have afforded over 200 million pounds' worth, and this figure is exceeded by the Australian colony of Victoria.

The origin of gold-bearing mineral veins is inseparably connected with that vexed question, the origin of mineral veins generally. By far the most common matrix of vein-gold is quartz or silica, but it is not the only one. To pass by the metals and metallic ores with which gold is found, there are several other minerals which serve as an envelope for the precious metal. Chief among them is lime. Some of the best mines of New South Wales are in calcareous veins. Sundry gold-reefs in Queensland, New South Wales, Victoria, and Bohemia are full of calcite. Dolomite occurs in Californian and Manitoban mines;

and apatite, aragonite, gypsum, selenite, and crystalline limestone have all proved auriferous, while in some cases neighbouring quartz has been barren. Felspar in Colorado and felsite magnesian slate in Newfoundland carry gold.

NUGGETS.

The physical conditions under which gold occurs are extremely variable. Popularly speaking, the most familiar form is the 'nugget,' or shapeless mass of appreciable size. These, however, constitute in the aggregate but a small proportion of the gold yielded by any field, and were much more common in the early days of placer-mining in California and Australia than they are now. One of the largest ever found, the 'Welcome' nugget, discovered in 1858 at Bakery Hill, Ballarat, weighed 2217 ounces 16 dwt., and sold for £10,500, whilst not a few have exceeded

Welcome Nugget.

1000 ounces. One found at Casson Hill, Calaveras county, California, in 1854, weighed 180 pounds. The 'Water Moon' nugget, found in Australia in 1852, weighed 223 pounds. The origin of these large nuggets has been a subject for discussion. Like all placer or alluvial gold, they have been in part at least derived from the auriferous veins traversing the rocks whose disintegration furnished the material forming the gravel beds in which the nuggets are found.

The famous nugget known as the 'Welcome Stranger' was discovered under singular circumstances in the Dunolly district of Victoria, which is one hundred and ten miles north-west of the capital, Melbourne, by two Cornish miners named Deeson and Oates. Their career is remarkable, as showing how fortune, after frowning for years, will suddenly smile on the objects of her apparent aversion. These two Cornishmen emigrated from England to Australia by the same vessel in 1854. They betook themselves to the far-famed Sandhurst Gold-field in Victoria; they worked together industriously for years, and yet only contrived to make a bare livelihood by their exertions. Thinking that change of place might possibly mean change of luck, they moved to the Dunolly Gold-field, and their spirits were considerably raised by the discovery of some small nuggets. But this was only a momentary gleam of sunshine, for their former ill-luck pursued them again, and pursued them even more relentlessly than before.

The time at last came, on the morning of Friday, February 5, 1869, when the storekeeper with whom they were accustomed to deal refused to supply them any longer with the necessaries of life until they liquidated the debt they had already incurred. For the first time in their lives they went hungry to work, and the spectacle of these two brave fellows fighting on an empty stomach against continued ill-luck must have moved the fickle goddess to pity and repentance. Gloomy and depressed as they naturally were, they plied their picks with indomitable perseverance, and while Deeson was breaking up the earth around the roots of a tree, his pick suddenly and sharply rebounded by reason of its having struck some very hard substance. 'Come and see what this is,' he called out to his mate. To their astonishment, 'this' turned out to be the 'Welcome Stranger' nugget; and thus two poverty-stricken Cornish miners became in a moment the possessors of the largest mass of gold that mortal eyes ever saw, or are likely to see again. Such a revolution of fortune is probably unique in the annals of the human race. Almost bewildered by the unexpected treasure they had found at their feet, Deeson and Oates removed the superincumbent clay, and there revealed to their wondering eyes was a lump of gold, a foot long and a foot broad, and so heavy that their joint strength could scarcely move it. A dray having been procured, the monster nugget was escorted by an admiring procession into the town of Dunolly, and carried into the local branch of the London Chartered Bank, where it was weighed, and found to contain $2268\frac{1}{2}$ ounces of gold. The Bank purchased the nugget for £9534, which the erstwhile so unlucky, but now so fortunate, pair of Cornish miners divided equally between them. Whether the storekeeper who refused them the materials for a breakfast that morning apologised for his harsh behaviour, history relates not, but the probability is that he was paid the precise amount of his debt and no more; whereas, had he acted in a more generous spirit towards two brothers in distress, he might have come in for a handsome present out of the proceeds of the 'Welcome Stranger.'

The 'Welcome' nugget above mentioned, found at Bakery Hill, Ballarat, in Victoria, on June 15, 1858, was nearly as large as the one just described, its weight being 2217 ounces 16 dwts. It was found at a depth of one hundred and eighty feet in a claim belonging to a party of twenty-four men, who disposed of it for £10,500. A smaller nugget, weighing 571 ounces, was found in close proximity to it. After being exhibited in Melbourne, the 'Welcome' nugget was brought to London and smelted in November 1859. The assay showed that it contained 99·20 per cent. of gold.

Another valuable nugget, which was brought to London and exhibited at the Crystal Palace, Sydenham, was the 'Blanche Barkly,' found by a party of four diggers on August 27, 1857, at Kingower, Victoria, just thirteen feet beneath the surface. It was twenty-eight inches long, ten inches broad in its widest part, and weighed 1743 ounces 13 dwts. It realised £6905, 12s. 6d. A peculiarity about this nugget was the manner in which it had eluded the efforts of previous parties to capture it. Three years before its discovery, a number of miners, judging the place to be a 'likely' locality, had sunk holes within a few feet of the spot where this golden mass was reposing, and yet they were not lucky enough to strike it. What a tantalising thought it must have been in after-years, when they reflected on the fact that they were once within an arm's length of £7000 without being fortunate enough to grasp the golden treasure! Kingower, like Dunolly, from which it is only a few miles distant, is a locality famous for its nuggets. One weighing 230 ounces was actually found on the surface covered with green moss; and pieces of gold have frequently been picked up there after heavy rains, the water washing away the thin coating of earth that had previously concealed them. Two men working in the Kingower district in 1860 found a very fine nugget, weighing 805 ounces, within a foot of the surface; and one of 715 ounces was unearthed at Daisy Hill at a depth of only three and a half feet.

A notable instance of rapid fortune was that of a party of four, who, having been but a few months in the colony of Victoria, were lucky enough to alight on a nugget weighing 1615 ounces. They immediately returned to

England with their prize and sold it for £5532, 7s. 4d. The place where they thus quickly made their 'pile,' to use an expressive colonialism, was Canadian Gully, at Ballarat, a very prolific nugget-ground. There was also found the 'Lady Hotham' nugget, called after the wife of Sir Charles Hotham, one of the early governors of Victoria. It was discovered on September 8, 1854, at a depth of 135 feet. Its weight was 1177 ounces; and near it were found a number of smaller nuggets of the aggregate weight of 2600 ounces, so that the total value of the gold extracted from this one claim was no less than £13,000. As showing the phenomenal richness of this locality, it may be added that on January 20, 1853, a party of three brought to the surface a solid mass of gold weighing 1117 ounces; and two days afterwards, in the same tunnel, a splendid pyramidal-shaped nugget weighing 1011 ounces was discovered; the conjoint value of the two being £7500.

A case somewhat similar to one already described was that of the 'Heron' nugget, a solid mass of gold to the amount of 1008 ounces, which was found at Fryer's Creek, Victoria, by two young men who had only been three months in the colony. They were offered £4000 for it in Victoria; but they preferred to bring it to England as a trophy, and there they sold it for £4080.

The 'Victoria' nugget, as its name suggests, was purchased by the Victorian government for presentation to Her Majesty. It was a very pretty specimen of 340 ounces, worth £1650, and was discovered at White Horse Gully, Sandhurst. Quite close to it, and within a foot of the surface, was found the 'Dascombe' nugget, weighing 330 ounces, which was also brought to London, and sold for £1500.

Just as a book should never be judged by its cover, so mineral substances should not be estimated by superficial indications. A neglect of this salutary precept was once very nearly resulting in the loss of a valuable Victorian nugget. A big lump of quartz was brought to the surface, and, as its exterior aspect presented only slight indications of the existence of gold, it was at first believed to be valueless; but as soon as the mass was broken up, there, embedded in the quartz, was a beautiful nugget of an oval shape.

New South Wales, the parent colony of the Australian group, has produced a considerable quantity of gold, but not many notable nuggets. Its most famous nugget was discovered by a native boy in June 1851 at Meroo Creek, near the present town of Bathurst. This black boy was in the employ of Dr Kerr as a shepherd, and one day, whilst minding his sheep, he casually came across three detached pieces of quartz. He tried to turn over the largest of the pieces with his stick; but he was astonished to find that the lump was much heavier than the ordinary quartz with which he was familiar. Bending down and looking closer, he saw a shining yellow mass lying near; and when he at last succeeded in lifting up the piece of quartz, his eyes expanded on observing that the whole of its under surface was of the same shining complexion. He probably did not realise the full value of his discovery; but he had sufficient sense to break off a few specimens and hasten to show them to his master. Dr Kerr set off at once to verify the discovery; and when he arrived at the spot, his most sanguine anticipations were fulfilled by the event. He found himself the possessor of 1272 ounces of gold; and he rewarded the author of his wealth, the little black boy, with a flock of sheep and as much land as was needed for their pasture.

METHODS OF MINING.

The more common form of alluvial gold is as grains, or scales, or dust, varying in size from that of ordinary gunpowder to a minuteness that is invisible to the naked eye. Sometimes indeed the particles are so small that they are known as 'paint' gold, forming a scarcely perceptible coating on fragments of rock. When the gold is very fine or in very thin scales, much of it is lost in the ordinary processes for treating gravels, by reason of the fact that it will actually float on water for a considerable distance.

From what has been already said it will be evident that gold-mining must be an industry presenting several distinct phases. These may be classed as alluvial mining, vein-mining, and the treatment of auriferous ores.

In alluvial mining natural agencies, such as frost, rain, &c., have, in the course of centuries, performed the arduous tasks of breaking up the matrix which held the gold, and washing away much of the valueless material, leaving the gold concentrated into a limited area by virtue of its great specific gravity. Hence it is never safe to assume that the portion of the veins remaining as such will yield anything like so great an equivalent of gold as the alluvials formed from the portion which has been disintegrated. As water has been the chief (but not the only) agent in distributing the gold and gravel constituting alluvial diggings or placers, the banks and beds of running streams in the neighbourhood of auriferous veins are likely spots for the prospector, who finds in the flowing water of the stream the means of separating the heavy grains of gold from the much lighter particles of rock, sand, and mud. Often the brook is made to yield the gold it transports by the simple expedient of placing in it obstacles which will arrest the gold without obstructing the lighter matters. Jason's golden fleece was probably a sheepskin which had been pegged down in the current of the Phasis till a quantity of gold grains had become entangled among the wool. To this day the same practice is followed with ox-hides in Brazil, and with sheepskins in Ladakh, Savoy, and Hungary. This may be deemed the simplest form of 'alluvial mining.' If the gold deposited in holes and behind bars in the bed of the stream is to be recovered, greater preparations are needed. Either the river-bed must be dredged by floating dredgers, worked by the stream or otherwise; or the gravel must be dug out for washing while the bed is left dry in hot weather; or the river must be diverted into another channel (natural or artificial) whilst its bed is being stripped. The first-named method is best adapted to large volumes of water, but probably is least productive of gold, passing over much that is buried in crevices in the solid bed-rock. The second plan is applicable only to small streams, and entails much labour. The third is most efficient, but very liable to serious interference by floods, which entail a heavy loss of plant.

In searching for placers it is necessary to bear in mind that the watercourses of the country have not always flowed in the channels they now occupy. During the long periods of geological time many and vast changes have taken place in the contour of the earth's surface. Hence it is not an uncommon circumstance to find beds of auriferous gravel occupying the summits of hills, which must, at the time the deposit was made, have represented the course of a stream. In the same way the remains of riverine accumulations are found forming 'terraces' or 'benches' on the flanks of hills. Lacustrine beds may similarly occur at altitudes far above the reach of any existing stream, having been the work of rivers long since passed away.

Another form of alluvial digging occurs in Western America and New Zealand, where the sea washes up auriferous sands. These are known as 'ocean placers' or 'beach diggings,' and are of minor importance.

Whilst most placers have been formed by flowing water, some owe their origin to the action of ice, and are really glacial moraines. Others are attributed to the effects of repeated frost and thaw in decomposing the rocks and causing rearrangement of the component parts. Yet another class of deposits is supposed to have been accumulated by an outpouring of volcanic mud. And, finally, experts declare that some of the rich *banket* beds of the Transvaal became auriferous by the infiltration of water containing a minute proportion of gold in solution.

In all cases the recovery of alluvial gold is in principle remarkably simple. It depends on the fact that the gold is about seven times as heavy, bulk for bulk, as the material forming the mass of the deposit. The medium for effecting the separation is water in motion. The apparatus in which it is applied may be a 'pan,' a 'cradle,' or a 'tom,' for operations on a very small scale, or a 'sluice,' which may be a paved ditch or a wooden 'flume' of great length, for large operations. The method is the same in all: flowing water removes the earthy matters, while obstructions of various kinds arrest the metal. As a rule, it is more advantageous to conduct the water to the material than to carry the material to water. In many cases a stream of water, conveyed by means of pipes, and acting under the influence of considerable pressure, is utilised for removing as well as washing the deposit. This method is known as 'piping' or 'hydraulicing' in America, where it has been chiefly developed, but is now forbidden in many localities, because the enormous masses of earth washed through the sluices have silted up rivers and harbours, and caused immense loss to the agricultural interest by burying the rich riverside lands under a deposit that will be sterile for many years to come. The plan permits of very economical working in large quantities, but is extremely wasteful of gold. The water-supply is of paramount importance, and has led to the construction of reservoirs and conduits, at very heavy cost, which in many

Hydraulic Gold-mining.

places will have a permanent value long after gold-sluicing has ceased. These large water-supply works are often in the hands of distinct parties from the miners, the latter purchasing the water they use. To give an example of the results attained in alluvial mining, it may be mentioned that in a three-months' working in one Victorian district in

1888, over 33,500 tons of wash-dirt were treated for an average yield of $18\frac{1}{2}$ grains of gold per ton, or, say, one part in 700,000. Where water cannot be obtained recourse is had to a fanning or winnowing process for separating the gold from the sand, which, however, is less efficacious.

Vein-mining for gold differs but little from working any other kind of metalliferous lode. When the vein-stuff has been raised it is reduced to a pulverulent condition, to liberate the gold from the gangue. In some cases roasting is first resorted to. This causes friability, and facilitates the subsequent comminution. When the gold is in a very fine state, too, it helps it to agglomerate. But if any pyrites are present the effect is most detrimental, the gold becoming coated with a film of sulphur or a glazing of iron oxide. The powdering of the vein-stuff is usually performed in stamp batteries, which consist of a number of falling hammers. While simple in principle, the apparatus is complicated in its working parts, and is probably destined to give way to the improved forms of crushing-rolls and centrifugal roller mills, which are less costly, simpler, more efficient, and do not flatten the gold particles so much. One of the most effective is that by Jordan. When the vein-stuff has been reduced to powder, it is akin to alluvial wash-dirt, and demands the same or similar contrivances for arresting the liberated gold and releasing the tailings—that is, mercury troughs, amalgamated plates, blanket strakes, &c.; but, in addition, provision is made for catching the other metalliferous constituents, such as pyrites, which almost always carry a valuable percentage of gold. These pyrites or 'sulphurets' are cleansed by concentration in various kinds of apparatus, all depending on the greater specific gravity of the portion sought to be saved.

Of the metals and minerals with which gold is found intimately associated in nature are the following: Antimony, arsenic, bismuth, cobalt, copper, iridium, iron, lead, manganese, nickel, osmium, palladium, platinum, selenium, silver, tellurium, tungsten, vanadium, and zinc, often as an alloy in the case of palladium, platinum, selenium, silver (always), and tellurium. The methods of separation vary with the nature of the ore and the conditions of the locality.

TREATMENT OF ORE AND GOLD IN THE TRANSVAAL.

The method of treatment of ore and gold in the Transvaal, the most perfect and effective known at the present time, has thus been described by Arthur Stenhouse:

The rock when hoisted out of the mine is first assorted, the waste rock being thrown on one side and the gold-bearing ore broken into lumps by a stone-breaker. The lumps of ore now pass by gravitation and feeders through a battery (or stamp mill), each stamp of which weighs about 1150 pounds, every stamp being lifted and dropped separately by the cam shaft at a speed of about 95 drops a minute. A stream of water is introduced, the ore is crushed into fine sand, and is carried by the water over a series of inclined copper plates, which are coated with quicksilver. The free gold in the sand at once amalgamates with the quicksilver on the plates, and the sand-laden stream continues on its course.

The sand, having now passed over the plates, is carried by launders on to the concentrators, or frue vanners. These concentrators separate and retain the heavy sand (or concentrates), whilst the lighter sand is carried by gravitation through a trough (or launder) to the cyanide vats.

The stream of water carrying the lighter sand empties

itself into the cyanide vats, and as each successive vat is filled up, the water is allowed to drain through the sand. A solution of cyanide of potassium is then pumped up and evenly distributed (by distributors) over the sand, and dissolves the gold in its progress, leaving pure sand alone in the vat. The gold-containing liquid (or solution) having left the vat, is led into a series of boxes filled with zinc shavings, the gold separates from the liquid, and settles on the zinc shavings in the shape of a small black powder. The cyanide solution now freed from the gold runs into the solution vats, and is restrengthened and ready for further use.

Gold Recovery.—In the mill or battery the copper plates are scraped daily, and the amalgams (that is, quicksilver and gold) are weighed and placed in the safe in charge of the battery manager. This amalgam is generally retorted once a week, that is to say, the quicksilver is evaporated (but not lost) and the gold is left in the retort. This retorted gold is then smelted into bars.

The concentrates recovered by the frue vanners are generally treated by chlorination (roasted). This process is gone through so that the iron can be separated from the gold. Concentrates are sometimes treated by cyanide, but the process, if cheaper, is slow and less effective. Chlorinated gold is also smelted into bars.

Cyanide.—The gold from the zinc shavings is recovered by retorting. It is afterwards melted into bars and called 'cyanide gold.'

Slimes (or float gold) are generally conserved in a dam, and when the quantity is sufficient they are treated by chlorination, or by a solution of cyanide of potassium.

After treatment all sand is still retained, and is really a small unbooked asset of the various gold-mining companies. The Rand undoubtedly is the best field to-day for students who wish to acquire the details of gold recovery. In no other country has science produced such excellent results. At least 95 per cent. of the gold in the ore can now be recovered, and scientific men from all countries are resident on the fields, and advantageous discoveries in the treatment of various ores are of almost daily occurrence.

STORY OF THE SOUTH AFRICAN GOLD-FIELDS.

There is material for the philosopher in the fact of gold-finding having occurred in connection with a part of the world to which King Solomon the Wise sent for supplies of gold and 'almug-trees,' for the mysterious Ophir has been located in Mashonaland, and the Queen of Sheba identified with the Sabia districts, which, though not in 'the Randt,' are curiously connected with the rise and progress of the mania.

Let us briefly trace that romantic history, merely mentioning by the way that, even in European history, African gold is no novelty, for the Portuguese brought back gold-dust (and negro slaves) from Cape Bojador four hundred and fifty years ago. The ruins of Mashonaland were discovered in 1864 by Karl Mauch, who also discovered the gold-field of Taté on the Zambesi, of which Livingstone had reported that the natives got gold there by washing, being too lazy to dig for it. When Karl Mauch came back to civilisation, people laughed at his stories of ruined cities in the centre of Africa as travellers' fables, but a number of Australian gold-diggers thought his report of the Taté gold-field good enough to follow up. So about 1867, a band of them went out and set up a small battery on the Taté River for crushing the quartz. This may be called the first serious attempt at gold-mining in South Africa since the days of the lost races who built the cities whose ruins Karl Mauch discovered and which Mr Theodore Bent has described. A Natal company assisted the Taté diggers with supplies, and enough gold was found to justify the floating of the Limpopo Mining Company in London. This was in 1868, and was practically the foundation of the 'Kaffir Circus,' though its founders knew it not. Sir John Swinburne was the moving spirit of this enterprise, and went out with a lot of expensive machinery, only to meet with a good deal of disappointment. The diamond discoveries in Griqualand soon drew away the gold-seekers, who found the working expenses too heavy to leave gold-mining profitable, and for a time the Taté fields were deserted. They were taken up again, however, twenty years later by a Kimberley enterprise, out of which developed the Taté Concession and Exploration Company, to whom the unfortunate potentate Lobengula granted a mining concession over no less than eight hundred thousand square miles of Matabeleland.

Just as the Australians were breaking ground on the Taté, Thomas Baines, the traveller, was making up his mind to test the truth of tales of gold in the far interior, which the Portuguese from Da Gama onwards had received from natives. In 1869 he set forth from Natal with a small expedition, and in 1870 received from Lobengula permission to dig for gold anywhere between the rivers Gwailo and Ganyona. Some seventeen years later this same concession was repeated to Mr Rudd, and became the basis from which sprang the great Chartered Company of British South Africa.

In the course of his journey, Baines encamped on the site of the present city of Johannesburg, without having the least idea of the wealth beneath him, and intent only upon that he hoped to find farther inland. On the map which he prepared of this journey is marked the 'farm of H. Hartley, pioneer of the gold-fields,' in the Witwatersrandt district. Hartley was known to the Boers as 'Oude Baas,' and was a famous elephant-hunter, but as ignorant as Baines himself that he was dwelling on the top of a gold-reef. And it was not in the Witwatersrandt, foremost as it now is, that the African gold boom began.

While the Taté diggers were pursuing their work and Baines his explorations, a Natalian named Button went, with an experienced Californian miner named Sutherland, to prospect for gold in the north-east of the Transvaal. They found it near Lydenburg, and companies were rapidly formed in Natal to work it. Such big nuggets were sent down that men hurried up, until soon there were some fifteen hundred actively at work on the Lydenburg field. The operations were fairly profitable, but the outbreak of the Zulu war, and then the Boer war, put an end to them for some years.

And now we come to one of the most romantic chapters in the golden history of South Africa, a history which was marked by hard and disheartening days what time the lucky diamond-seekers at Kimberley were swilling champagne, as if it were water, out of pewter beer-pots. There is more attraction for adventurers, however, in gold-seeking than in diamond-mining, for gold can be valued and realised at once, whereas diamonds may not be diamonds after all, and may be spoilt, lost, or stolen, before they can find a purchaser.

It is to be noted that much as the Transvaal Republic has benefited from gold-mining, the Boers were at first much averse to it, and threw all the obstacles they could in the way of the miners. And it was this attitude of the Boers, especially towards the Lydenburg pioneers, that led to the next development.

One of the tributaries of the Crocodile River (which

flows into Delagoa Bay) is the Kaap River, called also the River of the Little Crocodile, which waters a wide deep valley into which projects the spur of a hill which the Dutch pioneers called De Kaap (the cape). Beyond this cape-like spur the hills rise to a height of three thousand feet, and carry a wide plateau covered with innumerable boulders of fantastic shape—the Duivel's Kantoor. The mists gather in the valley and dash themselves against De Kaap like surf upon a headland; and the face of the hills is broken with caves and galleries as if by the action of the sea, but really by the action of the weather. Upon the high-lying plateau of the Duivel's Kantoor were a number of farms, the chief of which was held by one G. P. Moodie.

One day a Natal trader named Tom M'Laughlin had occasion to cross this plateau in the course of a long trek, and he picked up with curiosity some of the bits of quartz he passed, or kicked aside, on the way. On reaching Natal he showed these to an old Australian miner, who instantly started up-country and found more. The place was rich in gold, and machinery was as quickly as possible got up from Natal, on to Moodie's farm. On this farm was found the famous Pioneer Reef, and Moodie, who at one time would gladly have parted with his farm for a few hundreds, sold his holding to a Natal company for something like a quarter of a million. Then there was a rush of diggers and prospectors back from the Lydenburg district, and the De Kaap 'boom' set in. The beginning was in 1883, and two years later the whole Kaap valley and Kantoor plateau was declared a public gold-field. Two brothers called Barber came up and formed the centre of a settlement, now the town of Barberton. Every new reef sighted or vein discovered was the signal for launching a new company—not now in Natal only, but also in London, to which the gold-fever began to spread (but was checked again by the De Kaap reverses).

Some fifteen Natalians formed a syndicate to 'exploit' this country on their own account. Some were storekeepers in the colony, some wagon-traders, and some merely waiters on fortune. Only eleven of them had any money, and they supplied the wherewithal for the other four, who were sent up to prospect and dig. After six months of fruitless toil, the money was all done, and word was sent to the four that no more aid could be sent to them. They were 'down on their luck,' when as they returned to camp on what was intended to be their last evening there, one Edwin Bray savagely dug his pick into the rock as they walked gloomily along. But with one swing which he made came a turn in the fortunes of the band, and of the land, for he knocked off a bit of quartz so richly veined with gold as to betoken the existence of something superexcellent in the way of a 'reef.' All now turned on the rock with passionate eagerness, and in a very short time pegged out what was destined to be known as 'Bray's Golden Hole.'

But the syndicate were by this time pretty well cleaned out, and capital was needed to work the reef, and provide machinery, &c. So a small company was formed in Natal under the name of the Sheba Reef Gold-mining Company, divided into 15,000 shares of £1 each, the capital of £15,000 being equitably allotted among the fifteen members of the syndicate. Upon these shares they raised enough money on loan to pay for the crushing of 200 tons of quartz, which yielded eight ounces of gold to the ton, and at once provided them with working capital. Within a very few months the mine yielded 10,000 ounces of gold, and the original shares of £1 each ran up by leaps and bounds until they were eagerly competed for at £100 each. Within a year, the small share-capital (£15,000) of the original syndicate was worth in the market a million and a half sterling. This wonderful success led to the floating of a vast number of hopeless or bogus enterprises, and worthless properties were landed on the shoulders of the British public at fabulous prices. Yet, surrounded as it was by a crowd of fraudulent imitators, the great Sheba Mine has continued as one of the most wonderfully productive mines in South Africa. Millions have been lost in swindling and impossible undertakings in De Kaap, but the Sheba Mountain, in which was Bray's Golden Hole, has really proved a mountain of gold.

The De Kaap gold-field had sunk again under a cloud of suspicion, by reason of the company-swindling and share-gambling which followed upon the Sheba success, when another startling incident gave a fresh impetus to the golden madness.

Among the settlers in the Transvaal in the later seventies were two brothers called Struben, who had had some experience, though not much success, with the gold-seekers at Lydenburg, and who took up in 1884 the farm of Sterkfontein in the Witwatersrandt district. While attending to the farm they kept their eyes open for gold, and one day one of the brothers came upon gold-bearing conglomerates, which they followed up until they struck the famous 'Confidence Reef.' This remarkable reef at one time yielded as much as a thousand ounces of gold and silver to the ton of ore, and then suddenly gave out, being in reality not a 'reef' but a 'shoot.' There were other prospectors in the district, but none had struck it so rich as the Strubens, who purchased the adjacent farm to their own, and set up a battery to crush quartz, both for themselves and for the other gold-hunters. The farms were worth little in those days, being only suitable for grazing; but when prospectors and company promoters began to appear, first by units, then by tens, and then by hundreds, the Boers put up their prices, and speedily

Prospecting for Gold.

realised for their holdings ten and twenty times what they would have thought fabulous a year or two previously. And it was on one of these farms that the city of Johannesburg was destined to arise as if under a magician's wand, from a collection of huts, in eight years, to a city covering an area three miles by one and a half, with suburbs stretching many miles beyond, with handsome streets and luxurious houses, in the very heart of the desert.

It was one Sunday evening in 1886 that the great 'find' was made which laid the base of the prosperity of the Johannesburg-to-be. A farm-servant of the brothers Struben went over to visit a friend at a neighbouring farm, and as he trekked homeward in the evening, knocked off a bit of rock, the appearance of which led him to take it home to his employer. It corresponded with what Struben had himself found in another part, and following up both leads, revealed what became famous as the Main Reef, which was traced for miles east and west.

A lot of the 'conglomerate' was sent on to Kimberley to be analysed, and a thoughtful observer of the analysis there came to the conclusion that there must be more good stuff where that came from. So he mounted his horse and rode over to Barberton, where he caught a 'coach' which dropped him on the Rand, as it is now called. There he quietly acquired the Langlaagte farm for a few thousands, which the people on the spot thought was sheer madness on his part. But his name was J. B. Robinson, and he is now known in the 'Kaffir Circus' and elsewhere as one of the 'Gold Kings' of Africa. He gradually purchased other farms, and in a year or two floated the well-known Langlaagte Company with a capital of £450,000, to acquire what had cost him in all about £20,000. In five years this company turned out gold to the value of a million, and paid dividends to the amount of £330,000. The Robinson Company, formed a little later to acquire and work some other lots, in five years produced gold to the value of one and a half million, and paid to its shareholders some £570,000 in dividends. With these discoveries and successful enterprises the name and fame of 'the Rand' were established, and for years the district became the happy hunting-ground of the financiers and company promoters. The Rand, or Witwatersrandt, is the topmost plateau of the High Veldt of the Transvaal, at the watershed of the Limpopo and the Vaal; and on the summit of the plateau is the gold-city of Johannesburg, some five thousand seven hundred feet above the sea.

Soon the principal feature in Johannesburg was the Stock Exchange, and the main occupation of the inhabitants was the buying and selling of shares in mining companies, many of them bogus, at fabulous prices. The inevitable reaction came, until once resplendent 'brokers' could hardly raise the price of a 'drink;' though, to be sure, drinks and everything else cost a small fortune. To-day the city is the centre of a great mining industry, and the roar of the 'stamps' is heard all round it, night and day. From a haunt of gamblers and 'wild-catters,' it has grown into a comparatively sedate town of industry, commerce, and finance, and the gold-fever which maddened its populace has been transferred (not wholly, perhaps) to London and Paris.

The Stock Exchange of Johannesburg sprang into existence in 1887, and before the end of that year some sixty-eight mining companies were on its list, with an aggregate nominal capital of £3,000,000. During the 1895 'boom' in the market for mining shares in London and Paris, the market value of the shares of the group of South African companies was in the aggregate over £300,000,000! It is true that these are not all gold-mining shares, but the great majority are of companies either for or in connection with gold-mining. In 1887 the Transvaal produced only about 25,000 ounces of gold; in 1894 the output was 2,024,159 ounces; in 1895 it was 2,277,633 ounces.

Just before the Californian discoveries—namely, in 1849, the world's annual output of gold was only about £6,000,000. Then came the American and Australian booms, raising the quantity produced in 1853 to the value of £30,000,000. After 1853 there was a gradual decline to less than £20,000,000 in 1883. This was the lowest period, and then the De Kaap and other discoveries in Africa began to raise the total slowly again. Between 1883 and 1887 the El Callao mine in South America and the Mount Morgan in Australia helped greatly to enlarge the output, and then in 1807 the 'Randt' began to yield of its riches. The following are the estimates of a mining-expert of the world's gold production during 1890, £23,700,000; 1891, £26,130,000; 1892, £29,260,000; 1893, £31,110,000; 1894, £36,000,000; 1895, £40,000,000.

As to the future of the South African sources of supply, it is estimated by Messrs Hatch and Chalmers, mining engineers, who have published an exhaustive work on the subject, that before the end of the present century the Witwatersrandt mines alone will be yielding gold to the value of £20,000,000 annually; that early next century they will turn out £26,000,000 annually; and that the known resources of the district are equal to a total production within the next half century of £700,000,000, of which, probably, £200,000,000 will be clear profit over the cost of mining.

These estimates are considered excessive by some authorities; nevertheless it is to be remembered that the productivity of deep level mining has not yet been properly tested, that even the Transvaal itself has not yet been thoroughly exploited, and that there is every reason to believe that Matabeleland and Mashonaland are also rich in gold. But we have not to look to Africa alone. In Australia, besides the regular sources of supply which are being industriously developed, new deposits are being opened up in Western Australia at such a rate that some people predict that the 'Cinderella of the Colonies' will soon become the richest, or one of the richest, members of the family.

The following shows the contributions towards the world's gold supply on the basis of 1894:

United States	£7,950,000
Australasia	8,352,000
South Africa	8,054,000
British Columbia and South America	2,000,000
Russia	4,827,000
Other Countries	4,807,000
	£35,990,000

JOHANNESBURG—THE GOLDEN.

The railway journey from Capetown to Johannesburg of about three days is through a seemingly endless sandy country, with range succeeding range of distant mountains, all alike, and strikes a greater sense of vastness and desolation than an expanse of naked ocean itself. First and second class have sleeping accommodation, the third being kept for blacks and the lowest class Dutch. Well, we reach Johannesburg, which has not even yet, with all its wealth, a covered-in railway station; whilst by way of contrast in the progress of the place, just across the road is a huge club, with tennis, cricket, football, and cycling grounds, gymnasium, military band, halls for dancing, operas, and oratorios, &c., which will bear comparison with any you please. Its members are millionaires and clerks, lodgers and their lodging-house keepers, all equal there; for we have left behind caste, cliques, and cathedral cities, and are cosmopolitan, or, in a word, colonial. An institution like this gives us the state of society there in a nutshell, for, as wages are very high, any one in anything like lucrative employment can belong to it; and the grades in society are determined by money, and money only.

Johannesburg, the London of South Africa, which was a barren veldt previous to 1886, is now the centre of some one hundred thousand inhabitants, and increasing about as fast as bricks and mortar can be obtained. It is situated directly on top of the gold, and on looking down from the high ground above, it looks to an English eye like a huge, long-drawn-out mass of tin sheds, with its painted iron mine-chimneys running in a straight line all along the quartz gold-reef as far as you can see in either direction. The largest or main reef runs for thirty miles uninterruptedly, gold-bearing and honeycombed with mines throughout. This, even were it alone, could speak for the stability and continued prosperity of the Transvaal gold trade. In a mail-steamer arriving from the Cape there is sometimes as much as between £300,000 and £400,000 worth of gold, and the newspapers show that usually about £100,000 worth is consigned by each mail-boat.

As we enter the town we find fine and well-planned streets, crossed at places with deep gutters—gullies rather —to carry off the water, which is often in the heavy summer rains deeper than your knees. Crossing these at last trot, the driver never drawing rein, the novice is shot about, in his white-covered two-wheeled cab with its large springs, like a pea in a bladder. Indeed, one marvels at the daintily dressed *habitué* of the place being swung through similarly, quite unconcerned, and without rumpling a frill. We pass fine public buildings, very high houses and shops—somewhat jerry-built, it is true—but now being added to, or replaced by larger and more solid buildings. Indeed, bricks cannot be made fast enough for the demand, both there and in some of the outlying Transvaal towns where the 'gold boom' is on. There are lofty and handsome shops, with most costly contents, which can vie with London or Paris.

Let us watch from the high-raised stoep outside the Post-office, looking down over the huge market-square. What strikes us first are the two-wheeled two-horse cabs with white hoods, recklessly driven by Malays in the inseparable red fez, and these with the fast-trotting mule or horse wagons show the pace at which business or pleasure is followed. As a contrast comes the lumbering ox-wagon with ten or twelve span of oxen, a little Kaffir boy dragging and directing the leading couple by a thong round the horns, and the unamiable Dutch farmer revolving around, swearing, and using his fifteen-foot whip to keep the concern in motion at all. Then passes a body of some two hundred prisoners, Kaffirs, and a few whites leading, marched in fours by some dozen white-helmeted police and four or five mounted men, all paraded through the main streets, innocent and guilty alike, to the court-house, and many escaping *en route* as occasion offers. Well-dressed English men of business, and professional men, women in handsome and dainty costumes, hustle Jews of all degrees of wealth; carelessly dressed miners, and chaps in rags come in from prospecting or up-country, with the Dutchman everywhere in his greasy soft felt and blue tattered puggaree, Chinese shopkeepers, Italians, Poles, Germans; whilst outside in the roadways flows a continual stream of Kaffirs in hats and cast-off clothing of every sort imagination can picture, who are not allowed by law to walk upon the pavement.

GOLD-FIELDS OF COOLGARDIE.

It was at one time generally believed that the unexplored regions of the vast Eastern Division of Western Australia consisted merely of sandy desert or arid plains, producing at most scrub and spinifex or 'poison plants.' In recent years, however, a faith that the interior would prove rich in various mineral resources began to dawn, and rose in proportion as each report of a new 'find' was made to the government. But only a few ventured to cherish a hope that tracts of fertile country were lying beyond their ken, awaiting the advent of the explorer whose verdict upon the nature of the soil, or possibilities of obtaining water, would result in settlement, and prosperity, and civilisation.

By the opening up of the country surrounding Coolgardie—situated at a distance of three hundred and sixty-eight miles inland from Fremantle, the port of Perth—it has been proved that not only thousands of square miles of auriferous country are contained in these once despised 'back blocks,' but also large areas of rich pasturage and forest-lands.

At Coolgardie the country is undulating; and in the distance Mount Burgess makes a bold and striking feature in the landscape, isolated from the neighbouring low hills. A few miles to the south lies the vigorous little town, surrounded by a halo of tents. It is situated thirty-one degrees south, one hundred and twenty-one degrees east; the climate is therefore temperate, though very hot during the dry season. It has been judiciously laid out, and promises to be one of the prettiest inland towns in the colony. In the principal street all is bustle and activity: teams arriving from Southern Cross; camels unloading or being driven out by picturesque Afghans; diggers and prospectors setting out for distant 'rushes;' black piccaninnies rolling in the dust, or playing with their faithful kangaroo dogs—their dusky parents lolling near with characteristic indolence—and men of every nation and colour under heaven combine to give the scene a character all its own. In March 1896 Coolgardie was connected by rail with Perth.

There are good stores, numerous thriving hotels; and a hospital has lately been started in charge of two trained nurses. The spiritual needs of the population are supplied by Wesleyan services and Salvation Army meetings, and other agencies. As yet the public buildings are not architecturally imposing; the principal one is a galvanised-iron shed which does duty for a post-office. When the mail arrives, the two officials, with the aid of an obliging trooper, vainly endeavour to sort the letters and newspapers quickly enough to satisfy the crowd, all eager for news from home. During the hot dry months, Coolgardie has been almost cut off from the outside world. It was found necessary to limit the traffic between it and Southern Cross, owing to the great scarcity in the 'soaks' and wells along the road. Condensers have been erected at various stations close to the salt lakes, and the water is retailed by the gallon; by this means the road can be kept open till the wet season sets in.

Prospectors are energetically exploring the country in every direction around Coolgardie, and from all sides come glowing accounts of the quality of the land, which, besides being auriferous, is undoubtedly suitable for agricultural and pastoral purposes. To the eastward lie many thousands of acres of undulating pasture-land, wooded like a park with morrell, sandalwood, wild peach, zimlet-wood, salmon-gum, and other valuable timbers. The soil is a rich red loam, which with cultivation should equal the best wheat-growing districts of Victoria. So green and abundant is the grass that it has been described as looking like an immense wheat-field before the grain has formed. Several kinds of grass are to be found: the fine kangaroo variety; a species of wild oats; and a coarse jointed grass, all of which stock eat with relish, and thrive, it is said.

A Water-supply Department has been formed by the Western Australian government, and measures are being taken to obtain supplies of artesian water, as well as to construct a system of reservoirs and dams on a large scale.

Mr Bayley's discovery of Coolgardie might serve as an apt illustration of the 'early-bird' theory. While on a prospecting expedition in September 1892, he went one auspicious morning to look after his horse before breakfast. A gleaming object lying on the ground caught his eye. It was a nugget, weighing half an ounce. By noon, he, with his mate, had picked up twenty ounces of alluvial gold. In a couple of weeks they had a store of two hundred ounces. It was on a Sunday afternoon that they struck the now world-famed Reward Claim, and in a few hours they had picked off fifty ounces. Next morning they pegged out their prospecting area. But whilst thus profitably employed, they were unpleasantly surprised by the arrival of three miners who had followed up their tracks from Southern Cross. The discoverers worked on during the day at the cap of the reef, and by such primitive methods as the 'dolly-pot,' or pestle and mortar, easily obtained three hundred ounces of the precious metal. The unwelcome visitors stole two hundred ounces of the gold, a circumstance which obliged them to report their 'find' sooner than they would otherwise have done, fearing that, if they delayed, the thieves would do so instead, and claim the reward from the government.

On condition that they would not molest his mate during his absence, Mr Bayley agreed to say nothing about their having robbed him, and set out on his long ride to Southern Cross. He took with him five hundred and fifty-four ounces of gold with which to convince the Warden that his discovery was a genuine one. The field was declared open after his interview with the authorities.

DIAMONDS.

The diamond is a natural form of crystallised carbon, highly valued as a precious stone, but of much less value than the ruby. The lustre of the diamond is peculiar to itself, and hence termed 'adamantine.' In a natural condition, however, the surface often presents a dull, lead-gray, semi-metallic lustre. The high refractive and dispersive powers of the diamond produce, when the stone is judiciously cut, a brilliancy and 'fire' unequalled by any other stone. A large proportion of the incident light is in a well-cut diamond reflected from the inner surface of the stone. The diamond, especially when coloured, is highly phosphorescent, that is to say, after exposure to brilliant illumination it emits the rays which it has absorbed, and thus becomes self-luminous in the dark. Its excessive hardness serves to distinguish the diamond from other gem-stones: any stone which readily scratches ruby and sapphire must be a diamond. Notwithstanding its hardness the diamond is brittle, and hence the absurdity of the ancient test which professed to distinguish the diamond by its withstanding a heavy blow struck by a hammer when placed on an anvil.

In recent years, highly refined researches on this subject have been made by Dumas, Stas, Roscoe, and Friedel, all tending to prove that the diamond is practically pure carbon. Chemists have generally experimented, for the sake of economy, with impure specimens, and have thus obtained on combustion a considerable amount of ash, the nature of which has not been well ascertained. It has been shown, however, that the purer the diamond the smaller is the proportion of ash left on its combustion.

The art of cutting and polishing the diamond is said to have been discovered in 1456 by Louis de Berguem of Bruges. As now practised, the stone is first, if necessary, cleaved or split, and then 'bruted' or rubbed into shape. The faces of the stone thus 'cut' are ground and polished

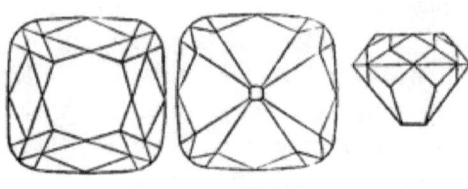

Square-cut Brilliant.

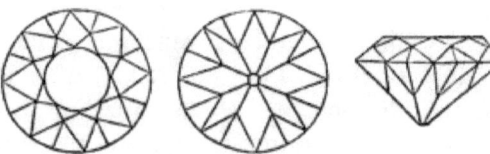

Round-cut Brilliant.

Rose-cut Diamond.

on flat metal discs, fed with diamond dust and oil, and revolving with great rapidity by steam-power. Antwerp comes first, then Amsterdam as the chief home of this industry, and the trade is chiefly in the hands of Jews; but diamond cutting and polishing are also now extensively carried on in London, Antwerp, &c. The common form of the diamond is either the *brilliant* or the *rose cut*. The brilliant resembles two truncated cones, base to base, the edge of the junction being called the *girdle*, the large plane on the top is the *table*, and the small face at the base the *culet;* the sides are covered with symmetrical facets. The rose has a flat base, with sides formed of rows of triangular facets rising as a low pyramid or hemisphere; but this form of diamond is daily becoming less fashionable, and is therefore of comparatively little value.

Although the term 'carat' is applied to diamonds as well as to gold, it does not mean the same thing. Used with regard to the metal, it expresses quality or fineness— 24-carat being pure gold; and 22-carat equal to coined gold. But applied to the diamond, carat means actual weight, and $151\frac{1}{2}$ carats are equal to one ounce troy.

India was formerly the only country which yielded diamonds in quantity, and thence were obtained all the great historical stones of antiquity. The chief diamond-producing districts are those in the Madras Presidency, on the Kistna and Godavari rivers, commonly though improperly termed the Golconda region; in the Central Provinces, including the mines of Sumbulpur; and in Bundelkhand, where the Panna mines are situated.

At present the diamond production of India is insignificant. It is notable, however, that in 1881 a fine diamond, weighing $67\frac{3}{8}$ carats, was found near Wajra Karur, in the Bellary district, Madras. The stone was cut into a brilliant weighing $24\frac{5}{8}$ carats, and is known as the 'Gordo-Norr.'

Brazil was not regarded as a diamond-yielding country until 1727, when the true nature of certain crystals found in the gold washings of the province of Minas Geraes was first detected. Diamonds occur not only in this province, but in Bahia, Goyaz, Matto Grosso, and Paraná. The geological conditions under which the mineral occurs have of late years been carefully studied by Professors Derby, Gorceix, and Chatrian. The diamonds are found in the sands and gravels of river-beds, associated with alluvial gold, specular iron ore, rutile, anatase, topaz, and tourmaline. In 1853 an extraordinary diamond was found by a negress in the river Bogagem, in Minas Geraes. It weighed $254\frac{1}{2}$ carats, and was cut into a brilliant of perfect water, weighing 125 carats. This brilliant, known as the 'Star of the South,' was sold to the Gaikwar of Baroda for £80,000.

Both the Indian and the Brazilian diamond-fields have of late years been eclipsed by the remarkable discoveries of South Africa. Although it was known in the last century that diamonds occurred in certain parts of South Africa, the fact was forgotten, and when in 1867 they were found near Hopetown, the discovery came upon the world as a surprise. A traveller named O'Reilly had rested himself at a farm in the Hopetown district, when his host, a man named Niekerk, brought him some nice-looking stones which he had got from the river. O'Reilly, when examining the pebbles, saw a diamond, which afterwards realised £500. Niekerk afterwards bought a diamond from a native for £400 which realised £10,000. The principal mines are situated in Griqualand West, but diamonds are also worked in the Orange River Free State, as at Jagersfontein. The stones were first procured from the 'river diggings' in the Vaal and Orange rivers. These sources have occasionally yielded large stones; one found in 1872 at Waldeck's Plant on the Vaal weighed $288\frac{3}{8}$ carats, and yielded a fine pale yellow brilliant, known as the 'Stewart.'

It was soon found that the diamonds of South Africa were not confined to the river gravels, and 'dry diggings' came to be established in the so-called 'pans.' The principal mines are those of Kimberley, De Beer's, Du Toit's Pan, and Bultfontein. The land here, previously

Kimberley Diamond-mine.

worth only a few pence per acre, soon rose to a fabulous price. At these localities the diamonds occur in a serpentinous breccia, filling pipes or 'chimneys,' generally regarded as volcanic ducts, which rise from unknown depths and burst through the surrounding shales. The 'blue ground,' or volcanic breccia containing fragments of various rocks cemented by a serpentinous paste, becomes altered by meteoric agents as it approaches the surface, and is converted into 'yellow earth.' At Kimberley the neighbouring schists, or 'reefs,' are associated with sheets of a basaltic rock, which are pierced by the pipes. About 2000 white men are employed in the industry, and about 4000 blacks, who earn, on an average, about £3 a week. In the year 1887 the production of the principal mines was over £4,000,000. The production for 1894 was somewhat less, while the total value of diamonds exported from 1867 to 1894 was about £70,000,000.

The great number of large stones found in the mines of South Africa, as compared with those of India and Brazil, is a striking peculiarity. In the earliest days of African mining a diamond of about 83 carats was obtained from a Boer. This stone, when cut, yielded a splendid colourless brilliant of $46\frac{1}{4}$ carats, known as the 'Star of South Africa,' or as the 'Dudley,' since it afterwards became the property of the Countess of Dudley, at a cost of £25,000. Some of the African stones are 'off coloured'—that is, of pale yellow or brown tints; but a large gem of singular purity was found at Kimberley in 1880. This is the famous 'blue-white' diamond of 150 carats, known from the name of its possessor as the 'Porter Rhodes.' At the De Beer's Mine was found, in 1889, the famous stone which was shown at the Paris Exposition. It weighed $428\frac{1}{2}$ carats in the rough, and $228\frac{1}{2}$ carats when cut. It measured one inch and seven-eighths in greatest length, and was about an inch and a half square.

Even larger than this remarkable stone is a diamond found in the Jagersfontein Mine in 1893, and named the 'Jagersfontein Excelsior.' This is now the largest and most valuable diamond in the world. It is of blue-white colour, very fine quality, and measures three inches at the thickest part. The gross weight of this unique stone was no less than $969\frac{1}{2}$ carats (or about $6\frac{1}{2}$ oz.), and the following are its recorded dimensions: Length, $2\frac{1}{2}$ inches; greatest width, 2 inches; smallest width, $1\frac{1}{2}$ inches; extreme girth in width, $5\frac{3}{8}$ inches; extreme girth in length, $6\frac{3}{4}$ inches. It is impossible to say what is the value of so phenomenal a gem. We do not know that an estimate has been even attempted; but it may easily be half a million if the cutting is successful. The diamond has, however, a black flaw in the centre. It is the property of a syndicate of London diamond merchants. The native who found it evaded the overseer, and ran to headquarters to secure the reward, which took the form of £100 in gold and a horse and cart.

Previous to this discovery, the most famous of the African diamonds was, perhaps, the 'Pam' or 'Jagersfontein' stone, not so much from its size, as because the Queen had ordered it to be sent to Osborne for her inspection with a view to purchase, when the untimely death of the Duke of Clarence put an end to the negotiations. The 'Pam' is only of 55 carats now; but it weighed 112 carats before being cut, and is a stone of remarkable purity and beauty. Its present value is computed at about twenty-five thousand pounds sterling.

The most valuable diamond in the world is (if it is a diamond) the famous 'Braganza' gem belonging to Portugal. It weighed in the rough state 1680 carats, and was valued at upwards of $5\frac{1}{2}$ millions sterling.

It has long been known that diamonds occur in Australia, but hitherto the Australian stones have been all of small size, and it is notable that these are much more difficult to cut, being harder than other diamonds. Although Victoria and South Australia have occasionally yielded diamonds, it is New South Wales that has been the principal producer. The chief diamond localities have been near Mudgee, on the Cudjegong River, and near Bingera, on the river Horton.

Borneo also yields diamonds. The stone known as the 'Matan' is said to have been found in 1787 in the Landak mines, near the west coast of Borneo. It is described as being an egg-shaped stone, indented on one side, and weighing, in its uncut state, 367 carats. Great doubt, however, exists as to the genuineness of this stone, and the Dutch experts who examined it a few years ago pronounced it to be simply rock-crystal. Among other diamond localities may be mentioned the Ural Mountains and several of the United States. The largest diamond yet recorded from North America was found at Manchester, Chesterfield county, Virginia. It weighed $23\frac{3}{4}$ carats, and yielded, when cut, a brilliant known as the 'Ou-i-nur,' which weighed, however, only $11\frac{3}{4}$ carats.

A few special diamonds, from their exceptional size or from the circumstances of their history, deserve notice. Of all the great diamonds, the 'Koh-i-nur' is perhaps the most interesting. While tradition carries it back to legendary times, it is known from history that the Sultan Ala-ed-din in 1304 acquired this gem on the defeat of the Rajah of Malwa, whose family had possessed it for many generations. In 1526 it passed by conquest to Humaiun, the son of Sultan Baber. When Aurungzebe subsequently possessed this stone, he used it as one of the eyes of the peacock adorning his famous peacock throne. On the conquest of Mohammed Shah by Nadir Shah in 1739, the great diamond was not found among the Delhi treasures, but learning that Mohammed carried it concealed in his turban, Nadir, on the grand ceremony of reinstating the Mogul emperor on the throne at the conclusion of peace, offered to exchange turbans, in token of reconciliation, and by this ruse obtained possession of the gem. It was when Nadir first saw the diamond on unfolding the turban, that he exclaimed 'Koh-i-nur,' or 'Mountain of Light,' the name by which the gem has ever since been known. At Nadir's death it passed to his unfortunate son, Shah Rokh, by whom it was ultimately given to Ahmed Shah, the founder of the Durani Afghan empire. By Ahmed it was bequeathed to his son, Taimur Shah; and from his descendants it passed, after a series of romantic incidents, to Runjit-Singh. On the death of Runjit, in 1839, the diamond was preserved in the treasury of Lahore, and on the annexation of the Punjab by the British in 1849, when the property of the state was confiscated to the East India Company, it was stipulated that the Koh-i-nur should be presented to the Queen of England. It was consequently taken in charge by Lord Dalhousie, who sent it to England in 1850. After the Great Exhibition of 1851, where it had been exhibited, it was injudiciously re-cut in London by Voorsanger, a skilful workman from Messrs Coster's factory at Amsterdam. The re-cutting occupied 38 days of 12 hours each, and the weight of the stone was reduced from $186\frac{1}{16}$ to $106\frac{1}{16}$ carats. The form is that of a shallow brilliant, too thin to display much fire. According to Lady Burton, it is believed to bring ill-luck to its possessor.

The 'Nizam' is the name of a stone said to have been found in the once famous diamond-mines of Golconda. Sir William Hunter, however, gives us to understand that there were really no diamond-mines at Golconda, and that the place won its name by cutting the stones found on the eastern borders of the Nizam's territory, and on a ridge of sandstone running down to the rivers Kistna and Godavery, in the Madras Presidency. However that may have been, both regions are now unproductive of valuable stones. The 'Nizam' diamond is said to weigh 340 carats, and to be worth £200,000; but we are unable to verify the figures.

The 'Great Table' is another Indian diamond, the present whereabouts of which is not known. It is said to weigh $242\frac{1}{2}$ carats, and that 500,000 rupees (or at par, £50,000) was once refused for it. The 'Great Table' is sometimes known as 'Tavernier's' diamond. It was the first blue diamond ever seen in Europe, and was brought, in 1642, from India by Tavernier. It was sold to Louis XIV. in 1668, and was described then as of a beautiful violet colour; but it was flat and badly cut. At what date it was re-cut we know not, but, as possessed by Louis Le Grand, it weighed only $67\frac{1}{2}$ carats. It was seized during the Revolution, and was placed in the Garde Meuble; but it disappeared, and has not been traced since. Some fifty years later, Mr Henry Hope purchased a blue diamond weighing some $44\frac{1}{2}$ carats (now known as the 'Hope' diamond), which it was conjectured may have been part of the 'Great Table.' It is preserved in the Green Vaults, Dresden, and is regarded as one of the most superb coloured diamonds known.

Another famous Indian diamond is the 'Great Mogul,' which appears to have been found about 1650, in the Kollur mine, on the Kistna. It was seen by the French jeweller Tavernier at the court of Aurungzebe in 1665, and is described as a round white rose-cut stone of 280 carats. Its subsequent history is unknown, and it is probable that at the sacking of Delhi by Nadir Shah in 1739 it was stolen and broken up. Some authorities have sought to identify the Great Mogul with the Koh-i-nur, and others with the Orloff.

The 'Orloff' is an Indian stone which was purchased at

Some of the Principal Diamonds of the World:
a, Great Mogul; b, Star of the South; c, Koh-i-nur; d, Regent; e, Orloff.
All actual size.

Amsterdam in 1776 by Prince Orloff for Catharine II. of Russia. The stone at one time formed the eye of an idol in a temple in the island of Seringham, in Mysore, whence it is said to have been stolen by a French soldier, who sold it to an English trader for £2000. The Englishman brought it home, and sold it for £12,000 to a Jew, who passed it on at a profit to an Armenian merchant. From the Armenian it was acquired, either by Catharine of Russia, or, for her, by one of her admirers, for £90,000 and a pension. It is now valued at £100,000. It weighs 193 carats, is about the size of a pigeon's egg, and is mounted in the imperial sceptre of the Czar.

Other famous stones are: The 'Austrian Yellow,' belonging to the crown of Austria, weighing $76\frac{1}{2}$ carats, and valued at £50,000; the 'Cumberland,' belonging to the crown of Hanover, weighing 32 carats, and worth at least £10,000; the 'English Dresden,' belonging to the Gaikwár of Baroda, weighing $76\frac{1}{2}$ carats, and valued at £40,000; the 'Nassak'—which the Marquis of Westminster wore on the hilt of his sword at the birthday ceremonial immediately after the Queen's accession—which weighs $78\frac{1}{2}$ carats, and is valued at £30,000.

The 'Regent' is a famous diamond preserved among the national jewels in Paris. It was found in 1701, at the Parteal mines, on the Kistna, by a slave, who escaped with it to the coast, where he sold it to an English skipper, by whom he was afterwards treacherously killed. Thomas Pitt, grandfather of the first Earl of Chatham, at that time governor of Fort St George, purchased the stone, and had it re-cut in London, whence it is often known as the 'Pitt.' Its original weight was 410 carats, but it was reduced in cutting to $136\frac{3}{4}$; the result, however, was a brilliant of fine water and excellent proportions. Pitt sold it in 1717, through the financier John Law, to the Duke of Orleans, then Regent of France during the minority of

Louis XV. The price paid was £135,000, and its value has since been estimated at £480,000. The stone is now among the French jewels in the Museum of Paris.

The large 'Sancy' is an historical diamond, about which many contradictory stories have been told. It appears that the Sancy was an Indian stone, purchased about 1570 by M. de Sancy, French ambassador at Constantinople. It passed temporarily into the possession of Henry III. and Henry IV. of France, and was eventually sold by Sancy to Queen Elizabeth of England. By James II. it was disposed of to Louis XIV., about 1695, for £25,000. At the beginning of the 19th century it passed to the Demidoff family in Russia, and by them it was sold in 1865 to Sir Jamsetjee Jeejeebhoy. In 1889 it was again in the market, the price asked being £20,000.

The Russian diamond, 'Moon of Mountains,' is set in the imperial sceptre, weighs 120 carats, and is valued at 450,000 roubles, or, say, about £75,000. The 'Mountain of Splendour,' belonging to the Shah of Persia, weighs 135 carats, and is valued at £145,000. In the Persian regalia there is said to be another diamond, called the 'Abbas Mirza,' weighing 130 carats, and worth £90,000.

THE HON. CECIL J. RHODES, THE DIAMOND KING.

We get a good insight into the character of Mr Rhodes from all his utterances and public acts; and an anecdote about him when busy with the work that made him famous as the 'Diamond King,' the amalgamation of the diamond-mines, shows up the man. He was looking at a map of Africa hung in the office of a Kimberley merchant. After looking at it closely for some time, he placed his hand over a large part of Southern and Central Africa, right across the continent, and turning to a friend at his side, said, 'There, all that British! That is my dream.' 'I give you ten years,' said his friend. When he was in power at the Cape, and the times were ripe, his dream was realised, and the shield of the great White Queen was thrown over North and South Zambesia, and railway and telegraphic communication was being pushed on towards the equator.

The Right Hon. Cecil John Rhodes is the fourth son of a clergyman, of Bishop Stortford, where he was born in 1853. He was educated at the local school, but his health being far from good, he was sent to Natal to join his elder brother, a planter there. Both brothers made for Kimberley at the first diamond rush, Cecil going into partnership as a diamond digger with Mr C. D. Rudd, who had also gone out to South Africa for his health. While at Kimberley, young Rhodes read sufficiently to enable him to pass at Oxford. His crowning achievement of the union of the De Beers Company and the Kimberley Central Company was not the work of a day, but it was accomplished largely through Mr Rhodes's financial skill, and became known as the De Beers Consolidated Mines, of which he was elected chairman and one of the life governors. The capital valuation of the company now stands at about twenty-five millions. Regular dividends of twenty-five per cent. have been paid for some years. It was natural that an influential man like Mr Rhodes should be sent to the Cape Parliament, and in 1889 he rose to be a member of the Cabinet. Another successful attempt at company promoting was his association with Mr Rudd in the Transvaal gold-fields. At first their mines on the Witwatersrandt did not turn out well; but it is long since they began to pay enormously, the net profits of 1894 being over two millions, while the market value of the concern is ten millions sterling.

Several gold prospectors had dealings with and concessions from Lobengula, in Matabeleland, before Mr Rudd and Mr Rhodes joined forces in 1888 and secured mineral concessions covering the whole of his kingdom. Then came the launching of the Chartered Company, incorporated in October 1889, with a capital of one million, which has since been raised to two and a half millions. Then Mashonaland was prospected, and forts built and roads were made, and the telegraph was carried on to Salisbury, giving connection with the Cape. When it was found that the settlers could not live in peace with Lobengula, a force under Dr Jameson, the administrator, broke the power of the Matabele in the autumn of 1893. The only serious affair was the deaths of forty-nine men of Wilson's column. Since that time the country has been slowly settled, and the railway is being pushed on to Buluwayo. Mr Rhodes has interested himself also in pushing on the telegraph system towards the Great Central African lakes, by way of Zumbo, in the Central African Protectorate, under the capable rule of Sir H. H. Johnston. Matabeleland is an excellent pastoral country, and if a sufficient number of agricultural emigrants could be got to remain and develop the territory, its future would be secured. Unfortunately, this class of emigrant has hitherto been lacking in South Africa—the gold and diamond fields have been too tempting—but in time, doubtless, the slow and sure sort of emigrant will find it to his interest to develop the land.

The residence of Mr Rhodes is at Groote Schnur, Rondebosch, near Cape Town. In the twelve hundred acres which surround the house there are charming views, and a natural Zoo, upon which he is said to have spent at least one hundred thousand pounds. He has thrown this place open to pleasure-seekers from the Cape for all time coming. He enjoys riding over his estate, and watching the visitors enjoying themselves. Lord Salisbury once termed him a 'remarkable man.' This is well borne out by all who have come in contact with him. 'He presents,' says the *African Review*, 'a character that is well worthy of analysis—that is a curious compound of generosity and almost repellent cynicism, of disinterestedness and ambition, of large aims that are dependent on things that are essentially trivial; the keen, hard-tempered character of a self-made man who has carved a career out of Kimberley finance and Cape Colonial politics. . . . Of giant force of mind and will, with practised judgment that nearly amounts to intuitive perception, with a grasp of cause and effect that is founded upon a microscopic observation of the laws of nature, he is decidedly a big man. He is a rarely accurate critic of his fellow-mortals.'

Dr Jameson prophesied, when in this country in 1895, that the annexation and occupation of Matabeleland and Mashonaland meant more than mere annexation of territory, but would lead to a commercial union, amalgamation, or federation of South African states. In Rhodesia, a country nearly as large as Europe, white men and women could live, and white children could be reared in health and vigour. Gold was to be found there, and coal and iron. The country has been settled since the power of Lobengula was broken, and the road and railway are doing their beneficent work. The revenue for 1894 nearly balanced the expenditure.

When Mashonaland and Matabeleland needed the railway, Mr Rhodes was still the key of the position. 'Krüger will not let us take the Kimberley line into his country? Very well,' in effect said Mr Rhodes, 'we will take it round him, and beyond, on the way to the Transvaal of the Zambesi.' And so the matter was arranged between the Imperial and Colonial government and the Chartered Company. So much land was to be given for taking the line to Vryburg, so much to Mafeking, in connection with the main trunk line from the Cape.

Dr Jameson's raid into Transvaal territory, early in 1896, ostensibly taken for the purpose of helping the people of Johannesburg, who complained of their treatment by the Boer government, and the complications which ensued, led to the resignation of Mr Rhodes as a member of the Cape government, when he turned his attention to the development of Rhodesia, the new and promising territory, which has been so named after him.

African Village.

CHAPTER VI.

BIG GUNS, SMALL-ARMS, AND AMMUNITION.

Woolwich Arsenal—Enfield Small-arms Factory—Lord Armstrong and the Elswick Works—Testing Guns at Shoeburyness—Hiram S. Maxim and the Maxim Machine Gun—The Colt Automatic Gun—Ironclads—Submarine Boats.

WOOLWICH ARSENAL.

SINCE early days, Woolwich has been an important centre for warships and war-material. Here ships were built and launched when England first began to have a navy of specially constructed men-of-war, for Henry VIII. established the Woolwich dockyard, and also appointed Commissioners of the navy, and formed the Navy Office. Some of the earliest three-deckers, or, as we may almost call them, five-deckers, were built at this dockyard; and of these the most famous was the *Great Harry*, so named after the king, which was launched here in 1514. For the period, the ship was a large one, being of a thousand tons burden; though we should not think much of her size now, when we have ironclads of over eleven thousand tons. There are models of her in the Greenwich Naval Museum, which is not far from Woolwich; and a curious lofty wooden castle she is, rising far up above the water-line, and offering a fair target, if the cannon of those days had any accuracy.

On June 3, 1559, Queen Elizabeth came down to Woolwich to witness the launch of a large ship called after her name. In 1637 a ship half as large again as the *Great Harry* was launched at Woolwich. She was the marvel of her days, and though named the *Royal Sovereign*, was more often called the *Golden Devil*, from the amount of mischief she wrought in the Dutch fleet. Her guns were probably of small size; but she carried enough of them on her three

The *Great Harry*.

flush-decks, her forecastle, her half-deck, her quarter-deck, and in her round-house; for in her lower tier were sixty ports; in the middle, thirty; in the third, twenty-six; in her forecastle were twelve; in her half-deck were fourteen. She was decorated in the emblematical style of the time with gilding and carvings; and these designs were the work of one Thomas Haywood, an actor, who has left us an account of the ship which he adorned, in a quarto volume published the same year in which she was launched. We can imagine what she looked like, with her lofty forecastle and poop, the latter provided with five lanterns, one of which, we are told, was large enough to contain ten persons.

Old Samuel Pepys gives us many references to Woolwich in his famous *Diary*. He paid frequent visits to the dockyard on his duties as Secretary to the Admiralty, and seems to have looked after his business well. For instance, on June 3, 1662, he writes: 'Povy and Sir W. Batten and I by water to Woolwich; and there saw an experiment made of Sir R. Ford's Holland yarn, about which we have lately had so much stir; and I have much concerned myself for our rope-maker, Mr Hughes, who represented it so bad; and we found it to be very bad, and broke sooner than, upon a fair trial, five threads of that against four of Riga yarn; and also that some of it had old stuff that had been tarred, covered over with new hemp, which is such a cheat as hath not been heard of.' The next month he is looking after the hemp again, and writes: 'To Woolwich to the rope-yard, and there looked over several sorts of hemp, and did fall upon my great survey of seeing the working and experiments of the strength and charge in the dressing of every sort; and I do think have brought it to so great a certainty, as I have done the king some service in it, and do purpose to get it ready against the Duke's coming to town to present to him.' He adds pathetically: 'I see it is impossible for the king to have things done as cheap as other men.'

Of as early date probably as the dockyard, was the 'Warren,' the name by which the Arsenal was formerly called. This establishment seems to have begun as a cannon-foundry, and such, indeed, it chiefly continues to be. Moreover, in other days when the dockyard flourished, stores of ships' cannon were kept here, ready to be placed on ships as soon as commissioned. But now that the dockyard is a thing of the past, and now that the large building-slips, workshops, and ropewalk are empty, the cannon at the Arsenal are chiefly those for the royal artillery and for forts. The dockyard has been closed since 1869; its broad roads are deserted, its workshops are silent, and its large sheds are only used for stores; but the Arsenal has increased in magnitude; and the 'Warren,' in which, before the establishment of the Plumstead magazines, powder was proved ('before the principal engineers and officers of the Board of Ordnance, to which many of the nobility and gentry were often invited, and afterwards sumptuously entertained by them'), has now become an enormous establishment, covering acres of ground, and containing workshops provided with the most complicated machinery, and foundries of enormous size. It is round this Arsenal that we propose to take the reader.

Having gained admittance, the visitor is put in charge of a guide. The tapping of the great furnace is a remarkable sight. A stream of molten steel runs into a huge tank which can contain four or five tons of metal, and this tank is dragged off by some score of men to fill the various moulds. It is remarkable, also, to see a huge steam-hammer of some forty tons' force welding a mass of metal at white-heat.

The Arsenal is divided into four departments — the Laboratory, the Gun Factory, the Gun-carriage Department, and the Stores; and of these four divisions, the first two contain the chief things not to be found in very many other places.

The Gun-carriage Department has workshops both for metal and wood work, and each branch contains many subdivisions. There is nothing, however, in this department which is peculiar to the Arsenal, with the exception, of course, of the special articles which are manufactured; that is to say, forging, steam-carpentering, wheel-making, and so on, are carried out as they would be executed elsewhere. The guides always make a point of showing the wheel-shoeing pit, as it is called, in which the tyre is put on a gun-wheel. The machinery in this department is very complete, especially in the carpenters' shops, where the lathes which work automatically, and turn wheel-spokes and such things according to a given pattern, and the steam-saws for cutting dovetails for sides of boxes, and other machinery, are all constructed on highly ingenious principles. With regard to the articles constructed, the trail of a gun may be followed in all stages of its construction until it appears complete with its wheels, and ready for the gun to be placed on it. Here, too, may be seen the ingenious Moncrieff gun-carriage, by which the gun is only raised above a fortification at the moment when it is fired, the 'sighting' being done from below by an arrangement of mirrors.

The Stores, again, are remarkable only for the quantity of material stowed away ready for use. For instance, there are ten thousand complete sets of harness for guns and baggage wagons always kept in stock. But when the visitor has just walked once through these storehouses, he will probably have seen all that he cares to see there.

It is, however, when we come to the Gun Factory that the special interest of the Arsenal begins. Imagine a huge mass of steel welded—for casting would not give sufficient strength—into the form of the trunk of a large fir-tree, and you have the first stage of a gun's existence. This solid mass is to form the tube of a cannon, and the solid core has to be removed by ingenious and powerful machinery. It takes a week or two to bore the interior of some of the larger guns. Some of the machines are constructed to bore a hole which is continually enlarged by successive tools; while others actually cut out a round solid mass from the interior. The tube has also to be subjected to the process of being turned both within and without, and it is then fit for the next process, which is that of cutting the grooves within it which give the required spin to the projectile, commonly called rifling. This is a delicate and intricate process, for the utility of the gun of course depends largely on the accuracy with which the grooves are made. The actual cutting is performed by a machine which travels up the tube at the required spiral; but as the work proceeds, the man in charge carefully examines the grooves along their whole length with the aid of a candle fixed at the end of a long rod which he pushes up the tube.

But when the tube has been bored, turned, and rifled, the gun is by no means finished. The tube by itself would be far too delicate for the large charges of powder employed; and, consequently, it has to be fitted at the breech end with two or three outer cases or jackets, the outside one of which bears the trunnions on which the gun rests. At last the gun is completed; and the next thing is to subject it to a severe test by firing from it a charge of powder proportioned to its size. For this purpose, it has to be taken to Plumstead Marshes, a portion of which forms the testing-ground and powder-magazines connected with the Arsenal. Lines of railway run down to the marshes, and the gun is mounted on a truck and dragged off by a locomotive to the place appointed for its trial. It may be mentioned that lines of railway run in all directions through the Arsenal, one of narrow gauge being introduced into most of the workshops, so that the visitor has to keep a lookout lest a tiny locomotive with a train of what may almost be called toy trucks should bear down upon him as he is walking along.—But to return to the gun. When it has been finally tested, cleaned, polished, and stamped, it is coated with a particular varnish, and is fit for service.

The next most interesting place to the Gun Factory is the Laboratory, where shells and bullets are manufactured. Shells are cast rough, and then finished off in a lathe. A band of copper now usually takes the place of the copper studs which were formerly inserted to enable the shell to fit into the rifled grooves. This band is expanded by the force of the explosion when the gun is fired, and fills up the grooves, so as to give the necessary spin to the shells. Shells are charged with their interior bullets at the Laboratory; but the powder is added down at the marshes. A shell when completed has become a very expensive article, especially if it is a large one. Some of those projectiles are so heavy that the guns from which they have to be fired are provided with small cranes for lifting them up to the breech. The shells are, like the guns, beautifully finished off and varnished, and then sent off to the stores.

Perhaps the most interesting place in the Laboratory department is the Pattern Room, which is a sort of museum where shot and shells of all sorts are to be seen, from the old-fashioned chain-shot, made of round balls fastened together, to the most perfect specimens of modern shells. Here, also, are to be seen those strange weapons of modern warfare called torpedoes, amongst them the famous 'fish torpedo,' which with its complicated mechanism may be almost described as an under-water ship. It is so constructed that it finds its way unseen and unheard, with its terrible charge of dynamite, to the side of a hostile vessel.

THE ENFIELD SMALL-ARMS FACTORY.

It is at Enfield, on the river Lea, some twelve miles down the Great Eastern Railway, that small-arms are manufactured, almost entirely, as required by our army.

Enfield Factory has not, like Woolwich Arsenal, an ancient history of its own. In the days of Henry VIII. and of Elizabeth, of the Duke of York and his faithful secretary, Samuel Pepys, Woolwich was famous for the production both of ships and of guns; but the small-arms factory on the borders of Essex dates only from the early part of this century. Its site seems to have been chosen regardless of any peculiar advantages for manufacturing purposes. It is simply a collection of workshops built in the flat meadows through which run the various branches, natural and artificial, of the lazy Lea; and the nearest town, about a mile and a half distant, is quiet and remote little Waltham, chiefly known for its Abbey Church, the burial-place of King Harold, which rises in its midst.

The situation of the Enfield Factory is, however, advantageous in this way: the canals form a safe means of water transit for the gunpowder which is manufactured in the adjacent mills at Waltham, and which is required at Enfield for use in the proving of the barrels of firearms; while the far-stretching marshes provide an apparently interminable range for carrying out the necessary experiments and trials with regard to the accuracy of the weapons manufactured.

Where one of the canals has been conducted into a square-shaped basin, the older and principal buildings of the manufactory have been located. They form a quadrangle of some extent; and here, too, are situated the offices and the quarters of the executive staff, which is composed partly of civilians and partly of military officers. Behind these, on the east side of the enclosure, and on the banks of one of the canals, are rows of workmen's cottages. Near the entrance gates are situated schools for the workmen's children; and at the other end of this street, as we may call it, is a church, which is served by the clergy of the parish of Enfield. On the west side extend north and south the flat meadows or marshes which form so convenient a spot for the testing and proving of the rifles.

All sorts of personal weapons required for the arming of a soldier in the English army are made here, not only firearms, such as rifles and revolvers, but lances, swords, and bayonets, the last having now become a sort of short sword. There is also one class of weapons which occupies a sort of intermediate position between those carried by the soldier himself and those drawn by horses—that of machine guns, as they are called, which, though not carried by men on their shoulders or in their hands, are drawn about by them on small carriages. These machine guns are classed with personal arms, because they are usually employed in connection with infantry; and also because—which is a far more important reason—the ammunition required for them is similar to that used in rifles. In fact, they are in principle only a collection of infantry rifles fastened together, or, as we shall see, a single rifle barrel with machinery attached which enables it to discharge with great rapidity.

There is one more general principle which we shall do well to bear in mind before we enter the factory. It is this, that of course the manufacture of small-arms is in as much a condition of uncertainty as that of larger warlike weapons in these days. What we see now may become obsolete in a very short time, and we shall be shown specimens of firearms which formed the universal weapons of the British army only a very few years ago, but are now as much out of date for practical purposes as cross-bows. Remembering this, let us go first when we enter to one of the offices, where we shall see arranged in a rack against the wall, amongst others, specimens of the old Enfield muzzle-loader, of the same weapon converted into a breech-loader, of the Martini-Henry rifle, and of the latest pattern of all, the magazine rifle. While, stored away in some out-of-the-way corner, it is just possible we might come across a specimen of the old smooth-bore or 'Brown Bess,' which formed the weapon of certain English linesmen so late as the beginning of the Crimean War.

The Enfield workshops are of course in appearance much like other workshops. There are the same processes of forging and casting, and the same machinery for hammering and turning and boring and drilling which we see elsewhere.

A rifle, as every one knows, consists of three portions—the wooden stock, the barrel, and the lock. The stock is usually made of walnut wood, and is manufactured in what we should perhaps describe as a carpenter's shop. Formerly, the stock of a rifle was formed out of one long piece of timber; but now the complicated machinery of the breech and lock cannot be contained in a hollow in the wood, as was formerly the case, but has to be enclosed in a steel case, to which the wooden butt and barrel support are screwed. To the rifles of the newest pattern there hangs, just below the lock, the magazine, in which are carried five or, in some cases, ten cartridges, which spring up into place in turn, ready to be discharged. In short, the rifle has become, as regards its rapidity of action, something similar to a revolver pistol. We shall find that a lock has in its manufacture to pass through an almost infinite number of processes, each part having to be forged or beaten out till the whole can be fitted together.

Let us pass on to the barrel-making shop. Rifle barrels are made from a solid round bar of steel, which is at first considerably shorter and stouter than the finished barrel will be. This steel bar is heated red-hot, and is passed between several pairs of rollers, which convert it outwardly into the required form. It has, however, afterwards to be bored and then rifled—that is, furnished with the spiral

K

grooves within, which gives the bullet the necessary spin. Of course the barrel is by far the most important portion of a firearm, and the barrels of rifles are, at Enfield, tested and proved in the most ingenious and searching manner. The first proof takes place after the barrel has been bored, but before it is rifled. The barrels are loaded with cartridges of considerably greater weight both in powder and bullet than those which will be used in them when they are ready for service, and are enclosed in a sort of strong box which has one side open. They are then discharged through the open side into a heap of sand, and examined; but it is a rare event to find a barrel that has not been able to bear this test. The second proof, which takes place after the rifling, is of a similar character.

But these proofs are only to test the strength of a barrel; the test of its accuracy is a much more delicate operation. Of course the machinery by which it is bored and rifled works with the most admirable precision; but yet it is necessary to put this machine-work to trial. There are, amongst others, two highly ingenious methods for doing this. In the one case it is placed on a stand which is so constructed that on it the barrel can be made to revolve rapidly. The barrel is pointed towards a window, and in front of it is a fixed sight. The workman looks through it while it is revolving; and if the sight remains steady to his eye, that is a proof that the barrel may be said to be straight. But there is yet another method. The mechanism of this testing apparatus is rather difficult to describe, but is something of this fashion. The barrel is made to revolve as before; but this time there is inserted in it a spindle, on which is fixed a short arm with a point which touches very lightly the interior of the barrel. If there is any inequality, or if the barrel is not perfectly straight, this short arm is of course shaken, and when this is the case, the motion is further communicated to a long arm at the end of which is an indicator, which is looked at by the workman through a magnifying glass.

Barrel, stock, and lock being at last completed and tested, the rifle is put together; but even then it is subjected to one more trial. This is carried out on the proof-ground in the marshes, and takes the form of an actual discharge of the weapon at a target. The rifle is screwed to a fixed and firm support, and then a certain number of rounds are fired at ranges of five hundred and one thousand yards respectively. In this test the hitting of the centre

Gatling Gun on Field Carriage.

of the target, or 'bull's-eye,' is not the end in view, as it is in ordinary target practice. That sort of shooting depends of course on the steadiness with which the marksman holds the rifle. In this case, however, the fixed *rest* may be directed on any portion of the target, and the *grip* will always be the same. The only object of the test is to see whether the rifle throws the bullet at each round on or near the same spot. A marker at the butt examines the position of each shot, and the smaller the space on which they strike, the better the weapon.

We have not yet spoken of the machine guns. These weapons are, as part of the regular equipment of armies, quite modern, though the idea of binding together a quantity of barrels and then discharging them at once, or with great rapidity one after another, is not altogether novel. Sometimes, instead of a number of barrels, one only is required, and the cartridges are discharged from short barrels or chambers which are brought in turn into position with the longer one. This is the ordinary revolver system; but modern machine guns are a great improvement on this method, and entirely dispense with

Nordenfelt-Palmcrantz Gun mounted on Ship's Bulwark.

the necessity of loading separate chambers. Machine guns have succeeded one another with extraordinary rapidity, and a gun seems only to be adopted in order to be superseded. Thus we have had during the last few years a series of these weapons bearing the names of Gatling, Gardner, Nordenfelt, and Maxim, described on a later page.

As we walk about the factory we see, besides the workmen, here and there groups of men in military uniform. These are armourer sergeants, who attend classes at which they are taught the mysterious mechanism of the breech-loaders and machine guns. In former days, Tommy Atkins could be instructed how to keep his weapon in order, lock and all; but now its complications are beyond the power of his understanding or of his fingers, perhaps of both, and he has to hand over his rifle to a more skilled superior when it is out of order. Truly, military matters, from the movement of the vast army corps of the present day down to the mechanism of the soldier's weapons, have become a highly technical matter.

LORD ARMSTRONG AND THE ELSWICK WORKS.

Sir W. G. Armstrong, the chairman and founder of this great firm of warship builders and makers of big guns at Elswick, Newcastle-on-Tyne, is the son of a Cumberland yeoman, and born at Newcastle in 1810. He early showed a turn for mechanical contrivances, and delicate youth as he was, when confined to the house he was quite happy making toys of old spinning-wheels and such-like things. He would also spend hours in a joiner's shop, copying the joiner's work, and making miniature engines. He had ample opportunity in his father's house of making himself acquainted with chemistry, electricity, and mechanics. In spite of his turn for mechanics, he was articled to a solicitor, who, at the finish of his apprenticeship, made him his partner. In his leisure hours he conducted his experiments. Fishing was also a favourite pastime with him, and in 1836, while rambling through Dent Dale, he saw a stream descending from a great height and driving only one single mill. This led him to think that there might be a more economical use of this water hydraulically, with the result that he produced a hydraulic engine, which was followed by the invention of a hydraulic crane for raising

LORD ARMSTRONG.

weights at harbours and in warehouses. It was soon adopted at the Albert Dock, Liverpool, and elsewhere.

Next he invented an apparatus for extracting electricity from steam, afterwards introduced into the Polytechnic Institution, London. Napoleon III. heard of this famous machine, and sent experts to examine it. Armstrong began to receive recognition; he was elected a member of the Royal Society in 1846, and a year later, aided by some friends, he began on a small scale the Elswick Engine-works in the suburbs of Newcastle, which have grown to be the largest concern of the kind in the country. At first the enterprise chiefly consisted in the manufacture of hydraulic cranes, engines, accumulators, and bridges.

The addition of ordnance and shipping, for which Armstrong became chiefly known, came later. Previous to the year 1853, the weapon used by the infantry portion of the British army was a clumsy smooth-bore musket, which was only effective up to three hundred yards at the farthest; the usual distance at which practice was made by the soldier seldom exceeding one hundred yards. In the above-named year, an arm was brought into use, termed, from the locality of its manufacture, the Enfield rifle. This weapon being lighter, and possessing a much greater range than the old small-arm, Brown Bess, as it was called, threatened very seriously to diminish the effect of field-artillery, if not to abolish that arm entirely, as, indeed, many infantry officers were sanguine enough to predict. Nor were they without good reason for their boasting, the only field-artillery consisting of 6-pounder brass guns for horse-artillery, 9-pounder guns for field-batteries, and sometimes 12-pounder and 18-pounder guns as batteries of position—that is to say, batteries used when the general of a force meant to make any stand in a suitable position; on these occasions, the guns were taken to the requisite places, and there left. Now, all these guns were smooth-bored; and as the range of the 6 and 9 pounders was limited in practice to about one thousand yards, it was a fair enough supposition that a company of concealed riflemen with their Enfield rifles could pick off the gunners and remain themselves comparatively secure, especially as their muskets being sighted up to, and effective at, eleven hundred yards, the guns also would be a good mark to aim at, and the riflemen hard to see, even if exposed.

Such was the state of affairs when Armstrong stepped in to the rescue of the artillery, and provided the British government with the rifled cannon now in use, and about which so much has been written.

Armstrong, during the Crimean War, made an explosive apparatus for blowing up ships sunk at Sebastopol. This led him to turn his attention to improvements in ordnance. He invented a kind of breech-loading cannon, and soon had an order for several field-pieces after the same pattern. He began with guns throwing 6 lb. and 18 lb. shot and shells, and afterwards 32 lb. shells; and the results at the time were deemed almost incredible. He had both reduced the weight of the gun by one-half, reduced the charge of powder, and his gun sent the shell about three times farther. His success led to his offering to government all his past inventions, and any that he might in the future discover. A post was created for him, that of Chief Engineer of Rifled Ordnance for seven years provisionally.

The founder of this great firm was knighted by the Queen in 1858, and made C.B. In 1887 he was raised to the peerage as Baron Armstrong of Cragside. His mansion and estate of Cragside is at Rothbury, and it is fitted up with the electric light and every convenience of wealth and taste. Armstrong's peculiar partnership between government and the Elswick Works was brought to a close in 1863, since which time the progress of the firm has been continuous. In 1882 an amalgamation took place between the Elswick Works and the firm of Charles Mitchell & Co., shipbuilders at Low Walker. Dr Mitchell, who was a native of Aberdeen, and a munificent donor to Newcastle and Aberdeen, was one of the directors of Armstrong, Mitchell, & Co. till his death in 1895.

This firm are now the leading warship builders in the world. Krupp's works at Essen (described in the earlier part of this book) are the only parallel to them in Europe. The engineering works, begun, as we have seen, in 1847, now occupy about nine acres; the ordnance works, founded ten years later, occupy about forty acres; while about five thousand men are employed. The shipbuilding yards are at Low Walker, nearer the sea. The hydraulic machinery for the Tower Bridge and the Manchester Ship Canal were both produced by this great firm.

Some years ago one of his biographers wrote: 'He entertains the great institutes of England when they visit his native city on royal lines, in regal splendour. His works at Elswick enjoy all modern improvements. His home at Jesmond is the abode of art, literature, and luxury. When his health complained under its heavy load, he cultivated agriculture, botany, and forestry for recreation; bought an estate at Rothbury, where the kindly invigorating air had healed him in days gone by; converted the barren hills into an earthly paradise; lighted his Cragside mansion with Swan's lamp and his own hydraulic power; applied water-power to his conservatory, that his plants might secure the sun. But amid all the luxuries which surround him, his life is as simple as nature; and now, at the ripe age of seventy-three, he maintains the freshness and elasticity of youth. He was wont to run like a deer along the moors of Allenheads to examine the target fired at by the original Armstrong gun.'

Lord Armstrong has been honoured both at home and

abroad, and has done much for the amenity of Newcastle; and Jesmond Dene, part of his Jesmond estate, was thrown open to the public by the Prince of Wales while his guest at Cragside. The high-level bridge, giving easy access to the park for the town, cost £20,000. Other benefactions have been £12,500 towards a museum; a hall for the literary society, a mechanics' institute, schools at Elswick, &c.

A recent purchase was at Bamborough, the ancient capital of the Northumbrian kings, where, nearer our own time, Grace Darling was born and died. Already great improvements are in progress there in the shape of workmen's houses; and the parish church is being restored. Bamborough Castle, which is also included in the purchase, is an imposing mass of masonry, standing on a pile of columnar basalt, which is mentioned early in history; there was a castle here as early as the fifth century. By the will of Lord Crewe it had been devoted as far back as 1721 to charitable purposes.

In the autumn of 1893, Lord Armstrong told the Elswick shareholders that he believed the time was coming when armoured ships would be as obsolete as mail-clad men. 'Do what we will,' he said, 'I believe that the means of attack will always overtake the means of defence, and that sooner or later armour will be abandoned.' His reason for this statement was the use of high explosives and quick-firing guns. In the future, light vessels of great speed, armed with quick-firing guns, are likely to be the order of the day. The life of a battleship, he also said, was far too valuable to be staked on the use of its ram; special ships should therefore be built for ramming. On another occasion he discussed the improvements in the manufacture of cordite which had made it possible to secure enormous power even with moderate-sized guns. With a 6-inch gun of 45 calibre, and a 100 lb. projectile, a velocity of nearly 3000 feet per second has been reached, giving an energy of 5884 tons, as against the 5254 tons of the 8-inch gun of ten years ago. This last gun could only fire four rounds in five minutes; now we hear of ten and eighteen rounds in three minutes. As to speed, some warships built for the Argentine Republic and for Japan had reached a speed of $26\frac{1}{4}$ miles an hour, and were at the time the fastest war-vessels afloat.

At the annual meeting of shareholders in 1895, Lord Armstrong said that the war-material which they supplied for the great naval war in the East thoroughly stood the test, and the quick-firing guns of the Japanese navy had greatly helped their victory. The heavily-armed high-speed cruisers also deserve a share of the credit, and these had been built by their firm.

In connection with an official inquiry it was found that in 1896 there were 18,000 men employed in the arsenal at Elswick alone, and that 13 ironclads and cruisers, and 1400 guns were being built.

TESTING GUNS AT SHOEBURYNESS.

It is at Shoeburyness, in the county of Essex, that experiments are carried out with the guns, large and small, manufactured at Woolwich and Enfield.

Shoeburyness has become a military centre, not because of any advantages afforded by its position on the sea, but because it consists of a large tract of dreary marshes flanked to the south and east by the far-stretching Maplin sands, which are almost entirely uncovered at low-water. These sands form the attraction from a scientific point of view.

The first connection of Shoeburyness with modern military matters appears to have been made so lately as the time of the Crimean War, when the flat rough marshland was employed as a camping ground for men and horses with the view of accustoming both to the hard work which lay before them in the East. This tract of country has thus become the property of the War Department, and that administrative body soon found another use for it, in which the half-submerged sands were to bear an important part. The idea was conceived that targets might be erected on these sands, and that the projectiles which were fired at them might be recovered at low-water. Hence the first connection of Shoeburyness with the artillery of the present day. A safe range can be found across the sands to almost any distance, and these marshes have therefore become the stage on which our great guns, such as Armstrongs and Whitworths, have made, so to speak, their first *début*.

To reach Shoeburyness we take the railway which runs along the south coast of Essex and the northern bank of the Thames. As we near the mouth of the estuary we pass Southend, beloved of *trippers*, with its pier stretching out in its length of over a mile, and then cross the base of the ness itself, when we reach the sea again. On the south-eastern face of the ness we are at our journey's end, and the railway also, so far as the general public is concerned, has come to a full stop. We walk through the little town or village, and on the farther side find what we may call the original settlement of gunnery experiments, now for the most part a group of barracks and quarters such as we might find at any military station. A few differences we notice, however, for, as we pass through the barrack-yard, we observe that one building is labelled 'Lecture-room,' and other evidences there are here and there that the artillerymen who are quartered here are not altogether engaged in their ordinary duties. We shall probably not linger long at the barracks, but we shall not fail to observe that the officers' quarters and mess-room occupy an extremely pleasant position on a wooded bank above the sea, and that at high-water the waves come rippling up to the very trees themselves. Farther on are the houses appropriated to married officers, all alike situated on the pleasant sea-bank.

We see in front of us huge wooden erections standing on the edge of the shore. These are conning-towers from which, when practice is going on, a view is obtained of the direction of the shot. Beneath them are the batteries from which the guns are fired, and here go on the courses of instruction in practical artillery work, which are necessary for newly joined officers.

But we have by no means seen the most important part of Shoeburyness when we have visited the barracks and the batteries. We notice that a line of rails winds its way in and out amongst guns and storehouses, and if we have timed our visit right we shall find a little miniature train just about to start for what is called *The New Range*. Taking our places in this train we shall be carried first through the village and past the terminus of the public line, and then along a private railway which winds along amongst the corn-fields, until we reach a retired spot on the sea-shore hemmed in by lofty trees. In this private place are carried on all the experiments for which Shoeburyness is famous, and here both guns and explosives are tested to their utmost capability.

It is not altogether an unpicturesque spot at which we have arrived. Grouped together in this immediate neighbourhood are certain nice old farmhouses and other buildings which have been taken possession of by the military. The space in front would no doubt be an admirable rabbit-warren, only the whole ground is now covered by guns of various sizes, targets, shields, breastworks, and models of portions of ironclad and other vessels. Amongst these run lines of rails by which guns and materials can be moved to any part of the ground; and in places there are overhead travelling cranes by which heavy cannon may be hoisted on to or off from their carriages or into trucks, as need may require; and we again see lofty conning-towers, though target practice at a distance is not carried on here to the same extent as it is in that portion of the establishment which we first visited. The work at *The New Range* is connected rather with experiments as to the force of explosives and the penetrating power of projectiles than with accuracy of aim and the direction of the shot.

We ought first to say a few words about modern explosives. Old-fashioned gunpowder, or *black* powder as it is now usually called, is composed, as everybody knows, of saltpetre, charcoal, and sulphur mixed together in the proportion usually of seventy-five, fifteen, and ten parts respectively.

Two chief varieties of the new brown powders are now made, and are known as 'slow-burning cocoa'—from the fact that cocoa-nut fibres were first employed in the experiments—and 'Prism brown I.' The former contains about four per cent. of sulphur, and burns rather more rapidly than the latter, which contains only two per cent. Baked straw is the material now used to supplant the charcoal, as it provides a form of cellulose which may be readily reduced to a fine state of division. The shape is still the perforated hexagonal prism introduced in America.

The burning of these powders is steady and the increase of pressure gradual, attaining a maximum when the bullet is about half-way down the barrel of the gun. The damage inflicted on the firing-chamber is very slight; perhaps as slight as ever will be obtained with such large charges of powder.

Uniformity of velocity is secured by ensuring that in

the making the proportions employed shall be accurate and the mixing complete. The prisms of any given class of powder are made exactly the same in weight and composition, and in consequence, a charge composed of a given number of prisms will give in every case almost exactly the same propelling force. It is thus that fine aiming adjustments are made possible, as two consecutive bullets of the same weight may be propelled almost exactly the same distance—varying only a few yards in a range of several miles—by equal weights of powder of uniform composition.

But explosives of the present day are composed of other substances. Cordite, of which we now hear so much, is made of nitro-glycerine, gun-cotton, and mineral jelly in the proportion of fifty-seven, thirty-eight, and five parts. It is also steeped in a preparation of acetone. Gun-cotton itself is dipped in a mixture of three parts of sulphuric to one of nitric acid. The force of cordite over gunpowder may be judged from the following facts. A cartridge containing seventy grains of black powder fired in the ordinary rifle of the army will give what is called a muzzle velocity of one thousand three hundred and fifty feet a second, while thirty grains only of cordite will give a velocity of two thousand feet. In larger arms, a little less than a pound of cordite fired in a twelve-pounder gun will give more velocity than four pounds of black powder fired in the same weapon. It need hardly be said that in the experiments at Shoeburyness it is the new-fashioned explosive which is chiefly used.

Let us examine one of the guns, a breech-loader, and see what improvements have been made which may conduce to rapidity of fire. We see that in the older pattern three motions were necessary to open the breech. First the bar which is fixed across the base of the block had to be removed, then a half turn had to be given to the block to free it in its bed, and then it had to be pulled forward. Firstly, it had to be thrown back on its hinge so as to open the gun from end to end. We are shown that in later patterns the cavity or bed into which the block fits is made in the form of a cone, so that the breech-block itself can be turned back without any preliminary motion forward. In artillery work, time is everything, and any one motion of the gunner's hands and arms saved is a point gained. Now let us look at the mechanism by which the recoil or backward movement of the gun is checked at the moment of firing. The gun slides in its cradle, and its recoil is counteracted by buffers which work in oil, something in the fashion of the oil springs which we see on doors. Iron spiral springs push the gun back again into place. Another interesting piece of mechanism is the electric machinery by which the gun is fired. When the recoil has taken place, the wire, along which runs the electric current, is pushed out of place, so that it is impossible to fire the gun, even though it be loaded, until it has been again fixed in its proper position on the cradle. Truly a modern cannon is a wonderful machine, and yet it is only a development from the sort of iron gas-pipe which was used in the middle ages. Hard by is a gun which has come to grief. In experiments which are carried on at Shoeburyness, guns are charged to their full, or, as in this case, more than their full strength. There is an ugly gash running down the outer case or jacket, as it is called, of the gun, and the latter has broken, and nearly jumped out of its cradle. Nursery phraseology certainly comes in strongly in the technical slang of gunnery when we have to do with *Woolwich Infants.*

After looking at the guns we naturally go on to look at the targets at which they are fired. Targets at *The New Range* are not so much marks as specimens of armour-plates and other protections. Some of these are built up with a strength which to the uninitiated appears to be proof against any attack. Here, for instance, we find a steel plate of eighteen inches in thickness, and behind this six inches of iron, the whole backed up by huge balks of timber. But notwithstanding its depth, the enormous mass has been dented and cracked, and in places pierced. When we look at plates which are not quite so thick, we see that the shells have formed what are pretty and regular patterns, for small triangles of metal have been splintered off and turned back, so that the aperture is decorated with a circle of leaves, and resembles a rose with the centre cut out. Where the shell has entered the plate before it bursts, the pattern remains very perfect; but when it explodes as it touches the surface, some of the encircling leaves are entirely cut off.

One target is pointed out to us which represents the iron casing of the vulnerable portions of a torpedo boat, consisting of engine-room, boilers, and coal-bunkers. These compartments have been riddled again and again. Even a service-rifle bullet can penetrate one side, and a shell of the smallest size will go through both, for torpedo boats are not very heavily built.

HIRAM S. MAXIM AND THE MAXIM MACHINE GUN.

Statisticians inform us that the entire loss of life in wars between so-called civilised countries from the year 1793 down to 1877 had reached the enormous amount of four million four hundred and seventy thousand. To many persons these figures convey a sad and salutary lesson. But, leaving the sentimental part of the subject aside, all will readily unite in admiring the wonderful mechanism which makes the Maxim Machine Gun an engine of terrible destructiveness. Stanley provided himself with this formidable weapon, to be used defensively in the expedition on which he started for the relief of Emin Bey. It obtained a gold medal at the Inventions Exhibition, and has been approved of, if not actually adopted, by many governments.

Its rate of firing—770 shots a minute—is at least three times as rapid as that of any other machine gun. It has only a single barrel, which, when the shot is fired, recoils a distance of three-quarters of an inch on the other parts of the gun. This recoil sets moving the machinery which

Rifle-calibre Maxim Gun.

automatically keeps up a continuous fire at the extraordinary rate of 12 rounds a second. Each recoil of the barrel has therefore to perform the necessary functions of extracting and ejecting the empty cartridge, or bringing up the next full one and placing it in its proper position in the barrel, of cocking the hammer, and pulling the trigger. As long as the firing continues, these functions are repeated round after round in succession. The barrel is provided with a water jacket, to prevent excessive heating; and is so mounted that it can be raised or lowered or set at any angle, or turned horizontally to the left or to the right. The bore is adapted to the present size of cartridges; and the maximum range is eighteen hundred yards. The gun can therefore be made to sweep a circle upwards of a mile in radius.

Nor is the gun excessively heavy, its total weight being only one hundred and six pounds, made up thus : Tripod, fifty pounds ; pivot (on which the gun turns and by which it is attached to the tripod), sixteen pounds ; gun and firing mechanism, forty pounds. The parts can be easily detached and conveniently folded for carriage, and may be put together again so quickly that, if the belt containing the cartridges is in position, the first shot can be delivered within ten seconds. It would therefore be extremely serviceable in preventing disaster through a body of troops being surprised. Reconnoitring parties, too, would deem it prudent to pay greater deference to an enemy's lonely sentry on advanced outpost duty if the latter were provided with this new Machine Gun, instead of the ordinary rifle.

Immediately below the barrel of the gun, a box is placed, containing the belt which carries the cartridges. The belts vary in length. Those commonly used are seven feet long, and capable of holding three hundred and thirty-three cartridges ; shorter ones hold one hundred and twenty cartridges ; but the several pieces can be joined together for continuous firing. Single shots can be fired at any time whether the belt is in position or not—in the former case by pressing a button, which prevents the recoil ; in the latter, by hand-loading in the ordinary way. To start firing, one end of the belt is inserted in the gun, the trigger is pulled by the hand once, after which the movement becomes continuous and automatic as long as the supply of cartridges lasts. At each recoil of the barrel, the belt is pushed sufficiently onward to bring the next cartridge into position ; the mechanism grasps this cartridge, draws it from the belt, and passes it on to the barrel. Should a faulty or an empty cartridge find its way in, and the gun does not go off in consequence, there is of course no recoil to keep up the repeating action, and the mechanism ceases to work until the obstruction is removed.

To devise and adjust the necessary parts of the machine with such precision that each part performs its proper function at the exact moment pre-arranged for it—to do all this while the gun fires at the enormous rate of six hundred rounds a minute, must have cost an immensity of thought, of labour, and of time.

The 'Colt Automatic Gun,' a new machine gun manufactured by the Colt Firearms Company, of Hartford, Connecticut, promised in 1896 to be a rival to the Maxim, as it fired 400 shots a minute.

Hiram S. Maxim was born in the state of Maine in 1840, and in his fourteenth year was apprenticed to a carriage-builder. From his father, who had a wood-working factory and mill, he learned the use of tools and derived his inventive turn of mind. After some experience in metal-working in his uncle's works at Fitchburg, he was in turn a philosophical instrument maker, and on the staff of some ironworkers and shipbuilders. About 1877 he became a consulting electrical engineer, a branch of science which he studied and became master of in a short time. Some of the earliest electric lights in the States were devised and erected by him. He was in England and Europe in 1880 in order to investigate electrical methods there. He was back in London in 1883, and after that visit, like Siemens, he made it his headquarters. What leisure he now had (1883–4) on hand he devoted to inventing his automatic machine gun, which should load and fire itself, and the British government was the first to recognise its merits and adopt it. The making of it has been taken over by the Maxim-Nordenfelt Gun

Company, which has a capital of about two millions sterling.

Like Edison he has taken out about a hundred different patents, some of which are connected with oil motors and smokeless gunpowder. His flying-machine, as described in his paper at the British Association in 1894, burns oil fuel, which developed three hundred and sixty horse-power. It was driven at sixty miles an hour horizontally, and the machine contained an aeroplane sloping six degrees to the horizon. The weight to be lifted was eight thousand pounds. After running nine hundred feet, the machine exerted an upward thrust of two thousand pounds greater than its own weight. The machine, after one thousand feet, broke loose; the steam was shut off, and it fell. The experiments have been conducted at Bexley, in Kent, where Mr Maxim had a light track of railway laid down, sixteen hundred feet long, on which the machine moved. The back part of the machine having been liberated from the check-rail too soon caused the accident at the experiment, and sent the whole machine off the track. There is sufficient evidence that it did rise from the ground, and Lords Rayleigh and Kelvin have become believers in its possibilities. This machine, as described at the time, with its four side sails and aeroplanes set, is over one hundred feet wide, and looks like a huge white bird with four wings instead of two. It is propelled by two large two-bladed screws, resembling the screw-propellers of a ship, driven by two powerful compound engines.

IRONCLADS.

A modern ironclad is an enormous piece of complicated mechanism. In order to protect this mechanism from hostile shot, the greater part of it is placed under water and covered by a thick steel deck; the remainder above water being protected by vast armour-plates varying from eight to twenty-four inches in thickness. From the exterior, an ironclad is by no means a thing of beauty; one writer has described it as 'a cross between a cooking apparatus and a railway station;' but in place of this ingenious parallel, imagine a low flat-looking mass on the water; from the centre rises a huge funnel, on either side of which are a turret and a superstructure running to the bow and stern; two short pole masts, with platforms on the top for machine guns, complete an object calculated to bring tears to the eyes of the veteran sailor who remembers the days of the grand old line-of-battle ship, with its tall tapering masts and white sails glistening in the sun. A stranger going on board one of our newest types of ironclads would lose himself amid the intricacies and apparent confusion of the numerous engines, passages, and compartments; it is a long time, in fact, before even the sailors find their way about these new ships; and the Admiralty allow a new ironclad to remain three months in harbour on first commissioning before going to sea, in order that the men may become acquainted with the uses of the several fittings on board, each ironclad that is built now being in many ways an improvement on its predecessor.

Those who have not been on board a modern ironclad can form no idea of the massiveness and solidity of the various fittings; the enormous guns, the rows of shot and shell, the huge bolts, bars, and beams seem to be meant for the use of giants, not men. Although crowded together in a comparatively small space, everything is in perfect order, and ready at any moment to be used for offensive or defensive purposes. It is not, perhaps, generally known that the captain of a man-of-war is ordered to keep his ship properly prepared for battle as well in time of peace as of war. Every evening before dark the quarters are cleared and every arrangement made for night-battle, to prevent surprise by a better prepared enemy. When at anchor in a harbour, especially at night, the ship is always prepared to repel any attempts of an enemy to board or attack with torpedoes or fireships. In addition to the daily and weekly drills and exercises, once every three months the crew are exercised at night-quarters, the time of course being kept secret by the captain, so that no preparations can be made beforehand, the exercise being intended to represent a surprise. In the dead of night, when only the officers of the watch and the sentries posted in the various parts of the ship are awake, the notes of a bugle vibrate between the decks; immediately, as if by magic, everything becomes alive; men are seen scrambling out of their hammocks, and lights flash in all directions; the huge shells are lifted by hydraulic power from the magazines, placed on trucks, and wheeled by means of railways to the turrets; men run here and there with rifles, boarding-pikes, axes, cases of powder and ammunition; others are engaged laying fire-hose along the decks, others closing the water-tight doors; while far down below, the engineers, stokers, and firemen are busy getting up steam for working the electric-light engines, turrets, &c. At the torpedo ports, the trained torpedo-men are placing the Whiteheads in their tubes; others are preparing cases of gun-cotton for boom-torpedoes. In ten minutes, however, all is again silent and each man stands at his station ready for action. The captain, followed by his principal officers, now walks round the quarters and inspects all the arrangements for battle, after which various exercises are gone through. A bugle sounds, and numbers of men rush away to certain parts of the ship to repel imaginary boarders; another bugle, and a large party immediately commence to work the pumps; another low, long blast is a warning that the ship is about to ram an enemy, and every man on board stretches himself flat on the decks until the shock of the (supposed) collision takes place. After a number of exercises have been gone through, the guns are secured, arms and stores returned to their places, the men tumble into their hammocks again, and are soon fast asleep.

It would be interesting to glance at some of the principal offensive and defensive capabilities of a modern ironclad. The first-class line-of-battle ship of fifty years ago carried as many as a hundred and thirty, what would

One of the 'Wooden Walls of Old England.' *The Duke of Wellington* Screw Line-of-Battle Ship. One hundred and thirty-one Guns.

be called in the present day, very light guns; in contrast to this, her Majesty's armour-plated barbette ram *Benbow* carries *two* guns weighing a hundred and ten tons each. These enormous weapons are forty-three feet eight inches long, and are capable of sending a shot weighing three quarters of a ton to a distance of seven miles. The effect of a shell from one of these guns piercing the armour of a ship and bursting would be very disastrous, and there are few, if any, ships whose armour, when fairly hit at a moderate distance, could withstand such a blow.

Guns, however, although terrible in effect, are now supplemented by other and more deadly means of offence. Foremost amongst these stands the Whitehead or Fish Torpedo. This infernal machine can be discharged from tubes in the side of a ship to a distance of a thousand yards under water at a speed of twenty-five miles per hour. Armed with its charge of gun-cotton it rushes forth on its mission; and, if successful in striking the ship against which it is aimed, explodes, and rends a large hole in her side, through which the water pours in huge quantities. In order to protect a man-of-war from this danger, she can be surrounded at short notice with thick wire-nettings, hanging from projecting side-spars, against which the torpedo explodes with harmless effect. These nettings are, however, principally intended for use when ships are at anchor in harbour at night; they could not well be employed in action with an enemy, as they offer such resistance to the water as to reduce the speed of the ship by four or five knots, and so encumber her as to render her liable to be rammed by a more active opponent.

All large ironclads now have two or three torpedo boats. These craft are constructed of steel one-sixteenth of an inch thick, and steam at a speed of sixteen knots, some of the larger kind reaching twenty or twenty-one knots an hour. Carrying two Whiteheads, they are valuable auxiliaries to the parent ship; their rapid movements, together with their dangerous freight, distracting the attention of an enemy.

Machine-guns, however, form a very effective remedy for them; a single torpedo boat attacking an ironclad would, directly she got within range, be riddled with Gardner and Nordenfelt shot, and sunk in about fifteen seconds. It is only when three or four approach in various

The *Majestic*.

directions, or during night attacks, that they become really dangerous. The electric search-lights, with which most large men-of-war are now provided, will show a torpedo boat at the distance of a mile on the darkest night; but there is of course always a chance of their getting close enough to a ship to discharge a torpedo before they are discovered.

The bow of many of our ironclads is constructed for the purpose of ramming (running down and sinking) an antagonist. To use a ram requires great speed and facilities for turning and manœuvring quickly; for the latter purposes, short ships are better than long ones. It would be a comparatively easy thing for a ship steaming fourteen knots to ram another that could only steam ten; a small ship might also outmanœuvre and ram a long one; but it would be extremely difficult, in fact almost impossible, for a ship to ram another vessel of equal speed and length. To secure facilities in turning and manœuvring, all our modern ships are built as short as possible, and have two screws, each worked by entirely separate sets of engines, so that one can go ahead whilst the other goes astern. If one set of engines is disabled, the other can still work independently, and a fair speed be maintained. We always think that two ships at close quarters trying to ram one another, must be like a game at chess, requiring the closest observation of your opponent's movements and the nicest judgment for your own, a wrong move being fatal to either.

It is the opinion of many naval men of authority that a modern naval battle would only occupy about half the time of a fight in the old Trafalgar days; that half the ships employed would be sunk, and that most of the remainder would be so battered as to be unfit for further service for months to come.

In connection with the Navy Estimates for 1896–7 it

was announced in the House of Commons that the following vessels would be constructed: 13 first-class battleships, 10 first-class cruisers, 16 second-class cruisers, 7 third-class cruisers, and 48 torpedo-boat destroyers.

SUBMARINE BOATS.

In 1864, during the American civil war, a submarine boat succeeded in sinking the Federal frigate *Housatonic*. This boat, however, was hardly an unqualified success, as, running into the hole made by its torpedo, it went down with the ship; and three crews had previously been lost while carrying out its initial experiments. Since then, many methods of submersion have been tried; but it is only within recent years that naval powers have awakened to the fact that a submersible boat, though by no means so formidable for offensive purposes as its name at first leads one to believe, is a factor which might have to be taken into consideration in the next naval war.

Modern types of these boats are the Holland, Nordenfelt, Tuck, and Goubet. The Holland boat comes to us from over the Atlantic, and is peculiar in its weapon of offence. It is fifty feet long, eight feet in diameter, and is driven by a petroleum engine carrying sufficient fuel for two days' run. The diving is effected by means of two horizontal rudders, one on each side of the stern. This only allows of submersion when the boat is in motion; and the boat cannot be horizontal while submerged. It carries ten-inch gelatine blasting shells, fired from a pneumatic gun twenty feet long, whose radius of action is two hundred yards under water and one thousand yards above. The use of gelatine is also objectionable, as the confined space and the vibration of the boat prevent such explosives being carried without some risk of premature explosion. It is for this reason that gun-cotton is adopted in torpedo work, as it will not explode on concussion, and is little affected by change of temperature.

The principal features of the Nordenfelt boat are its method of submersion and its propulsion by steam. The boat is one hundred and twenty-five feet long, twelve feet beam, and displaces two hundred and fifty tons when entirely submerged, one hundred and sixty tons when running on the surface. Her propelling machinery consists of two double cylinder compound engines, with a horse-power of one thousand, and propelling the boat at fifteen knots on the surface. The submersion of the boat is effected by means of two horizontal propellers working in wells at each end. Two conning-towers project about two feet above the deck, of one-inch steel, surmounted by glass domes, protected with steel bars, for purposes of observation. The boat usually runs on the surface with these towers showing, unless the buoyancy, which is never less than half a ton, is overcome by the horizontal propellers, when the boat becomes partially or totally submerged according to their speed. To ascend to the surface it is only necessary to stop the horizontal propellers, which also stop automatically on reaching a set depth. In the forward tower are the firing keys, machinery and valves necessary for driving or steering the vessel, for controlling the horizontal propellers, and for discharging the White-head torpedoes. Four of these are carried, and they are discharged with powder from two tubes in the bows. In the conning-tower are also placed the instruments indicating the depth, level, and course. When the boat is awash, the funnels have to be unshipped and the boat closed up before submersion. The length of time, twenty-five minutes, required for this operation is an objection to this boat, though when submerged it does not get unpleasantly hot. The temperature after a three hours' submerged run was only ninety degrees Fahrenheit. The crew consists of a captain and eight men.

The Tuck also comes from America. It is of iron, cigar-shaped, thirty feet long and six feet in diameter. It is submerged by means of a horizontal rudder in the stern and a horizontal propeller acting vertically amidships beneath the boat. It is driven by electricity, supplied from storage batteries packed closely in the bows. Compressed air is carried in reservoirs, but a supply is usually obtained when the boat is not far from the surface, by means of an iron pipe twenty feet long, which usually lies on deck, but which can be raised to an upright position by

Section of the Goubet Submarine Boat.

gearing from within. The top then rises above the surface of the water, and by opening a valve in the foot and attaching a pump, fresh air is drawn into the interior. The crew need not exceed three men.

The Goubet class are of iron, sixteen feet long, three feet wide, and about six feet deep. The motive power is a Siemens motor driven by storage batteries. Fifty of these boats were purchased by the Russian government. They have no rudder, but a universal joint in the screw shaft permits of the screw being moved through an arc of ninety degrees. The torpedo is carried outside the boat, secured by a catch worked from inside. On arriving under the enemy, the torpedo is released, and striking the ship's bottom, is held there by spikes. The boat then withdraws, unreeling a connecting wire; and when at a safe distance, fires. The absence of a rudder, however, causes erratic steering, and the spikes with which the torpedo is fitted might fail to stick in steel-bottomed ships.

Submarine boats cannot be driven under water at a speed exceeding six knots. If driven beyond, they are inclined to dive, and in deep water, before the corrective forces against a dive have had time to act, might reach a depth where the pressure would drive in the sides or compress them to a sufficient extent to seriously reduce the displacement. In shallow water, the boat might be driven on to the bottom, and if it be clay, held there, an accident attended with fatal consequences in the case of one boat.

It is also difficult to direct the course of a submarine boat; and it is doubtful whether the advantage of not being seen counteracts the disadvantage of not being able to see. According to Mr Nordenfelt in a lecture on Submarine Boats, 'The mirror of the surface throws a strong light into the boat; you cannot see forward at all, and you cannot see far astern; it is as black as ink outside; you can only see a sort of segment.' This means that you cannot safely advance at a great speed under water. It is impossible to think of a submarine boat as a boat that actually manœuvres and does its work under water. The boat should run awash, and you can then see where you are. When we consider, then, that a boat totally submerged cannot be driven over six knots, and cannot be properly directed; when we consider the speeds of seventeen and eighteen knots attained by modern battleships, we arrive at the conclusion that boats totally submerged are useless against modern battleships in motion. Running awash, they could be tackled by torpedo catchers and torpedo boats.

CHAPTER VII.

EVOLUTION OF THE CYCLE.

In praise of Cycling—Number of Cycles in Use—Medical Opinions—Pioneers in the Invention—James Starley—Cycling Tours.

IR WALTER SCOTT once told a friend that if he did not see the heather once a year he would die. He saw it much oftener than once a year. When the building and planting of Abbotsford had become a passion with him, and when the vacation came round in connection with his duties in the Court of Session, he would not stay ten minutes longer in Edinburgh than he could help. Sometimes his carriage would be waiting in Parliament Square to bear him off as swiftly as possible to Abbotsford. John Locke says there is a good vein of poetry buried in the breast of most business men; there is at least in the breast of most men, strong or latent, a longing, a passion for freedom, for change. When the buds swell and burst; when the May-blossom breaks forth on the hawthorn, and makes a spring snowstorm in the valley; when the cuckoo is heard, and the lark rains down his drops of melody above the springing clods; when the lambs gambol in the green fields, and the hives are murmurous with their drowsy insect hum—the awakening comes in man, too, for freedom, freshness, change. They

are happy who can enjoy such, and be rested and refreshed; for millions are chained to the oar, and know not what they miss, and millions more have not had their eyes or their desires awakened to what they miss. Lowell expresses the feeling:

> What man would live coffined with brick and stone,
>   Imprisoned from the healing touch of air,
>   And cramped with selfish landmarks everywhere,
> When all before him stretches, furrowless and lone,
> The unmapped prairie none can fence or own?
> What man would read and read the self-same faces,
>   And like the marbles which the windmill grinds,
>   Rub smooth for ever with the same smooth minds,
> This year retracing last year's, every year's, dull traces,
> When there are woods and unpenfolded spaces?
>
> .   .   .   .
>
> To change and change is life, to move and never rest:
> Not what we are, but what we hope, is best.
> The wild, free woods make no man halt or blind;
>   Cities rob men of eyes and hands and feet.

We want, then, to recover our eyes, and hands, and feet, remembering the story of eyes and no eyes. For this end, few things are better than a day now and then in the open air, in order to bring a man to himself. The best stimulant in the world is mountain air, and the grandest restorative music the rhythmic beat of the waves along the shore.

The cyclist covers a wonderful stretch of country, going and returning, and comes back refreshed too, though tired, thinking that nobody in the universe can have had a better or pleasanter holiday than he has enjoyed. He has whizzed along leafy lanes, with glimpses of running streams to right and left; he has heard the musical monotony of the hill burns as he rested on the bridge; he has awakened sleepy villages, and enjoyed his repasts at country inns. And so the cyclist has a ready power to give himself the requisite and healthful change of scene.

CYCLING.

The pastime of cycling, at first only patronised by athletic youth, has now spread to every class of the community. The vast improvement in machines, and the health and exhilaration to be gained by the exercise, have had much to do with its popularity alike with aristocracy and democracy. Like golf, it has come to stay, although many who take cycling up for amusement will drop it again as they would do anything else. But there will always remain a strong and increasing contingent, fully aware, by practical experience, of its health and pleasure giving powers, who will place it second to no existing recreation. And so the cyclist gets gleams and glances of beauty from many a nook and corner of the land, where railway, coach, or his unaided pedestrian powers would never carry him. It has widened a twenty-mile radius to a forty-mile radius, and increased man's locomotive powers threefold. Let no one imagine that there is not a considerable amount of exertion and fatigue, and sometimes hardship. But it is of a wholesome kind, when kept within limits, and physically, morally, and socially, the benefits that cycling confers on the men of the present day are almost unbounded.

Truly, we have here a great leveller; as one says: 'It puts the poor man on a level with the rich, enabling him to "sing the song of the open road" as freely as the millionaire, and to widen his knowledge by visiting the regions near to or far from his home, observing how other men live. He could not afford a railway journey and sojourn in these places, and he could not walk through them without tiring sufficiently to destroy in a measure the pleasure which he sought. But he can ride through twenty, thirty, fifty, even seventy miles of country in a day, without serious fatigue, and with no expense save his board and lodging.' This is very well put. Another enthusiast has said: 'If you want to come as near flying as we are likely to get in this generation, learn to ride on a pneumatic bicycle.' 'Sum up,' says another, 'when summer is done, all the glorious days you have had, the splendid bits of scenery which have become a possession for ever, your adventures worth telling, and see how you have been gladdened and enriched.'

An enthusiastic journalist who had been burning the candle at both ends betook himself to the wheel, and found it of so much service to body and mind that he straightway, in the columns of his newspaper, began to advise the whole world to learn the bicycle. He could hardly tell the difference it had made to his feelings and general health, and he knew of no exercise which brought so easily such a universal return in good health, good spirits, and amusement. Mr G. Lacy Hillier, of the Badminton volume on Cycling, confirms this. The cyclist seems to enter into the spirit of Emerson's saying as thoroughly as Thoreau might have done: 'Give me health and a day, and I will make the pomp of empires ridiculous.' Many overdo the exercise, then renounce it, or give it a bad name; others, by over-rapid riding in towns, make themselves public nuisances, and vastly increase the dangers of overcrowded streets. The sensible cyclist rides for health, increase of knowledge, and amusement.

Though at one time Mr Ruskin was prepared to spend all his best bad language in abusing the wheel, the world has gone its own way, and the careering multitudes in Battersea Park and elsewhere, on country and suburban roads, in crowded towns, have been the means of creating new manufactures, which have vastly benefited our home industries. Mr H. J. Lawson, inventor of the rear-driving safety, lately estimated the annual output of cycles at over a million, and the money spent at over ten millions. But in the absence of statistics this is only guesswork. The periodical called *Invention* has stated that in 1884 there were 8 bicycle factories, which turned out 6000 machines. In 1895 there were about 400 factories, with an estimated output of 650,000 bicycles. The bicycle tax in France is, said to yield not less than £80,000 a year. In the United States, where cycling has become a greater craze than with us, two hundred and fifty thousand cycles at least were purchased in 1894; in 1895 more than four hundred thousand changed hands. When the proposal was made some time ago to impose a tax on cycles, it was calculated that there were at least eight hundred thousand riders in the United Kingdom. Now the number is estimated at over a million. The past few seasons have witnessed quite a 'boom' in cycling and a great increase in the number of riders. Ladies have taken more rapidly to the pastime in America and France than in England. The rubber and then the pneumatic or inflated tyre have wrought a marvellous revolution; the high 'ordinary,' the tricycle, and the heavy 'solid,' and even the 'cushion,' have in most cases been relegated to the home of old iron. The Pneumatic Tyre Company, with a capital of four millions sterling, when in full swing, turns out twenty-five thousand tyres per week. The profits of this concern in 1896 were at the rate of £432,000 a year. Coventry, Birmingham, Wolverhampton, London, and other towns, have largely benefited by the cycle trade.

Sir B. W. Richardson has often called attention to the benefit of cycling in the case of dwellers in towns. Dr Turner finds that nothing neutralises better the poison introduced into the blood through faulty digestion than gentle and continued exercise on the wheel. Mr A. J. Watson, the English amateur one-mile and five-mile champion in 1895, declared that he never suffered from any ill effects, save perhaps during the hard days in winter, when prevented from riding. Dr Andrew Wilson once quoted a budget of correspondence from ladies who had tried the wheel, all of which was in the same direction, provided that overstrain was avoided. Where the heart is weak, cycling should be left alone. The muscles of the legs are developed and the circumference of the chest increased in the case of healthy riders.

Here are a few hints by a medical man: 'Never ride within half an hour of a meal, either before or after. Wheel the machine up any hill the mounting of which on the wheel causes any real effort. See that the clothing round the stomach, neck, and chest is loose. Have the handle-bar sufficiently raised to prevent stooping. Be as sparing as possible of taking fluids during a long ride. Unless the wind, road, &c., be favourable, never ride more than ten miles an hour, save for very short distances, and never smoke while riding.'

The cycle as we know it did not burst upon the world in all its present completeness, but has been a gradual evolution, the work of many a busy hand and brain, guided by experience. As far back as 1767 we find that Richard Lovell Edgeworth had something of the nature of a velocipede; and about the same date, William Murdoch, inventor of gas for illuminating purposes, had a wooden horse of his own invention upon which he rode to school at Cumnock.

The French appear to be entitled to whatever of credit attaches to the original invention of the hobby-horse, a miserable steed at best, which wore out the toes of a pair of boots at every journey. M. Blanchard, the celebrated aëronaut, and M. Masurier conjointly manufactured the first of these machines in 1779, which was then described as 'a wonder which drove all Paris mad.' The Dandy-horse of 1818, the two wheels on which the rider sat astride, tipping the ground with his feet in order to propel the machine, was laughed out of existence. In 1840, a blacksmith named Kirkpatrick Macmillan, of Courthill, parish of Keir, Dumfriesshire, made a cycle on which he rode to Glasgow, and caused a big sensation on the way. This worthy man died in 1878, aged 68. The notable fact regarding Macmillan's cycle is, that he had adapted cranks and levers to the old dandy or hobby-horse. Gavin Dalziel, of Lesmahagow, Lanarkshire, had a bicycle of his own invention in daily use in 1846. The French are probably justified, moreover, in claiming as their own the development of the crude invention into the present velocipede, for, in 1862, a M. Rivière, a French subject residing in England, deposited in the British Patent Office a minute specification of a bicycle. His description was, however, unaccompanied by any drawing or sketch, and he seems to have taken no further steps in the matter than to register a theory which he never carried into practice. Subsequently, the bicycle was re-invented by the French and by the Americans almost simultaneously, and indeed, both nations claim priority in introducing it. It came into public notoriety at the French International Exhibition of 1867, from which time the rage for them gradually developed itself, until in 1869 Paris became enthusiastic over velocipedes. Extensive foundries were soon established in Paris for the sole purpose of supplying the ironwork, while some scores of large manufactories taxed their utmost resources to meet the daily increasing demand for these vehicles.

There was a revival of cycling between 1867-69. An ingenious Frenchman, M. Michaux, had some years before fitted pedals and a transverse handle to the front wheel of what came to be irreverently known as the 'boneshaker.' This embryo bicycle had a considerable vogue, and was introduced to Mr Charles Spencer's gymnasium in London in 1868. Spencer was in Paris in 1868, in company with Mr R. Turner, representative of the Coventry Machinists' Company, and they were each admiring the graceful evolutions of Henri Tascard on his velocipede over the broad asphalt paths of the Luxemburg Gardens. 'Charlie, do you think you could do that?' said Turner. Spencer said he thought he would have a trial, and would take home a machine that very night. He accordingly brought over a machine to London, practised riding stealthily in some of the most out-of-the-way London streets, and soon gained sufficient confidence to appear in public. Mr John Mayall, jun., photographer, Regent Street, witnessed the arrival of one of the first bicycles at Spencer's gymnasium, in Old Street, St Luke's. 'It produced but little impression upon me,' he says, 'and certainly did not strike me as being a new means of locomotion. A slender young man, whom I soon came to know as Mr Turner of Paris, followed the packing-case and superintended its opening. The gymnasium was cleared, Mr Turner took off his coat, grasped the handles of the machine, and, with a short run, to my intense surprise, vaulted on to it, and putting his feet on the treadle made the circuit of the room. We were some half-a-dozen spectators, and I shall never forget our astonishment at the sight of Mr Turner whirling himself round the room—sitting on a bar above a pair of wheels in a line, that ought, as we inadvertently supposed, to fall down as soon as he jumped off the ground.'

It is almost laughable, now, to read how Spencer at first always rode on the pavement, and how politely everybody cleared out of his way. Even Policeman X helped to make a passage for him. Some wiseacre, on being quizzed as to the uses of this strange new machine, would reply, 'Why, it is a machine for measuring roads, of course;' and a street arab would shout, 'Oh, crikey, Bill, 'ere's a lark. A swell a ridin' on two wheels. Mind how you fall, sir,' &c. Spencer's speed at first was but five miles an hour. Soon there were many inquiries for this wonderful new aid to locomotion. Spencer and Turner entered heartily into the business. An order for 500 machines was given to the Coventry Machinists' Company in the end of 1868. This was the firm with which Mr James Starley, inventor of the 'Coventry Tricycle,' was connected, and this order helped the start of what has grown to be an enormous and beneficial industry to the town of Coventry.

The account of feats of long-distance riding, of forty and fifty miles a day, got abroad—the feat by Turner, Spencer, and Mayall particularly, in riding to Brighton and back in a day, in February 1869, further popularised cycling. Charles Dickens and James Payn were amongst those who were bitten by the velocipede 'mania.'

Yet the bone-shaker craze might have died a natural death but for the introduction of the rubber tyre and other improvements. Mr James Starley, of Coventry, through whose inventive genius the tricycle was evolved from the bicycle, was also an improver and pioneer. Starley says of his improvements: 'I regarded the rider as the motive force; and believing it absolutely necessary that he should be so placed that he could exert the greatest amount of power on his pedals, with the least amount of fatigue to himself—believing, also, that the machine of the future must be so made that such essentials as the crank-shaft, pedals, seat, and handles could easily be made adjustable — I decided to change my shape, make my wheels of a good rolling size, place my crank-shaft as near the ground as safety would permit, connect my back wheel with my crank by means of a chain, so that the gear might be adjusted and varied at pleasure, and a short, strong man could ride with a fifty, a sixty, a seventy, or even a higher gear, while a tall, weak man could ride with a lower gear than the short, strong one; to give my saddle a vertical adjustment so that it could be raised or lowered at will; so to place my handles that they could be set forward or backward, raised or lowered, as might be desired; and finally, to make it impossible for the pedalling to interfere with the steering.' In the 'Rover' bicycle he gave an impetus to the early history of the machine, which has been crowned in the pneumatic tyre, the invention of John Boyd Dunlop, born at Dreghorn, Ayrshire, in 1840. Mr Dunlop was engaged as a veterinary surgeon near Belfast, where he built himself an air-wheel from ordinary thin rubber sheets, with rubber valve and plug. Mr C. K. Welch followed with the detachable tyre. The big, ungainly looking wheels were at first laughed at, but when pneumatic tyred machines won race after race, they became the rage. And when the company formed to make the Dunlop tyre sold their interest in the concern, in 1896 it was worth about £3,000,000. The capital originally subscribed was £260,000, and £658,000 had been paid in dividends.

A cycling tour is health-giving and enjoyable when gone about rationally and prudently. It is pleasant to plan, and no less so to carry out, as it is always the unexpected which happens. There are halts by the wayside, conversations with rustics, fine views; and every part of the brain and blood is oxygenated, giving that kind of wholesome intoxication which Thoreau said he gained by living in the open air. One's own country is explored as it has never been explored before. Some wheelmen have been credited with seven and eight thousand miles in a single season. Others, more ambitious, have made a track round the globe. Mr Thomas Stevens, starting from San Francisco in April 1884, occupied three years in going round the world. Mr T. Allen and Mr L. Sachtleben, two American students, as a practical finish to a theoretical education, occupied three years in riding round the world—15,404 miles on the wheel. They climbed Mount Ararat by the way, and interviewed Li Hung Chang, the Chinese viceroy. The wheel ridden by these 'foreign devils' was described by one Chinaman as 'a little mule that you drive by the ears, and kick in the sides to make him go.'

Mr Frank G. Lenz, who started from America in June 1892 to ride round the world, was unfortunately killed by six Kurds, sixty-five miles from Erzeroum, between the villages of Kurtali and Dahar, on May 10, 1894. There have been many interesting shorter rides. Mr Walter Goddard of Leeds, and Mr James Edmund of Brixton, started from London and rode entirely round Europe on wheels; Mr Hugh Callan rode from Glasgow to the river Jordan; Mr R. L. Jefferson, in 1894, rode from London to Constantinople, between March 10 and May 19. In 1895 the same gentleman rode from London to Moscow, 4281 miles, and had nothing good to say of Russian inns or roads. A lady of sixty has done seventy miles in one day; while an English lady tourist did twelve hundred miles in her various ups and downs between London and Glasgow during one holiday.

The lighter the machine, the more expensive it is. Racing-machines are built as light as twenty pounds in weight. Some of the swiftest road-riders patronise machines of twenty-six or twenty-seven pounds; but for all-round work, one of thirty-three pounds, without lamp or bell, is a good average machine. As to speed, we have had 460 miles in the twenty-four hours on the racing-track, and 377 miles on the road. Huret, a French rider, has done 515 miles between one midnight and another; the Swiss cyclist Lesna has done 28 miles an hour; while Mr Mills and Mr T. A. Edge, in a ride from Land's End to John o' Groat's on a tandem, beat all previous records, doing the journey in three days four hours and forty-six minutes.

A very sensible American rider, when on tour, starts shortly after breakfast, and with a brief rest for lunch, has his day's work of about fifty miles over by four P.M. Then he changes underclothing—a most important and never-to-be-forgotten matter—has dinner, and an enjoyable ramble over the town or village where he stays over-night. But he is a luxurious dog, and not many will carry such an abundant kit in the triangular bag below the handle bar. Imagine three light outing shirts, three suits, gauze underclothing, a dark flannel bicycle suit, laced tanned gaiters, light-weight rubber coat, comb; clothes, hair, and tooth brushes; soap and towel, writing-pad and pencil, map and matches, and tool bag! Many a cyclist carries a hand camera, and brings home a permanent record of his journeys.

It has been well said that many a boy will start in life with a more vigorous constitution because of the bicycle, and many a man who is growing old too fast by neglect of active exercise will find himself rejuvenated by the same agency. Only let the getting over a certain distance within a certain time not be the main object. And winter riding, when the roads permit, need not be neglected, for nothing is more invigorating than a winter ride. The doctors tell us that as long as one can ride with the mouth shut, the heart is all right. A fillip should be given to the appetite; whenever this is destroyed, and sleeplessness ensues, cycling is being overdone.

Cycling, of course, as we have already said, is not all pleasure or romance. There is a considerable amount of hard work, with head-winds, rain, mud, hills, and misadventures through punctures of the tyre. This last may happen at the most inopportune time; but the cyclist is generally a philosopher, and sets about his repairs with a cool and easy mind.

A word in closing about accidents, which are often due

to carelessness and recklessness. A cyclist has no right to ride at ten or fourteen miles an hour in a crowded thoroughfare. He takes his life—and other people's!—in his hands if he does so. No less is caution needed on hills, the twists and turns in which are unseen or unfamiliar, and where the bottom of the incline cannot be seen. As the saying goes, 'Better be a coward for half an hour than a corpse for the rest of your lifetime.' But experience is the best guide, and no hard-and-fast rules can be laid down for exceptional circumstances.

The Dandy-horse.

CHAPTER VIII.

STEAMERS AND SAILING-SHIPS.

Early Shipping—Mediterranean Trade—Rise of the P. and O. and other Lines—Transatlantic Lines—India and the East—Early Steamships—First Steamer to cross the Atlantic—Rise of Atlantic Shipping Lines—The *Great Eastern* and the New Cunarders *Campania* and *Lucania* compared—Sailing-ships.

THE CARRYING-TRADE OF THE WORLD.

F all the industries of the world, that which is concerned with the interchange of the products of nations is suffused with the most interest for the largest number of people. Not only is the number of those who go down into the sea in ships, and who do business on the great waters, legion, but three-fourths of the population of the globe are more or less dependent on their enterprise. The ocean-carrying trade we are accustomed to date from the time of the Phœnicians; and certainly the Phœnicians were daring mariners, if not exactly scientific navigators, and their ships were pretty well acquainted with the waters of Europe and the coasts of Africa. But the Phœnicians were rather merchant-adventurers on their own account than ocean-carriers, as, for instance, the Arabians were on the other side of Africa, acting as the intermediaries of the trade between Egypt and East Africa and India. In the early

days, too, there is reason to believe that the Chinese were extensive ocean-carriers, sending their junks both to the Arabian Gulf and to the ports of Hindustan, long before Alexander the Great invaded India. But there is nothing more remarkable in the history of maritime commerce than the manner in which it has changed hands.

Even down to the beginning of the present century, almost the whole of the carrying-trade of the Baltic and the Mediterranean was in the hands of the Danes, Norwegians, and Germans, while our own harbours were crowded with foreign ships. This was one of the effects of our peculiar Navigation Laws, under which foreigners were so protected that there was hardly a trade open to British vessels. It is, indeed, just ninety years since British ship-owners made a formal and earnest appeal to the government to remove the existing shackles on the foreign trade of the country, and to promote the development of commerce with the American and West Indian colonies. One argument of the time was the necessity for recovering and developing the Mediterranean trade, as affording one of the best avenues for the employment of shipping and the promotion of international commerce. It was a trade of which England had a very considerable share in the time of Henry VII., who may very fairly be regarded as the founder of British merchant shipping. He not only built ships for himself for trading purposes, but encouraged others to do so, and even lent them money for the purpose. And it was to the Mediterranean that he chiefly directed his attention, in eager competition with the argosies of Venice and Genoa. There resulted a perfect fleet of what were called 'tall ships' engaged in carrying woollen fabrics and other British products to Italy, Sicily, Syria, and the Levant, and in bringing home cargoes of silk, cotton, wool, carpets, oil, spices, and wine.

Steam has worked a change in favour of this country

nowhere more remarkable than in the Mediterranean trade. When the trade began to revive for sailing-vessels, by a removal of some of the irksome restrictions, Lisbon was the most important port on the Iberian Peninsula for British shipping. There was a weekly mail service by sailing-packets between Falmouth and Lisbon, until the Admiralty put on a steamer. Some time in the 'thirties,' two young Scotchmen named Brodie Wilcox and Arthur Anderson had a small fleet of sailing-vessels engaged in the Peninsular trade, and in the year 1834 they chartered the steamer *Royal Tar* from the Dublin and London Steam-packet Company. This was the beginning of the great Peninsular and Oriental Steam Navigation Company, destined to revolutionise the carrying-trade both of the Mediterranean and the East. When the Spanish government negotiated for a line of steamers to be established between England and Spain, Wilcox and Anderson took up the project, organised a small company, and acquired some steamers, which at first did not pay. They persevered, however, until shippers saw the superiority of the new vessels to the old sailers, and at last the Peninsular Company obtained the first mail-contract ever entered into by the English government. This was in 1837; the Cunard and Royal Mail (West Indian) lines were not established until 1840. In a couple of years the Peninsular Company extended their line through the Straits to Malta and Alexandria, and again to Corfu and the Levant. In 1840 they applied for and obtained a charter as the Peninsular and Oriental Steam-navigation Company, with the object of establishing a line of steamers on the other side of the Isthmus of Suez, from which have developed the great ramifications to India, China, Japan, the Straits Settlements, and Australia. It was, indeed, through the Mediterranean that we obtained our first hold on the Eastern carrying-trade.

In considering the development of maritime commerce, it is always to be remembered that the design of Columbus and the early navigators in sailing westwards was not to find America, but to find a new way to India and Far Cathay. Mighty as America has become in the world's economy, its first occupation was only an incident in the struggle for the trade of the Far East. But with the occupation of America came two new developments in this carrying-trade—namely, one across the Atlantic, and one upon and across the Pacific. To the eventful year in which so many great enterprises were founded—namely, 1840—we trace the beginning of steam-carrying on the Pacific, for in that year William Wheelwright took or sent the first steamer round Cape Horn, as the pioneer of the great Pacific Steam-navigation Company. Within about a dozen years thereafter, the Americans had some fifty steamers constantly engaged on the Pacific coast of the two Continents, besides those of the English company. Out of one of those Pacific lines grew Commodore Vanderbilt's Nicaragua Transit Company, a double service of two lines of steamers, one on each side of the Continent, with an overland connection through Nicaragua. Out of another grew the New York and San Francisco line, connecting overland across the Isthmus of Panama— where M. de Lesseps did *not* succeed in cutting a Canal. And out of yet another of those Pacific enterprises, all stimulated by Wheelwright's success, grew in the course of years a line between San Francisco and Hawaii, and another between San Francisco and Australia. Some forty years ago the boats of this last-named line used to run down to Panama to pick up passengers and traffic from Europe, and it is interesting to recall that at that period the design was greatly favoured of a regular steam service between England and Australia *viâ* Panama. A company was projected for the purpose; but it came to nothing, for various reasons not necessary to enter upon here. But as long ago as the early fifties, when the Panama Railway was in course of construction, there were eight separate lines of steamers on the Atlantic meeting at Aspinwall, and five on the Pacific meeting at Panama. Later on, when the Americans had completed their iron-roads from ocean to ocean across their own dominions, they started lines of steamers from San Francisco to China and Japan. And later still, when the Canadian Pacific Railway was completed across Canada, a British line of ships was started across the Pacific to Far Cathay, and afterwards to Australia and New Zealand. So that the dream of the old navigators has, after all, been practically realised.

The repeal of the corn laws gave an immense impetus to British shipping, by opening up new lines of traffic in grain with the ports of the Baltic, the Black Sea, and Egypt; and the extension of steamer communication created another new carrying-business in the transport of coals abroad to innumerable coaling stations. Thus demand goes on creating supply, and supply in turn creating new demand.

From the old fruit and grain sailers of the Mediterranean trade have developed such extensive concerns as the Cunard line (one of whose beginnings was a service of steamers between Liverpool and Havre), which now covers the whole Mediterranean, and extends across the Atlantic to New York and Boston; the Anchor line, which began with a couple of boats running between the Clyde and the Peninsula, and now covers all the Mediterranean and Adriatic, and extends from India to America; the Bibby line, which began with a steamer between Liverpool and Marseilles, and now covers every part of the Mediterranean (Leyland line), and spreads out to Burma and the Straits. These are but a few of many examples of how the great carrying-lines of the world, east and west, have developed from modest enterprises in mid-Europe. And even now the goods traffic between the Mediterranean and the United Kingdom, North Europe and America, is less in the hands of these great lines than in that of the vast fleets of ocean tramps, both sail and steam.

One of the most wonderful developments in the carrying-trade of the world is the concern known as the Messageries Maritimes of France — now probably the largest steamer-owning copartnery in the world. Prior to the Crimean War, there was an enterprise called the Messageries Impériales, which was engaged in the land-carriage of mails through France. In 1851 this company entered into a contract with the French government for the conveyance of mails to Italy, Egypt, Greece, and the Levant; and as years went on, the mail subsidies became so heavy that the enterprise was practically a national one. During the war, the Messageries Company's vessels were in such demand as transports, &c., that the company had to rapidly create a new fleet for mail purposes. With peace came the difficulty of employing the enormously augmented fleet. New lines of mail and cargo boats were therefore successively established between France and the Danube and Black Sea; Bordeaux and Brazil and the River Plate; Marseilles and India and China, &c. In fact, the Messageries Company's ramifications now extend from France to Great Britain, South America, the whole of the Mediterranean, the Levant, the Black Sea, the Red Sea, the Indian Ocean and the China Seas, and the South Pacific.

Few people, perhaps, have any conception of the numbers of regular and highly organised lines of steamers now connecting Europe and America. Besides the Messageries, the Austro-Hungarian Lloyd's and the Italian mail lines run between the Mediterranean and the River Plate. Argentina and Brazil are connected with different parts of Europe by about a dozen lines. Between the United States and Europe there are now about thirty distinct regular lines of steamers carrying goods and passengers; and about a dozen more carrying goods only. Four of these lines are direct with Germany, two with France, two with Holland, two with Belgium, one with Denmark, and two with Italy, one of which is under the British flag. All the rest of the passenger lines and most of the cargo lines run between the United Kingdom and the United States. As for the 'tramps' steaming and sailing between North America and Europe, they are of all nations; but again the majority fly the British flag, though once upon a time the American-built clippers, of graceful lines and 'sky-scraping' masts, used to monopolise the American carrying-trade under the stars and stripes. Once upon a time, too, these beautiful American clippers had the bulk of the China tea-trade, and of the Anglo-Australian general trade. But they were run off the face of the waters by the Navigation Laws of America and the shipping enterprise of Britain. The great and growing trade between the United States and India, too, is now nearly all carried in British vessels; and a large part of the regular steam service between New York and the West Indies is under the British flag. That a change will take place when America repeals the laws which forbid Americans to own vessels built abroad or manned by foreigners is pretty certain.

With regard to India, the growth in the carrying-trade has been enormous since Vasco da Gama, four hundred years ago, found his way round the Cape of Good Hope to Calicut. For an entire century, down to 1600, the Portuguese monopolised the trade of the East, and as many as two and three hundred of their ships would often be gathered together in the port of Goa, taking in cargo for different Eastern and European ports. To-day, Goa is a deserted port, and the Portuguese flag is rarely seen—a ship or two per annum now being sufficient for all the trade between Portugal and India. In the century of Portuguese prosperity the English flag was hardly known in Eastern waters. It was the Dutch who drove out the Portuguese; and the reason why the Dutch were tempted out to India was because the rich cargoes brought home by the Portuguese could not be disposed of in Portugal, and had to be taken to Amsterdam, or Rotterdam, or Antwerp, where the opulent Dutch merchants purchased them for redistribution throughout Europe. This is how the Dutch came into direct relations with the Indian trade before the English, and why Barentz and others tried to find a near way to India for the Dutch vessels by way of the north of Europe and Asia. Failing in the north, the Dutch followed the Portuguese round the Cape, and reaching Sumatra, founded the wide domain of Netherlands-India. This occupation was effected before 1600; and between that year and 1670 they expelled the Portuguese from every part of the Eastern Archipelago, from Malacca, from Ceylon, from the Malabar Coast, and from Macassar.

The Dutch in turn enjoyed a monopoly of the Indian trade for about a hundred years. Then with the rise of Clive came the downfall of the Dutch, and by 1811 they were stripped of every possession they had in the East. Later, we gave them back Java and Sumatra, with which Holland now does a large trade, reserved exclusively to Dutch vessels. But in India proper the Dutch have not a single possession, and it is doubtful if in all the Indian Peninsula there are now a hundred Dutchmen resident.

Two immense streams of trade are constantly setting to and from India and Europe through the Suez Canal and round the Cape. Not only is the bulk of that trade conducted by the well-known Peninsular and Oriental, British

India, City, Clan, Anchor, and other lines (though the Messageries Maritimes, North German Lloyd's, and other foreign lines have no mean share), but the whole coast-line of India is served by the steamers of the British-India and Asiatic lines; and British vessels conduct the most of the carrying-trade between India and Australia, China, Japan, the Straits, Mauritius, &c.

A new carrying-trade was created when the Australasian colonies were founded one after the other—in the taking out of home manufactures, implements, machinery, &c., and bringing back wool and tallow; and then gold, wheat, fruit, and frozen meat. This colonial trade is now divided between sailers and steamers, and in the steamer traffic some of the foreign lines are eagerly bidding for a share. Similarly, a new carrying-trade has been of quite recent years developed by the opening up of South Africa, and this is practically all in British hands.

An important item of international carriage of recent development is the mineral oil of America and Russia. The carriage of these oils is a trade of itself. Another special branch of the world's carrying-trade is connected with the sea-fisheries. All the fishing-grounds of the Atlantic and North Sea may be said to be now connected with the consuming markets by services of steamers. The cod-fishers off the Banks of Newfoundland transfer their dried and salted fish to vessels which speed them to the good Catholics of Spain and France and Italy, just as the steam auxiliaries bring to London the harvests gathered by the boats on the Dogger Bank.

Of late years not unsuccessful efforts have been made, especially by Captain Wiggins, to establish direct communication between Great Britain and the arctic coasts of Russia once every summer. And hopes are entertained that on the completion of the railway from Winnipeg to Fort Churchill, the greatly shorter sea-route *via* Hudson

Strait and Hudson Bay may greatly facilitate communication with Manitoba and the Canadian North-west.

It is computed that on the great ocean highways there are not fewer than ten thousand large and highly-powered steamers constantly employed. If it be wondered how sailing-vessels can maintain a place at all in the race of competition in the world's carrying-trade, a word of explanation may be offered. Do not suppose that only rough and low-valued cargo is left for the sailers. They still have the bulk of the cotton and wheat and other valuable products, not only because they can carry more cheaply, but because transport by sailing-vessels gives the merchant a wider choice of market. Cargoes of staple products can always be sold 'to arrive' at some given port, and it is cheaper to put them afloat than to warehouse them ashore and wait for an order.

What, then, are the proportions borne by the several maritime nations in this great international carrying-trade? The question is not one which can be answered with absolute precision, but the tables of the Marine Department of the Board of Trade enable one to find an approximate answer. In 1893 the tonnage of steam and sailing vessels of all nationalities in the foreign trade entering and clearing at ports in the United Kingdom was 74,632,847, of which 54,148,664 tons were British, and 20,484,183 tons were foreign. In the foreign total, the largest proportions were Norwegian, German, Dutch, Swedish, Danish, and French. The Teutonic races have thus the most of the ocean-carrying; the United States proportion of the above total was small.

So far the United Kingdom. Now let us see what part British shipping plays in the foreign trade of other countries. We find that the total tonnage of the British Empire was 10,365,567. The other principal maritime countries owned 12,000,000 tons. Therefore, roughly speaking, the British Empire owns about five-elevenths of the entire shipping of the world. Even so recently as thirty years ago, about two-thirds of the ocean-carrying trade was performed by sailing-vessels; to-day, about four-fifths of it is performed by steamers.

THE FIRST STEAMER TO CROSS THE ATLANTIC.

The earliest steamers the world ever saw, not reckoning the experimental craft constructed by such men as Fulton, Bell, Symington, and Watt, were those employed in the transatlantic trade. As far back as the year 1819, the Yankee paddle-steamer *Savannah*, of three hundred tons burden, crossed from the port of that name, in Georgia, to Liverpool. She occupied twenty-five days upon the passage; but, as she was fully rigged, and under all sail during at least two-thirds of the voyage, the merit of her performance, as an illustration of the superiority of the engine over canvas, is somewhat doubtful. Yet she was beyond dispute the first steamer to accomplish a long sea-voyage, and to the Americans belong the credit of her exploit. Indeed, from the time of their last war with us, down to within a quarter of a century ago, our Yankee neighbours generally seemed to be a little ahead of this country in maritime matters. They taught us a lesson in shipbuilding by their famous Baltimore clippers, and they were the first to demonstrate in a practical manner, and to the complete capsizal of the learned Dr Lardner's theories, the possibility of employing steam for the purposes of ocean navigation.

Although in 1838 the *Sirius* and the *Great Western* successfully made the journey from England to America, yet five years before that date, Canadian enterprise accomplished the feat of bridging the Atlantic Ocean with a little vessel propelled wholly by steam. This was the *Royal William*, whose beautiful model was exhibited at the British Naval Exhibition in London, where she attracted the attention and curiosity of the first seamen in the empire. The *Royal William*—named in honour of the reigning sovereign—was built in the city of Quebec by a Scotchman, James Goudie, who had served his time and learned his art at Greenock. The keel was laid in the autumn of 1830; and her builder, then in his twenty-second year, writes: 'As I had the drawings and the form of the ship, at the time a novelty in construction, it devolved upon me to lay off and expand the draft to its full dimensions on the floor of the loft, where I made several alterations in the lines as improvements. The steamship being duly commenced, the work progressed rapidly; and in May following was duly launched, and before a large concourse of people was christened the *Royal William*. She was then taken to Montreal to have her engines, where I continued to superintend the finishing of the cabins and deck-work. When completed, she had her trial trip, which proved quite satisfactory. Being late in the season before being completed, she only made a few trips to Halifax.'

The launching of this steamer was a great event in Quebec. The Governor-general, Lord Aylmer, and his wife were present, the latter giving the vessel her name. Military bands supplied the music, and the shipping in the harbour was gay with bunting. The city itself wore a holiday look. The *Royal William*, propelled by steam alone, traded between Quebec and Halifax. While at the last-named place, she attracted the notice of Mr Samuel Cunard, afterwards Sir Samuel, the founder of the great trans-continental line which bears his name. It is said that the *Royal William* convinced him that steam was the coming force for ocean navigation. He asked many questions about her, took down the answers in his notebook, and subsequently became a large stockholder in the craft.

The cholera of 1832 paralysed business in Canada, and trade was at a standstill for a time. Like other enterprises at this date, the *Royal William* experienced reverses, and she was doomed to be sold at sheriff's sale. Some Quebec gentlemen bought her in, and resolved to send her to England to be sold. In 1833 the eventful voyage to Britain was made successfully, and without mishap of any kind. The *Royal William's* proportions were as follows: Builder's measurement, 1370 tons; steamboat measurement, as per Act of Parliament, 830 tons; length of keel, 146 feet; length of deck from head to taffrail, 176 feet; breadth of beam inside the paddle-boxes, 29 feet 4 inches; outside, 43 feet 10 inches; depth of hold, 17 feet 9 inches. On the 4th of August 1833, commanded by Captain John M'Dougall, she left Quebec, *via* Pictou, Nova Scotia, for London, under steam, at five o'clock in the morning. She made the passage in twenty-five days. Her supply of coal was 254 chaldrons, or over 330 tons. Her captain wrote: 'She is justly entitled to be considered the first steamer that crossed the Atlantic by steam, having steamed the whole way across.'

About the end of September 1833, the *Royal William* was disposed of for ten thousand pounds sterling, and chartered to the Portuguese government to take out troops for Dom Pedro's service. Portugal was asked to purchase her for the navy; but the admiral of the fleet, not thinking well of the scheme, declined to entertain the proposition. Captain M'Dougall was master of the steamer all this time. He returned with her to London with invalids and disbanded Portuguese soldiers, and laid her up off Deptford Victualling Office. In July, orders came to fit out the *Royal William* to run between Oporto and Lisbon. One trip was made between these ports, and also a trip to Cadiz for specie for the Portuguese government.

On his return to Lisbon, Captain M'Dougall was ordered to sell the steamer to the Spanish government, through Don Evanston Castor da Perez, then the Spanish ambassador to the court of Lisbon. The transaction was completed on the 10th of September 1834, when the *Royal William* became the *Ysabel Segunda*, and the first war-steamer the Spaniards ever possessed. She was ordered to the north coast of Spain against Don Carlos. Captain M'Dougall accepted the rank and pay of a Commander, and, by special proviso, was guaranteed six hundred pounds per annum, and the contract to supply the squadron with provisions from Lisbon. The *Ysabel Segunda* proceeded to the north coast; and about the latter part of 1834 she returned to Gravesend, to be delivered up to the British government, to be converted into a war-steamer at the Imperial Dockyard. The crew and officers were transferred to the *Royal Tar*, chartered and armed as a war-steamer, with six long thirty-two pounders, and named the *Reyna Governadoza*, the name intended for the *City of Edinburgh* steamer, which was chartered to form part of the squadron. When completed, she relieved the *Royal Tar* and took her name.

In his interesting letter, from which these facts are drawn, to Robert Christie, the Canadian historian, Captain M'Dougall thus completes the story of the pioneer Atlantic steamer: 'The *Ysabel Segunda*, when completed at Sheerness Dockyard, took out General Alava, the Spanish ambassador, and General Evans and most of his staff officers, to Saint Andero, and afterwards to St Sebastian, having hoisted the Commodore's broad pennant again at Saint Andero; and was afterwards employed in cruising between that port and Fuente Arabia, and acting in concert with the Legion against Don Carlos until the time of their service expired in 1837. She was then sent to Portsmouth with a part of those discharged from the service, and from thence she was taken to London, and detained in the City Canal by Commodore Henry until the claims of the officers and crew on the Spanish government were settled, which was ultimately accomplished by bills, and the officers and crew discharged from the Spanish service about the latter end of 1837, and *Ysabel Segunda* delivered up to the Spanish ambassador, and after having her engines repaired, returned to Spain, and was soon afterwards sent to Bordeaux, in France, to have the hull repaired. But on being surveyed, it was found that the timbers were so much decayed that it was decided to build a new vessel to receive the engines, which was built there, and called by the same name, and now [1853] forms one of the royal steam-navy of Spain, while her predecessor was converted into a hulk at Bordeaux.'

This, in brief, is the history of the steamer which played so important a rôle in the maritime annals of Canada, England, and Spain. Her model is safely stored in the rooms of the Literary and Historical Society of Quebec, where it is an object of profound veneration. At the request of the government, a copy of the model was made, and formed part of the Canadian exhibit to the World's Fair at Chicago in 1893.

It was not, however, until five years later that the successful passages of two memorable vessels from England to America fairly established the era of what has been called the Atlantic steam-ferry. These ships were respectively the *Sirius* and the *Great Western*. The former was a craft of about 700 tons burden, with engines of three hundred and twenty horse-power: she sailed from Cork on the 4th of April 1838, under the command of Lieutenant Roberts, R.N., bound for New York. The latter vessel was a steamer of 1340 tons, builders' measurement, with engines of four hundred and forty horse-power: she was commanded by Captain Hoskins, R.N., and sailed from Bristol on the 8th of April in the same year, bound likewise for New York. The *Sirius*, it was calculated, had a start of her competitor by about seven hundred nautical miles; but it was known that her utmost capabilities of speed scarcely exceeded eight knots an hour; whilst the *Great Western*, on her trial trip from Blackwall to Gravesend, ran eleven knots an hour without difficulty.

The issue of the race was therefore awaited with the utmost curiosity on both sides of the Atlantic. Contemporary records usually afford good evidence of the significance of past events, and the interest in this novel ocean match was prodigious, to judge from the accounts with which the Liverpool and New York papers of the day teemed. The following is in brief the narrative of the voyage of these two famous ships across the Western Ocean. The *Sirius*, after leaving Cork on the 4th of April, encountered very heavy weather, which greatly retarded her progress. She arrived, however, off Sandy Hook on the evening of Sunday, the 22d of April; but going aground, she did not get into the North River until the following morning. When it was known that she had arrived, New York grew instantly agitated with excitement.

'The news,' ran the account published by the *Journal of Commerce* in the United States, 'spread like wildfire through the city, and the river became literally dotted all over with boats conveying the curious to and from the stranger. There seemed to be a universal voice in congratulation, and every visage was illuminated with delight. A tacit conviction seemed to pervade every bosom that a most doubtful problem had been satisfactorily solved; visions of future advantage to science, to commerce, to moral philosophy, began to float before the "mind's eye;"

curiosity to travel through the old country, and to inspect ancient institutions, began to stimulate the inquiring.

'Whilst all this was going on, suddenly there was seen over Governor's Island a dense black cloud of smoke spreading itself upward, and betokening another arrival. On it came with great rapidity, and about three o'clock in the afternoon its cause was made fully manifest to the accumulated multitudes at the Battery. It was the steamship *Great Western*, of about 1600 tons burden (*sic*) [the difference probably lies between the net and the gross tonnage], under the command of Lieutenant Hoskins, R.N. She had left Bristol on the 8th inst., and on the 23d was making her triumphant entry into the port of New York. This immense moving mass was propelled at a rapid rate through the waters of the Bay; she passed swiftly and gracefully round the *Sirius*, exchanging salutes with her, and then proceeded to her destined anchorage in the East River. If the public mind was stimulated by the arrival of the *Sirius*, it became almost intoxicated with delight upon view of the superb *Great Western*. The latter vessel was only fourteen clear days out; and neither vessel had sustained a damage worth mentioning, notwithstanding that both had to encounter very heavy weather. The *Sirius* was spoken with on the 14th of April in latitude 45° north, longitude 37° west. The *Great Western* was spoken on the 15th of April in latitude 46° 26' north, longitude 37° west. At these respective dates the *Great Western* had run 1305 miles in seven days from King Road; and the *Sirius* 1305 miles in ten days from Cork. The *Great Western* averaged $186\frac{1}{2}$ miles per day, and the *Sirius* $130\frac{1}{2}$ miles; *Great Western* gained on the *Sirius* fifty-six miles per day. The *Great Western* averaged seven and three-quarter miles per hour; the *Sirius* barely averaged five and a half miles per hour.'

Such was the first voyage made across the Atlantic by

these two early steamships, and there is something of the true philosophy of history to be found in the interest which their advent created. It is worthy of passing note to learn what ultimately became of these celebrated vessels. The *Sirius*, not proving staunch enough for the Atlantic surges, was sent to open steam-communication between London and St Petersburg, in which trade she was for several years successfully employed. The *Great Western* plied regularly from Bristol to New York until the year 1847, when she was sold to the Royal Mail Company, and ran as one of their crack ships until 1857, in which year she was broken up at Vauxhall as being obsolete and unable profitably to compete with the new class of steamers being built.

The success of these two vessels may be said to have completely established steam as a condition of the trans-atlantic navigation of the future. 'In October 1838,' says Lindsay, in his *History of Merchant Shipping*, 'Sir John Tobin, a well-known merchant of Liverpool, seeing the importance of the intercourse now rapidly increasing between the Old and New Worlds, despatched on his own account a steamer to New York. She was built at Liverpool, after which place she was named, and made the passage outwards in sixteen and a half days. It was now clearly proved that the service could be performed, not merely with profit to those who engaged in it, but with a regularity and speed which the finest description of sailing-vessels could not be expected to accomplish. If any doubts still existed on these important points, the second voyage of the *Great Western* set them at rest, she having on this occasion accomplished the outward passage in fourteen days sixteen hours, bringing with her the advices of the fastest American sailing-ships which had sailed from New York long before her, and thus proving the necessity of having the mails in future conveyed by steamers.'

In fact, as early as October 1838, the British government, being satisfied of the superiority of steam-packets over sailing-ships, issued advertisements inviting tenders for the conveyance of the American mails by the former class of vessels. The owners of the *Great Western*, big with confidence in the reputation of that ship, applied for the contract; but, not a little to their chagrin, it was awarded to Mr (afterwards Sir Samuel) Cunard, who as far back as 1830 had proposed the establishment of a steam mail service across the Atlantic. The terms of the original contract were, that for the sum of fifty-five thousand pounds per annum, Messrs Cunard, Burns, and MacIver should supply three ships suitable for the purpose, and accomplish two voyages each month between Liverpool and the United States, leaving England at certain periods; but shortly afterwards it was deemed more expedient to name fixed dates of departure on both sides of the Western Ocean. Subsequently, another ship was required to be added to the service, and the amount of the subsidy was raised to eighty-one thousand pounds a year. The steam mail service between Liverpool, Halifax, and Boston was regularly established in 1840, the first vessel engaged in it being the *Britannia*, the pioneer ship of the present Cunard line.

We get an admirable idea of what these early steamships were from Dickens's account of this same *Britannia*, which was the vessel he crossed to America in on his first visit to that country in 1842. In one of his letters to John Forster, describing a storm they were overtaken by, he unconsciously reflects the wondering regard with which the world still viewed the triumphant achievements of the marine engine. 'For two or three hours,' he writes, 'we gave it up as a lost thing. This was not the exaggerated apprehension of a landsman merely. The head-engineer, who had been in one or the other of the Cunard vessels since they began running, had never seen such stress of weather; and I afterwards heard Captain Hewitt say that nothing but a steamer, and one of that strength, could have kept her course and stood it out. A sailing-vessel must have beaten off and driven where she would; while through all the fury of that gale they actually made fifty-four miles headlong through the tempest, straight on end, not varying their track in the least.' What would the skipper of one of the modern 'Atlantic greyhounds' think of such a feat? And, more interesting speculation still, what must Dickens himself have thought of the performances he lived to witness as against this astonishing accomplishment on the part of the old *Britannia* ?

There exists a tendency to ridicule the early steamers as they appear in portraits, with their huge paddle-boxes; tall, thin, dog-eared funnels; and heavily-rigged masts, as though their engines were regarded as quite auxiliary to their sail-power, and by no means to be relied upon. Contrasted with some of the leviathans of the present day, the steamers of half a century ago are no longer calculated to strike an awe into the beholder; but, in truth, some very fine vessels were built whilst the marine engine was still quite in its infancy. In a volume of the *Railway Magazine* for 1839 is an account of what are termed colossal steamers. 'An immense steamer,' runs the description, 'upwards of two hundred feet long, was lately launched at Bristol, for plying between England and America; but the one now building at Carling & Co.'s, Limehouse, for the American Steam-navigation Company, surpasses anything of the kind hitherto made. She is to be named after our Queen, the *Victoria ;* will cost from eighty to one hundred thousand pounds, has about one hundred and fifty men now employed daily upon her, and is expected to be finished in November next. The extreme length is about 253 feet; but she is 237 feet between the perpendiculars, 40¼ feet beam between the paddle-boxes, and twenty-seven feet one inch deep from the floor to the inner side of the spar-deck. The engines are two, of 250 horse-power each, with six feet four inch cylinders, and seven feet stroke. They are to be fitted with Hall's patent condensers, in addition to the common ones. She displaces at sixteen feet 2740 tons of water; her computed tonnage is 1800 tons. At the water-line every additional inch displaces eighteen and a half tons. The average speed is expected to be about two hundred nautical miles a day, and consumption of coal about thirty tons. The best Welsh coal is to be used. It is calculated she will make the outward passage to New York in eighteen days, and the homeward in twelve, consuming 540 tons of coal out, and 360 home. Expectation is on tiptoe for the first voyage of this gigantic steamer, alongside of which other steamers look like little fishing-boats.'

The next route on which steam-navigation was opened, following upon that of the North Atlantic passage, was between Great Britain and India. The steamers of the Honourable Company had indeed doubled the Cape nearly two years before the *Sirius* and *Great Western* sailed upon their first trip. The *Nautical Magazine* for 1836 contains the original prospectus issued by a syndicate of London merchants upon the subject of steam-communication with the East Indies. As an illustration of the almost incredible strides that have been made in ocean travelling since that period, this piece of literature is most instructive. The circular opens by announcing that it is proposed to establish steam traffic with India, extending, perhaps, even to Australia! It points out in sanguine terms how those distant parts of the earth, by the contemplated arrangement, 'will be reached at the outset in the short period of seventy-three days; and, when experience is obtained, this time will in all probability be reduced by one-third; shortening the distance by the route in question, from England to Australia, in forty days' steaming, at ten miles an hour. If two days be allowed for stoppages at stations, not averaging more than a thousand miles apart throughout the line, the whole time for passing between the extreme points would only be sixty days, but a relay of vessels will follow, if the undertaking be matured, in which case twenty-four hours will be ample time at the depots, and a communication may be expected to be established, and kept up throughout the year, between England and Australia, in fifty days. It is reasonably expected that Bombay will be reached in forty-eight days, Madras in fifty-five, Calcutta in fifty-nine, Penang in fifty-seven, Singapore in sixty, Batavia in sixty-two, Canton in sixty-eight, and Mauritius in fifty-four days.'

The *Nautical Magazine* writer gravely comments upon this scheme as quite plausible. He is indeed inclined to be anticipatory. Instead of seventy-three days to Australia, he is of opinion that the voyage may ultimately be accomplished in fifty, and that the table of time generally may be reduced by about one-third throughout; although, to qualify his somewhat daring speculations, he admits that it is well to base the calculations on the safe side. But the Honourable East India Company asserted their prerogatives, and put a stop to the scheme of the New Bengal Steam Company, as the undertaking was to have been called. This raised a strong feeling of dissatisfaction, and the Court of Directors was obliged to provide a substitute in lieu of the new line they had refused to sanction. Their own homely, lubberly craft were quite unequal to the requirements of 'prompt despatch' which even then was beginning to agitate the public mind. The possibility of establishing steam-communication between England and India had been clearly demonstrated as early as the year 1825, when the *Enterprise*, of 480 tons and 120 horse-power, sailed from London on the 16th of August, and arrived in Calcutta on the seventh of December. She was the first steamer to make the passage from this country to our great Eastern Empire; the first, indeed, ever to double the stormy headland of the Cape.

But it was not until the people of India began to petition and the merchants of London to clamour for the adoption of steam-power in the Indian navigation that the conservative old magnates of John Company were stimulated into action. Lieutenant Waghorn's Overland Route had almost entirely superseded the sea-voyage by way of the Cape; but the want of an efficient packet service between London and Alexandria, and Suez and Bombay, was greatly felt. Accordingly, in December 1836, the steamship *Atalanta* was despatched from Falmouth to ply on the Indian side of the route. She was a vessel of 630 tons burden, with engines of 210 horse-power, and was built at Blackwall by the once famous firm of Wigram & Green. The orders of Captain Campbell, who commanded her, were that he was to steam the whole distance, only resorting to sail-power in case of a failure of machinery, in order fully to test the superiority of the marine engine over canvas. She sustained an average speed of about eight knots an hour during the entire passage, and but for her repeated stoppages would undoubtedly have accomplished the quickest voyage yet made to India. She was followed, in March 1837, by the *Bernice*, of 680 tons and 230 horse-power. This vessel, which likewise made the run without the assistance of her sails, left Falmouth on March 17, and arrived at Bombay on the 13th of June.

As the race between the *Sirius* and the *Great Western* may be said to have inaugurated the steam-navigation of the Atlantic, so did the voyages of the *Atalanta* and *Bernice* first establish regular communication by steamers between Great Britain and India. True, there had been desultory efforts of enterprise prior to this time, and the pioneer of the Peninsular and Oriental steamers, the *Royal Tar*, had sailed some three years before; but there was no continual service. The *Times* of November 11, 1838, pointed out the approaching change. 'Scarcely,' it says, 'has the wonder created in the world by the appearance of the *Great Western* and *British Queen* begun to subside, when we are again called upon to admire the rapid strides of enterprise by the notice of an iron steamship, the first of a line of steamers to ply between England and Calcutta, to be called the *Queen of the East*, 2618 tons, and 600 horse-power. This magnificent vessel is designed by Mr W. D. Holmes, engineer to the Bengal Steam Committee, for a communication between England and India. Great praise is due to Captain Barber, late of the Honourable East India Company's service, the agent in London for the Steam Committee in Bengal, who has given every encouragement to Mr Holmes in carrying forward his splendid undertaking. When these vessels are ready, we understand the voyage between Falmouth and Calcutta will be made in thirty days.'

From this time ocean steamers multiplied rapidly. One after another of the now famous shipping firms sprang up, beginning with the Cunard and the Peninsular and Oriental lines. The first British steamship was registered at London in the year 1814: in 1842 there were 940 steamers registered; and already was the decay of the sailing-ship so largely anticipated, that Mr Sydney Herbert, in a Committee of the House of Commons, had this same year pointed out 'that the introduction of steamers, and the consequent displacement of the Leith smacks,

Margate hoys, &c., would diminish the nursery for seamen by lessening the number of sailing-vessels.'

THE NEW CUNARDERS.

Less than fifty years ago the Eastern Steam-navigation Company having failed to obtain the contract to carry the mails from Plymouth to India and Australia—in vessels of from twelve hundred to two thousand tons, with engines of from four to six hundred horse-power, which were never built—began to consider a new enterprise, suggested by the late Isambard K. Brunel. This was to build the largest steamer ever yet constructed, to trade with India round the Cape of Good Hope. The general commercial idea was, that this leviathan vessel was to carry leviathan cargoes at large freights and great speed, to Ceylon, where the goods and passengers would be rapidly trans-shipped to smaller swift steamers for conveyance to various destinations in India, China, and Australia. The general mechanical idea was, that in order to obtain great velocity in steamers it was only necessary to make them large—that, in fact, there need be no limit to the size of a vessel beyond what might be imposed by the tenacity of material. On what was called the tubular principle, Brunel argued—and proved to the satisfaction of numerous experts and capitalists—that it was possible to construct a vessel of six times the capacity of the largest vessel then afloat that would steam at a speed unattainable by smaller vessels, while carrying, besides cargo, all the coal she would require for the longest voyage.

Thus originated the *Great Eastern*, which never went to India, which ruined two or three companies in succession, which cost £120,000 to launch, which probably earned more as a show than ever she did as an ocean-carrier—

except in the matter of telegraph cables—and which ignobly ended a disastrous career by being sold for £16,000, and broken up at New Ferry, on the Mersey.

We are now entering upon a new era of big ships, in which such a monster as the *Great Eastern* would be no longer a wonder. Two additions to the Cunard fleet, the *Campania* (1892) and *Lucania* (1893), are within a trifle as large as she, but with infinitely more powerful engines and incomparably greater speed.

We need not suppose, however, that the idea of big ocean steamers has been the monopoly of this country. So long ago as 1850 or thereabouts, Mr Randall, a famous American shipbuilder, designed, drafted, and constructed the model of a steamer for transatlantic service, 500 feet long by 58 feet beam, to measure 8000 tons. A company was formed in Philadelphia in 1860 to carry out the project; but the civil war broke out soon after, and she was never built.

The *Great Eastern* was launched in January 1858, and her principal dimensions were these: Length between perpendiculars, 680 feet; breadth of beam, 83 feet; length of principal saloons, 400 feet; tonnage capacity for cargo and coals, 18,000 tons; weight of ship as launched, 12,000 tons; accommodation for passengers, (1) 800, (2) 2000, (3) 1200 = 4000; total horse-power, 7650. She had both screw and paddles for propulsion, and her displacement was 32,160 tons.

By this time the Cunard Company had been eighteen years in existence. They started in 1840 with the *Britannia*—quickly followed by the *Acadia*, *Columbia*, and *Caledonia*, all more or less alike—which was a paddle-steamer of wood, 207 feet long, 34 feet broad, 22 feet deep, and of 1156 tons, with side-lever engines developing 740 indicated horse-power, which propelled the vessel at the average speed of nine knots an hour.

There was accommodation for 225 tons of cargo and 115 cabin passengers—no steerage in those days—who paid thirty-four guineas to Halifax and thirty-eight guineas to Boston, for passage, including provisions and wine.

At the time of the *Great Eastern* the latest type of Cunarder was the *Persia*, and it is interesting to note the development in the interim. This vessel was 380 feet long, 45 feet broad, 31 feet deep, of 3870 tons, with engines developing 4000 indicated horse-power, propelling at the rate of thirteen and a half knots an hour. The *Persia* and the *Scotia*, sister-ships, were the last of the Atlantic side-wheelers. In 1862 the first screw-steamer was added to the Cunard fleet. This was the *China*, built by the Napiers of Glasgow, 326 feet long by 40½ feet broad, and 27½ feet deep, of 2600 tons, and with an average speed of about twelve knots.

Such was the type of Cunarder in the early days of the *Great Eastern*, whose dimensions have now been nearly reached. The *Campania*, however, was not built with a view to outshine that huge failure, but is the outcome of a wholly different competition. The *Campania* and the *Lucania* represent the highest development of marine architecture and engineering skill, and are the product of long years of rivalry for the possession of the 'blue ribbon' of the transatlantic race.

The competition is of ancient date, if we go back to the days when the American 'Collins' Company tried to run the Cunard Company off the waters; and during the half-century since the inauguration of steam service the Cunard Company have sometimes held and sometimes lost the highest place for speed. The period of steam-racing—the age of 'Atlantic greyhounds'—may be said to have begun in the year 1879, when the Cunard *Gallia*, the Guion *Arizona*, and the White Star *Britannic* and *Germanic* had all entered upon their famous careers. It is matter of

The *Great Eastern* and the *Persia*.

history now how the *Arizona*—called the 'Fairfield Flyer,' because she was built by Messrs John Elder & Company, of Fairfield, Glasgow—beat the record in an eastward run of seven days twelve and a half hours, and a westward run of seven days ten and three-quarter hours. To beat the *Arizona*, the Cunard Company built the *Servia*, of 8500 tons and 10,300 horse-power; but she in turn was beaten by another Fairfield Flyer, the *Alaska*, under the Guion flag. The race continued year by year, as vessels of increasing size and power were entered by the competing companies. While all the lines compete in swiftness, luxury, and efficiency, the keenest rivalry is now between the Cunard and the White Star companies. And just as the *Campania* and *Lucania* were built to eclipse the renowned *Teutonic* and *Majestic*, so the owners of these boats prepared to surpass even the two Cunarders we describe.

Let us now see something of these marvels of marine architecture. They are sister-ships, both built on the Clyde by the Fairfield Shipbuilding and Engineering Company, and both laid down almost simultaneously. They are almost identical in dimensions and appointments, and therefore we may confine our description to the *Campania*, which was the first of the twins to be ready for sea.

This largest vessel afloat does not mark any new departure in general type, as the *Great Eastern* did in differing from all types of construction then familiar. In outward appearance, the *Campania*, as she lies upon the water, and as seen at a sufficient distance, is just like numbers of other vessels we have all seen. Nor does her immense size at first impress the observer, because of the beautiful proportions on which she is planned. Her lines are eminently what the nautical enthusiast calls 'sweet;' and in her own class of naval art she is as perfect a specimen of architectural beauty as the finest of the grand old clippers which used to 'walk the waters as a thing of life.' The colossal size of St Peter's at Rome does not strike you as you enter, because of the exquisite proportions. And so with the *Campania*—you need to see an ordinary merchant-ship, or even a full-blown liner, alongside before you can realise how vast she is.

Yet she is only 60 feet shorter than the mammoth *Great Eastern*, and measures 620 feet in length, 65 feet 3 inches in breadth, and 43 feet in depth from the upper deck. Her tonnage is 12,000, while that of the *Great Eastern* was 18,000; but then her horse-power is 30,000 as against the *Great Eastern's* 7650!

This enormous development of engine-power is perhaps the most remarkable feature about these two new vessels. Each of them is fitted with two sets of the most powerful triple-expansion engines ever put together. A visit to the engine-room is a liberal education in the mechanical arts, and even to the eye of the uninitiated there is the predominant impression of perfect order in the bewildering arrangement of pipes, rods, cranks, levers, wheels, and cylinders. The two sets of engines are placed in two separate rooms on each side of a centre-line bulkhead fitted with water-tight doors for intercommunication. Each set has five inverted cylinders which have exactly the same stroke, and work on three cranks. Two of the cylinders are high-pressure, one is intermediate, and two are low-pressure. Besides the main engines, there are engines for reversing, for driving the centrifugal pumps for the condensers, for the electric light, for the refrigerating chambers, and for a number of other purposes—all perfect in appointment and finish. In fact, in these vast engine-rooms one is best able to realise not only the immense size and power of the vessel, but also the perfection to which human ingenuity has attained after generations of ceaseless toil—and yet it is only half a century since the *Britannia* began the transatlantic race.

Each of the various engines has its own steam-supplier. The main engines are fed by twelve double-ended boilers, arranged in rows of six on each side of a water-tight bulkhead. The boilers are heated by ninety-six furnaces, and each set of six boilers has a funnel with the diameter of an ordinary railway tunnel. In the construction of these boilers some eight hundred tons of steel were required, the plates weighing four tons each, with a thickness of an inch and a half. From these mighty machines will be developed a power equal to that of 30,000 horses! Compare this with the *Great Eastern's* 7650 horse-power, or even with the later 'greyhounds.' The greatest power developed by the two previous additions to the Cunard fleet, the *Etruria* and *Umbria*, is about 14,000 horses, which is the utmost recorded by any single-screw engines. The *City of Paris* has a power of 18,500, and the *Teutonic* a power of 18,000 by twin-screw engines. The *Campania*, therefore, is upwards of half as much again more powerful than the largest, swiftest, and most powerful of her predecessors.

These engines of the *Campania* work two long propeller-shafts, each carried through an aperture in the stern close to the centre-line, and fitted to a screw. Unlike other twin-screw vessels, the propellers and shafts are, as it were, carried within the hull, and not in separate structures. Abaft of the screws, the rudder is completely submerged, and is a great mass of steel-plating weighing about twenty-four tons.

With a straight stem, an elliptic stern, two huge funnels, and a couple of pole-masts—intended more for signalling purposes than for canvas—the *Campania* looks thoroughly business-like, and has none of the over-elaborated get-up of the *Great Eastern*, with her double system of propulsion and small forest of masts. The bulwarks are close fore and aft; and from the upper deck rise two tiers of houses, the roofs of which form the promenade deck and the shade deck. In the structure of the hull and decks enormous strength has been given, with special protection at vital parts, as the vessel is built in compliance with the Admiralty requirements for armed cruisers. Below the line of vision are four other complete tiers of beams, plated with steel sheathed in wood, on which rest upper, main, lower, and orlop decks. The last is for cargo, refrigerating-chambers, stores, &c.—all the others are devoted to the accommodation of passengers.

The *Campania* is fitted to carry 460 first-class passengers, 280 second-class, and 700 steerage passengers—in all, 1440, besides a crew of 400. She has cargo-space for 1600 tons, which seems a trifle in comparison with her size, but then it is to be remembered that the fuel consumption of those 96 furnaces is enormous, and requires the carrying of a very heavy cargo of coals for internal consumption.

The accommodation for passengers is probably the most perfect that has yet been provided on an ocean steamer, for here the experience of all previous developments has been utilised. The dining-room is an apartment 100 feet long and 64 feet broad, furnished in handsome dark old mahogany, to seat 430 persons. The upholstery is tastefully designed, and the fittings generally are elegant; but the peculiar feature is a splendid dome rising to a height of thirty-three feet from the floor to the upper deck, and designed to light both the dining-room and the drawing-room on the deck above it. The grand staircase which conducts to these apartments is of teak-wood; the drawing-room is in satin-wood relieved with cedar and painted frieze panels. The smoking-room on the promenade deck is as unlike a ship's cabin as can be imagined; it is, in

The *Campania*.

fact, a reproduction of an old baronial hall of the Elizabethan age, with oaken furniture and carvings. The other public apartments, library, boudoir, &c., are all more remarkable for quiet taste and artistic effect than for the gorgeousness of gilded saloons affected on some lines, but the prevailing feeling is one of luxurious comfort. The staterooms for first-class passengers occupy the main, upper, and promenade decks, and they are as much like real bedrooms as the old type of 'berths' are not. Besides the single bedrooms, there are suites of rooms for families or parties, finely appointed with ornamental woods, rich carpets, and with brass bedsteads instead of the old wooden bunks. All the sleeping-rooms are as light, lofty, and well ventilated as the sleeping-rooms on the old liners were the reverse.

The first-class passengers are placed amidships; the second-class are placed aft; and the steerage, forward. The steerage accommodation is superior to anything yet provided in that class; while the second-class accommodation is quite up to the usual first-class, with spacious, beautifully furnished staterooms, a handsome dining-room in oak, an elegant drawing-room in satin-wood, and a cosy smoking-room. Indeed, some of the second-class apartments look as if they were intended to be utilised for first-class passengers in times of extra pressure.

These are details of interest to possible passengers and to those who have already experienced the comforts and discomforts of the Atlantic voyage. But the great interest of the ship, of course, is in her immense size and enormous power. The navigating-bridge from which the officer in charge will direct operations, is no less than sixty feet above the water-level, and from there one obtains a survey unique of its kind. The towering height, the vast expanse of deck, the huge circumference of the funnels, the forest of ventilators indicative of the hives of industry below, the great lighthouse structures which take the place of the old angle-bedded side-lights—everything beneath you speaks of power and speed, of strength and security.

The following table shows at a glance how the *Campania* compares with her largest predecessors in point of size and power:

	Tonnage.	Length in feet.	Breadth in feet.	Horse-power.
Great Eastern	18,900	682	82	7,650
Britannic	5,000	455	46	5,500
Arizona	5,150	450	45	6,300
Servia	8,500	515	52	10,300
Alaska	6,400	500	50	10,500
City of Rome	8,000	545	52	11,800
Aurania	7,270	470	57	8,500
Oregon	7,375	500	54	7,375
America	5,528	432	51	7,354
Umbria	7,700	501	57	14,320
Etruria	7,800	520	57	14,500
City of Paris	10,500	560	63	18,500
Teutonic	9,860	582	$57\frac{1}{2}$	18,000
Normannia	—	520	$57\frac{1}{4}$	16,350
Campania } Lucania }	12,950	620	65	30,000

As to speed, the record of course has been broken. In 1850 the average passage of a Cunarder westward was thirteen days, and eastward twelve days sixteen hours; in 1890, the average was reduced to seven days fifteen hours twenty-three minutes, and seven days four hours and fifty-two minutes, respectively. The fastest individual passages down to 1891 were made by the *Etruria*, westwards in six days one hour and forty-seven minutes; and by the *Umbria*, eastwards in six days three hours and seventeen minutes. But these were beaten by the *Teutonic*, which reduced the homeward record to five days and twenty-one hours; and by the *City of Paris*, which reduced the outward passage to five days and sixteen hours. Roughly speaking, these new Cunarders are about ten times the size and forty times the power of the pioneers of the fleet, and the *Campania* will run every twenty minutes almost as many miles as the *Britannia* could laboriously make in an hour.

Is it possible that within the next fifty years we shall be able to make the voyage to New York in three days? The old *Britannia* took fourteen days to Boston, and it was not until 1852 that the ten days' record to New York was broken by the 'Collins' Company. If, then, in forty years we reduced the record from ten to five, who can say that the limit of speed has yet been reached?

SAILING-SHIPS.

A modern sailing-ship replete with labour-saving appliances is a veritable triumph of the naval architect's art, and an excellent object lesson on man's power over the forces of nature. If Christopher Columbus could revisit our planet from the shades, he would doubtless be astonished by a critical comparison between the tiny wooden caravel with which he discovered a New World, and a leviathan four-masted steel sailing-ship, now navigated in comparative comfort to every possible port where freight is obtainable. Wooden cargo-carrying craft impelled by the unbought wind are surely diminishing in numbers; and in the near future it is not improbable that a stately sailing-ship will be as seldom seen on the waste of waters as a screw steamship was half a century ago. Even looking leisurely backward down the imposing vista of the last thirty years of the Victorian era, it will be readily perceived with what marvellous mastery iron and steel have supplanted, not only wood in the hulls, masts, and yards of sailing-ships, but also hemp in their rigging.

A radical revolution has been effected in the form, size, and construction of these cargo-carriers during such a rela-

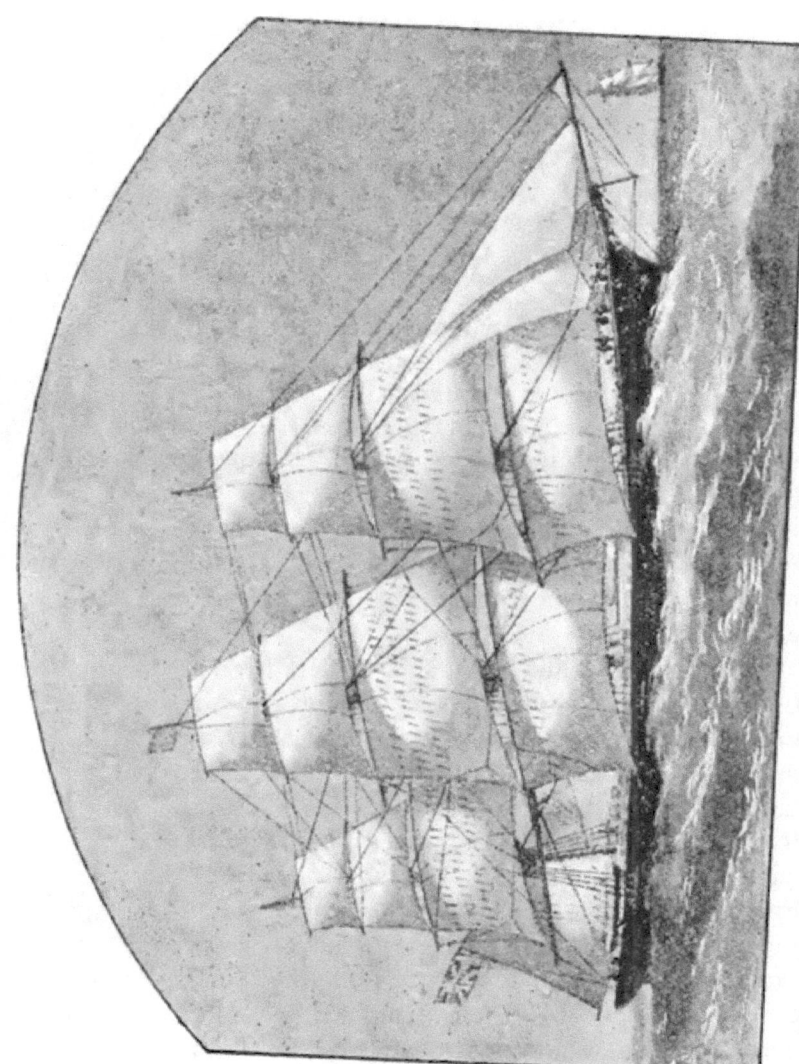

Clipper Sailing-ship of 1850–60.

tively insignificant interval, and the end is not yet. The old-fashioned type of wooden merchantman remained practically invariable for more than a hundred years; but change is all-powerful at present, so that a vessel is almost of a bygone age before she shall have completed her maiden voyage. It would appear, however, that the limit of size has been reached. Ship-owning firms and shipbuilders will probably soon be compelled to keep the modern steel sailing-ship within more moderate dimensions. Vessels of exceptionally large carrying capacity are in demand owing to the fact that experience proves them to be the best kind for affording a fair return to the capital invested. Salvage appliances and docks do not keep pace with the requirements of such leviathans; so that underwriters evince an increasing dislike to big ships, and the premium for insurance rises accordingly, to compensate for extra risk.

Many mariners and some shipbuilders were at one time quick to express a pronounced opinion that it was quite unnatural for an iron ship to remain afloat. Wood was made to swim, but iron to sink, said these sincere but mistaken admirers of the good old days. Their misgivings have proved to be without foundation in fact, for iron ships have ousted wooden craft almost utterly from the ocean-carrying traffic. Iron has also reached its meridian altitude, and steel is rapidly rising above the horizon of progress. The shipbuilding yards of Nova Scotia, Canada, the United States of America, and British Columbia, however, still launch wooden sailing-vessels, although in decreasing numbers, and, as a rule, of inconsiderable tonnage.

It seems scarcely credible that only as recently as 1870 there were not more than ten sailing-ships afloat of two thousand tons register and upwards under the red ensign of the British mercantile marine. To-day we have more than that number of splendid steel sailing-ships, each having a register tonnage in excess of three thousand. During the twelve months of 1892 there were turned out from one yard alone on the Clyde, that of Messrs Russell & Co., no fewer than thirteen huge sailing-vessels, varying in register tonnage from two thousand three hundred to three thousand five hundred! One of the largest wooden sailing-ships afloat in 1870 was the *British Empire*, of two thousand seven hundred tons register, which, under the command of Captain A. Pearson, was an ark of safety to the families of European residents in Bombay during the Indian Mutiny. She had been originally intended for a steamship, and this will account for her exceptional dimensions. The shipbuilding firm of A. Sewall & Co., of Bath, Maine, U.S.A., in 1889 built the *Rappahannock*, of 3054 tons register; in 1890, the *Shenandoah*, 3258 tons; in 1891, the *Susquehanna*, 2629 tons; and in 1892, the *Roanoke*, of 3400 tons register.

Several cities claim to be the birthplace of Homer, and there exists similar rivalry with respect to the first iron ship. This at least is certain, that the first iron vessel classed by Lloyd's was the British barque *Ironsides*, in 1838. She was but 271 tons register. The Clyde stands *facile princeps* in this most important branch of industry. Vessels built on the banks of that river have rendered a praiseworthy account of themselves on every sea and under every flag. No other country, save ourselves, launched any iron or steel ships of 2000 tons register or above, but preferred to obtain them from our shipbuilding yards. The so-called protection of native industry principle prevailing in America precludes ship-owners over there from taking advantage directly of the cheapest market. Several of the large sailers, however, built on the Clyde for citizens of the United States are therefore necessarily sailed under the British, Hawaiian, or some flag other than that of the country to which they actually belong.

The number of seamen carried per one hundred tons in the modern four-masted sailing-ship is cut down to the uttermost limit consistent with safety; and, as a consequence, dismasting and tedious passages are not infrequent. The *Hawaiian Isles*, 2097 tons register, a United States ship under a foreign flag, bound to California with a cargo of coal, found it impossible to weather Cape Horn by reason of violent westerly gales. She was turned round, ran along the lone Southern Ocean, before the 'brave west winds' so admirably described by Maury, and eventually reached her destination by the route leading south of Australia. She was one hundred and eighty-nine days on the passage, and no fewer than sixty guineas per cent. had been freely paid for her re-insurance. A similar ship, the *John Ena*, carrying a substantial cargo of 4222 tons of coal from Barry to San Francisco, also encountered bad weather, made a long passage, and twenty guineas per cent. was paid on her for re-insurance. Another new ship, the *Achnashie*, 2476 tons register, got into still more serious difficulty under like circumstances. She had to put back to Cape Town, damaged and leaky, after attempting in vain to contend against the bitter blast off Cape Horn. There, her cargo was discharged, and she went into dry-dock for the absolutely necessary repairs. The *Austrasia*, 2718 tons register, was almost totally dismasted near the island of Tristan da Cunha, in the South Atlantic, on her maiden passage, while bound from Liverpool to Calcutta with a cargo of salt. By dint of sterling seamanship she was brought to Rio Janeiro in safety, returned to Liverpool under improvised masts, discharged her cargo, refitted, took in quite a different cargo at London, and sailed for California. The *Somali*, 3537 tons register, the largest sailing-ship launched in 1892, was dismasted in the China Sea. Everything above the lower masts had to be made for her on the Clyde; yet, within fifteen days of the order being received by Messrs Russell & Co., the spars and gear were completed and shipped for passage to the *Somali* at Hong-kong. Underwriters suffer severely with such ships.

One of the largest sailing-ships afloat is the French five-master, *La France*, launched in 1890 on the Clyde, and owned by Messrs A. D. Bordes et Fils, who possess a large fleet of sailing-vessels. In 1891 she came from Iquique to Dunkirk in one hundred and five days with 6000 tons of nitrate; yet she was stopped on the Tyne when proceeding to sea with 5500 tons of coal, and compelled to take out 500 tons on the ground that she was overladen. There is not a single five-masted sailing-ship under the British flag. The United States has two five-masters, the *Louis* of 830 tons, and the *Gov. Ames* of 1778 tons, both fore-and-aft schooners, a rig peculiar to the American coast. Ships having five masts can be counted on the fingers of one hand; but, strange to say, the steamship *Coptic*, of the Shaw, Savill, & Albion Co., on her way to New Zealand, in December 1890, passed the *Gov. Ames* in fourteen degrees south, thirty-four degrees west, bound for California; and two days later, in six degrees south, thirty-one degrees west, the French five-master, *La France*, bound south. Passengers and crew of the *Coptic* might travel over many a weary league of sea, and never again be afforded two such excellent object lessons in the growth of sailing-ships in quick succession.

Some large sailing-ships experience a decided difficulty in obtaining freights that will repay expenses, even ignoring a margin for profit, and we are reluctantly compelled to confess that the days of sailing-ships are almost numbered. The cry for huge sailers is an evidence that steam is determining the dimensions of the most modern cargo-carriers under sail.

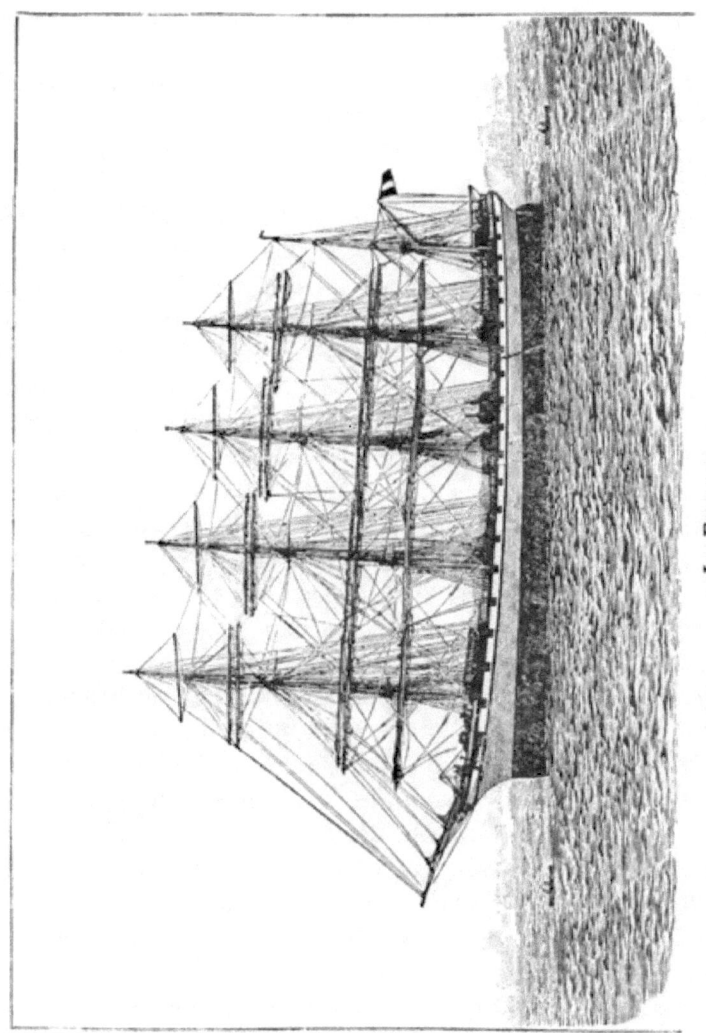

La France.

CHAPTER IX.

POST-OFFICE—TELEGRAPH—TELEPHONE—PHONOGRAPH.

Rowland Hill and Penny Postage—A Visit to the Post-office—The Post-office on Wheels—Early Telegraphs—Wheatstone and Morse—The State and the Telegraphs—Atlantic Cables—Telephones—Edison and the Phonograph.

THE STORY OF ROWLAND HILL AND PENNY POSTAGE.

THE story of Penny Postage and its inception by Sir Rowland Hill is full of romantic interest, and that great social reform, introduced more than fifty years ago, has unquestionably spread its beneficial influence over every country in which a postal system of any kind exists.

The Hill family were, we know, in those bygone days far from being well off, and were often hard put to to find the money to pay the high postage on letters which they received. Born in 1795, Rowland Hill was considerably past middle life before he entertained any idea of practising his reforming hand on the Post-office, and had passed a busy existence chiefly as a schoolmaster, in which capacity he had indulged in many schemes, scholastic and otherwise, with more or less success. At the time that his attention was first directed to Post-office matters, he was employed as Secretary of the Commissioners for the Colonisation of South Australia. He was no doubt attracted to the subject of postal reform by the frequent discussions which were then taking place in parliament in regard to the matter. Mr Wallace of Kelly, the member for Greenock, who was the champion of the cause in the House of Commons, was fierce in his denunciation of the existing abuses and irregularities of the post, and subsequently proved a strong and able advocate of the scheme for postage reform.

Once arrested by the subject which has since made his life famous, Rowland Hill went to work in a very systematic manner. Firstly, he read very carefully all the Reports relative to the Post-office; then he placed himself in communication with Mr Wallace and the Postmaster-general, both of whom readily supplied him with all necessary information. In this manner he made himself acquainted with his subject, with the result that, in 1837, he published his famous pamphlet on *Post-office Reform: its Importance and Practicability*, the first edition being circulated privately amongst the members of parliament and official people; while some months later a second edition was published which was given to the public.

We have to remember that at this time the postage charges were enormously high, that they depended not upon weight alone, but also upon the number of enclosures, and that they varied according to distance. Thus, for example, a letter under one ounce in weight and with one enclosure (that is, sheet or scrap of paper) posted in London for delivery within the metropolitan area, or even, we believe, fifteen miles out, cost 2d.; if for delivery thirty miles out, 3d.; eighty miles out, 4d.; and so on. Again, as showing how the charges according to enclosure operated, a letter with a single enclosure from London to Edinburgh was charged 1s. $1\frac{1}{2}$d.; if double, 2s. 3d.; and if treble, 3s. $4\frac{1}{2}$d. Moreover, the charges were not consistently made, for whereas an Edinburgh letter (posted in London) was charged 1s. 1½d., a letter for Louth, which cost the Post-office fifty times as much as the former letter, was only charged 10d.

The public, however, found means of their own of remedying the evil, which, if not wholly legitimate, were under the circumstances to be regarded with some degree of leniency. Letter-smuggling was a not unnatural result of the high and disproportionate charges referred to, and was almost openly adopted to an extent that is hardly credible. Thus, many Manchester merchants—Mr Cobden amongst the number—stated before the Post-office Inquiry Committee appointed in 1838, their belief that four-fifths of the letters written in that town did not pass through the Post-office. A carrier in Scotland confessed to having carried sixty letters daily for a number of years, and knew of others who carried five hundred daily. A Glasgow publisher and bookseller said he sent and received fifty letters or circulars daily, and added that he was not caught until he had sent twenty thousand letters otherwise than through the post! There were also other methods of evading the postage rates at work. Letters were smuggled in newspapers, which in these days passed free within a stated period through the post, the postage being covered by the stamp-duty impressed on the papers. Invisible ink, too, was used for inditing messages on the newspapers themselves; while the use of certain pre-arranged codes on the covers of letters was likewise systematically adopted, the addressees, after turning the letters over and learning from the covers all they desired to know, declining to take in the letters on the ground that they could not afford to pay the postage.

The system of 'franking' letters in the high-postage days led to an appalling abuse of that privilege, which belonged to peers and members of the House of Commons. It was no doubt originally allowed to enable members to correspond with their constituents; but under the circumstances it is perhaps not surprising that the plan soon became abused, and was ultimately used to cover all kinds of correspondence, not only members' but other people's as well. At one time, indeed, all sorts of curious packages passed free under the franking privilege, such as dogs, a cow, parcels of lace, bales of stockings, boxes of medicine, flitches of bacon, &c. Sometimes, indeed, franked covers were actually sold; and they have even been known to be given in lieu of wages to servants, who speedily converted them into ready money.

This abuse, taken together with the illicit traffic in letters, so openly and widely carried on, formed of course a most important argument in favour of the proposals for cheap postage formulated by Rowland Hill, and no doubt did much to damage the cause of his opponents. But there is one other abuse to which Londoners were subject which may just be mentioned. At that time the Twopenny Post was in operation in the English metropolis, and would have fairly served the inhabitants in postal matters if it had not been for the practice which existed of allowing commercial houses and other firms who were willing to pay for the privilege to have their letters picked out from the general heap and delivered by special postmen, and so enable them to get their correspondence an hour earlier than those who did not pay the 'quarterage,' as it was called, of five shillings (per quarter), and which, it appears, went into the pockets of the postmen concerned, many of whom, we are told, and it can easily be understood, thus made incomes of from three to four hundred pounds a year. However beneficial such a system was to commerce and trade in London, it operated most unfairly on ordinary correspondents, and it was certainly not the least of the evils which the introduction of Penny Postage swept away.

It is not necessary to enter at any length into all the arguments that weighed with Rowland Hill in propounding his great scheme. It need only be very briefly stated that the great point to which he applied himself was the cost to the Post-office of receiving, transmitting, and delivering a letter. Having roughly and, as subsequently proved, not inaccurately calculated the average postage at sixpence farthing per letter, he then went to work to ascertain the expenses of management; and the result of his investigations showed that, no matter what distance had to be traversed, the average cost of each letter to the government was less than one-tenth of a penny! From this there was only one conclusion that could well be forced on his mind, and that was a uniform rate of postage. Having solved this great problem, there were many other matters of adjustment and improvement to which his attention had to be given. He was, for example, not long in deciding that the charge according to enclosures was an iniquitous one, and that a just and fair tax could only be made according to weight. Then, again, he clearly saw that the principle of throwing the postage on the recipients of letters was an improper one, while it was also a burden on the Post-office employees. The prepayment of postage became necessarily a feature of his plan; but he experienced some difficulty in arriving at a feasible method of adopting it. At first he considered that this might be carried out by payment of money over the counter; but he subsequently came to the conclusion that the purposes of the public and the Post-office would be better served by the use of some kind of stamp or stamped covers for letters, and this arrangement he brought forward and fully explained before the Commissioners of Post-office Inquiry, referring to it as 'Mr Knight's excellent suggestion.' Charles Knight had suggested the idea of stamps for prepayment in 1833-34. The following extract from the Commissioners' Report, which gives a brief description of the proposed arrangement, may perhaps be read with interest at the present time:

'That stamped covers, or sheets of paper, or small vignette stamps—the latter, if used, to be gummed on the face of the letter—be supplied to the public from the Stamp-office, and sold at such a price as to include the postage. Letters so stamped to be treated in all respects as franks. That each should have the weight it is entitled to carry legibly printed upon the stamp. That the stamp of the receiving-house should be struck upon the superscription or duty stamp, to prevent the latter being used a second time. The vignette stamps being portable, persons could carry them in their pocket-books.'

The proposed arrangement met with approval from the Commissioners, and also from the Committee on Postage in 1837 and 1838; and, in consequence, the Penny Postage Act of 1840 contained a clause providing for the use of such stamps and stamped covers.

Such were the main points of Rowland Hill's plan, which was so logical and reasonable in all its features, and so intelligible to the popular mind, that it can be readily understood how heartily it was embraced by the general public. But popular as his scheme was with the mass of the people, it encountered the bitterest opposition from many quarters; and in successfully carrying it through, Rowland Hill had, like most other great reformers, to overcome huge difficulties and obstacles. It is very amusing at this distance of time, when we have become so accustomed to the immense advantages of Penny Postage as to view them almost as part of the ordinary conditions of life, to recall some of the arguments used fifty years ago against the measure. Lord Lichfield, as Postmaster-general, in adverting to the scheme in the House of Lords, described it thus: 'Of all the wild visionary schemes which I have ever heard of, it is the most extravagant;' and endorsed this statement six months later when he had given more attention to the subject, being 'even still more firmly of the same opinion.' On a subsequent occasion he contended that the mails would have to carry twelve times as much in weight as before, and therefore the charge would be twelve times the amount then paid. 'The walls of the Post-office,' he exclaimed, 'would burst; the whole area in which the building stands would not be large enough to receive the clerks and letters.' Outside the Post-office, too, as well as by both the government and opposition, much animosity was exhibited against the proposal.

If, however, the opposition against the introduction of Penny Postage was strong, the advocacy of the plan was no less powerful, while, moreover, it was thoroughly backed by popular opinion. Complaints as to the high rates of postage flowed in, and parliament was nearly inundated with petitions in favour of the scheme, which also received much literary support. The Mercantile Committee during all the time of agitation actively spread information of the progress of the measure, with a view to rouse the public to a sense of its importance. The *Post* circular kept circulating; and handbills, fly-sheets, and pictorial illustrations were freely distributed. One print took a dramatic form, representing 'A Scene at Windsor Castle,' in which the Queen, being in the Council Chamber, is made to say: 'Mothers pawning their clothes to pay the postage of a child's letter! Every subject studying how to evade the postage without caring for the law!'—(To Lord Melbourne): 'I trust, my lord, you have commanded the attendance of the Postmaster-general and Mr Rowland Hill, as I directed, in order that I may hear the reasons of both about this universal Penny Postage plan, which appears to me likely to remove all these great evils.' After the interview takes place, the Queen is made to record the opinion that the plan 'would confer a great boon on the poorer classes of my subjects, and would be the greatest benefit to religion, morals, to general knowledge, and to trade.' This *jeu d'esprit*, which was published by the London Committee, was circulated by thousands, and proved extremely useful in bringing the burning question home in an attractive form to the masses of the nation.

The agitation as to Rowland Hill's scheme lasted for two years, and with such vehemence that the period has become an epoch in the history of this country. The end of the story of this memorable reform is soon told; for an agitation which may be said to have shaken the nation to its core and was felt from end to end of the kingdom could have but one conclusion, and that a successful one. A Parliamentary Committee was appointed to inquire into the whole matter; and after a session of sixty-three days, reported in favour of Penny Postage. That was in August 1838. Next year a Bill for Cheap Postage passed through parliament with slight opposition; and on the 12th of November 1839 the Treasury issued a Minute authorising a uniform rate of fourpence for inland letters. This was, however, merely a temporary measure, in which Rowland Hill concurred, and was resorted to chiefly to accustom the Post-office clerks to a uniform rate and the system of charging by weight. The full measure of the Penny Postage scheme was accomplished a few months later on, when, on the 10th of January 1840, the uniform rate of One Penny for letters not exceeding half an ounce in weight was officially introduced.

Such in brief is the story of Penny Postage, which has caused such a revolution not only in the postal arrangements of this country, but in the conditions of all sections and grades of society. In the first year of its operation the number of letters posted was more than doubled, the number sent in 1840 being 169,000,000, as against 82,000,000 posted in 1839, including 6,500,000 letters sent under the franking privilege, which was abolished with the introduction of the Penny Postage system. In 1851 the number of letters posted in Great Britain and Ireland had risen to 670,000,000; while in 1895 the quantity sent reached the fabulous number of 1771 millions, or about forty-five letters per head of the population. This refers to letters pure and simple. If we take into account post-cards, newspapers, book-packets, &c., the aggregate number of postal packets posted in 1895 will be found to fall not far short of 1134 millions. Truly may it be said that the results of Penny Postage have been stupendous. But more than this; the net revenue derived from postage has long, long since exceeded that which accrued under the old system.

The story of Penny Postage would be incomplete if we did not add a word as to how the great reformer fared at the hands of his country. With the introduction of his scheme he of course became associated with the Post-office, although at first he held a Treasury appointment, from which, however, after about three years' service, he was dismissed on the ground that his work was finished. Public indignation was aroused at this treatment of one who had already done so much for his country; and the nation seemed to think that the right place for Rowland Hill was at the Post-office, where further useful reforms might well be expected to follow from one who had begun so well. At all events, in 1846 he was restored to office, being appointed Secretary to the Postmaster-general, and eight years later he became Chief Secretary of the Post-office, an appointment which he held for ten years, when, from failing health, he retired with full pay into private life, full of years and honours. Soon after his dismissal from the Treasury, a grateful country subscribed and presented him with the sum of fifteen thousand pounds; and on his retirement, parliament voted him the sum of twenty thousand pounds. In 1860 he received at Her Majesty's hands the dignity of Knight Commander of the Bath; and both before and after his retirement he was the recipient of many minor honours. In 1879 Sir Rowland Hill was presented with the freedom of the City of London; but he was an old man then, and only lived a few months to enjoy this civic honour. He had a public funeral, and was accorded a niche in the temple of fame at Westminster.

A VISIT TO THE POST-OFFICE.

Without a personal visit to the Post-office, it is perhaps difficult to gain any correct impression of its immensity, or of the perfect discipline and order which prevade the buildings devoted to postal and telegraphic work. It is a visit which should be made by every one interested, if possible. They would then marvel that we get our letters and papers in the short time we do, if they were to see the thousands upon thousands that are poured into St Martin's-le-Grand day by day. The General Post-office never sleeps save on Sunday between twelve and half-past one. The work is never at a standstill.

We began our visit to St Martin's-le-Grand by inspecting what is known as the 'blind' department, where letters with indistinct, incomplete, and wrongly spelt addresses are puzzled out by those specially trained in solving such mysteries. Scrap-books are kept in this department, into which the curious and amusing addresses originally inscribed on the face of letters transmitted through the Post-office are copied and preserved. Whilst we were looking at these a post-card was handed in to one of the officials merely addressed Jackson. Whether the sender thought it would go around to the various Jacksons in London, we know not, but anyway it was decided to take the trouble to return it to the sender, advising him that it was insufficiently addressed. The trouble careless persons give the Post-office is inconceivable, and the way some try to cheat in the manner of registering letters needs to be seen to be believed.

From the 'blind' department we were conducted to the 'hospital,' where badly done up letters and parcels which have come to grief are doctored and made sufficiently secure to reach their destination. When it is recollected that postage is so cheap, the outside public might at least take the trouble to do up letters and parcels properly without putting the Post-office to the enormous trouble thus caused—needless trouble sustained without a murmur and without extra charge. Some are put into fresh envelopes, others are sealing-waxed where slits have occurred, and others are properly tied up with string. All this trouble might be saved by a little forethought on the part of the senders.

The number of samples that different firms send through the post each day is astonishing. It is said that 1,504,000 pattern and sample packets are posted annually in the metropolis. In addition to those just mentioned, alpaca, corduroy, gloves, ribbons, plush, whalebone, muslin, linen, biscuits, oilcakes, pepper, yeast, toilet soap, sperm candles, mustard, raisins, &c., are sent by sample post. One firm alone posted 125,418 packets containing spice.

The time to visit the sorting process at the Post-office is between half-past five and eight o'clock in the evening. At closing time the letters are simply poured by thousands into the baskets waiting to receive them, and each one as soon as full is wheeled off in an instant to the sorters and other officials waiting to deal with them. When they have been deposited on the innumerable tables, the first process is to face the letters—not so easy a task when the shapes and sizes of the letters are so varied. As soon as the facing process is over, they are passed as quick as lightning on to the stampers, who proceed to deface the Queen's head. The noise whilst this process is being gone through is deafening. Some stampers have a hand-machine, whilst others are making a trial of a treadle stamping-machine which stamps some four hundred letters per minute. From the stampers the letters pass on to the sorters. Whilst all this is proceeding, the visitor should step up into the gallery for a minute or two and look down on the busy scene below. It is a sight well worth seeing and not likely to be forgotten—the thousands of letters heaped on the tables, and the hundreds of workers as hard at work as it is possible for them to be. The envelopes are separated and placed in the several pigeon-holes which indicate the various directions they are to travel. Liverpool, Manchester, Birmingham, Edinburgh, and Glasgow have special receptacles for themselves, as the first three cities have on an average fifteen thousand letters a day despatched to each; and further, there are eight despatches a day to these places, eleven thousand per day go to Glasgow, and between eight and nine thousand to Edinburgh. All official letters—that is, 'On Her Majesty's Service'—have a special table to themselves. Some eighty-nine thousand Savings-bank books pass through St Martin's-le-Grand daily. Some sorters get through between forty and fifty letters a minute, whilst a new-comer will not be able to manage more than twenty or thirty.

The nights on which various mails go out are extra busy ones, especially Friday evening, when the Indian, Chinese, and Australian mails are sent. The reduction of the postage has made an enormous difference in the contents of the mail-bags to these parts of the world. It may be interesting here to note how the mails are dealt with at Brindisi. Van after van conveys the mail-bags from the train to the ship, where two gangways are put off from the shore to the ship's side. Lascars run up one and down the other with the bags. Each lascar has a smooth flat stick like a ruler, and as he deposits his mail-bag on a long bench over the hold, he gives up his stick to a man standing by. When five lascars have arrived, the sticks go into one compartment of a small wooden box; and when the box is full—that is, when a hundred have been put in—the box is carried off and another brought forward. Three hundred and ninety-two bags is a good average, and they take just under forty minutes to put on board. The French and Italian mails are included in these; but no other European mails go by the Peninsular and Oriental Company. At Aden, two sorters come on board and spend their days in some postal cabins sorting the mails for the different parts of India, &c. The bags in which these mails are enclosed are only used once. They are made in one of our convict prisons, and fresh ones are distributed each week both outward and homeward.

Turning from the General Post-office South, which is now exclusively utilised for letters and papers, we proceed to the General Post-office North, which is devoted solely to the telegraph department. The Savings-bank department was originally in the same building as the telegraph; but owing to the rapid increase in both departments, the Savings-bank has been removed to Queen Victoria Street. Coldbath-Fields Prison was converted into a home for the Parcel Post. Some three thousand male and female clerks are employed in the telegraph department alone. The top floor of the building is devoted to the metropolitan districts. A telegram sent from one suburb of London to another is bound to pass through St Martin's-le-Grand; it cannot be sent direct. The second floor deals with the provinces. The pneumatic tube is now used a great deal; and by means of it some fifty telegrams can be sent on at once, and not singly, as would be the case if the telegraphic instrument was the only instrument in use. The tube is mostly used at the branch offices.

The press is a great user both of the postal and telegraphic department. In the postal department the representatives can call for letters at any hour, provided their letters are enclosed in a distinctive-coloured envelope, such as bright red or orange. Of course this privilege has to be paid for. In the telegraph department the press can obtain their 'private wires' after six in the evening, as the wires are no longer required for commercial purposes. The plan adopted in sending the same message to every provincial town which has a daily journal is the following: all along the route the operators are advised of the fact, and whilst the message is only actually delivered at its final destination, the words are caught as they pass each town by means of the 'sounder.' By this ingenious arrangement, dozens of towns are placed in direct communication with the central office whence the message is despatched. To carry on our telegraphic arrangements three miles of shelves are needed, on which are deposited forty thousand batteries.

THE POST-OFFICE ON WHEELS.

The particular portion of the 'Post-office on Wheels' which we purpose describing is the Special Mail which leaves London from Euston Station daily. We have selected this mail, not only because all the duties appertaining to the Travelling Post-office are performed therein, but also because it is the most important mail in the United Kingdom, probably in the whole world. In the Special Mail, the post-office vehicles are forty-two feet in length, and one of thirty-two feet. There is a gangway communication between all the carriages, so that the officers on duty can pass from one to another throughout the entire length without going outside. All the carriages are lighted with gas.

The pair-horse vans which convey the London bags for provincial towns come dashing into the station in rapid succession, and as there are only fifteen minutes before the train starts, no time is to be lost. The bags are quickly removed from the vans, the name of each being called out in the process, thus enabling an officer who stands near to tick them off on a printed list with which he is provided. They are then stowed away in the respective carriages in appointed places.

Having proceeded to the principal sorting carriage, we see that there are some thousands of the letters which have come from the London offices still to be disposed of. They lie on the desks in large bundles; but every minute there is a perceptible diminution of their numbers by means of the vigorous attacks of the men engaged. From end to end of one side of the carriage—that farthest from the platform—rows of sorting-boxes, or 'pigeon-holes,' are fixed nearly up to the roof, starting from the sorting-table, which is about three feet from the floor. The boxes into which the ordinary letters are sorted are divided into sets, numbered consecutively from 1 to 45, and one sorter works at each set. The numbers on the boxes are in accordance with a prescribed plan, each number representing the names of certain towns, and into such boxes the letters for those towns are sorted. The plan mentioned is carried out as follows: Suppose we say that No. 10

represents Rugby, of course when the mail-bag for that town is despatched the box is empty. It is then used, say, for Crewe, and when the bag for that place is gone the box again becomes empty. It is then used for some other town farther down the line, and so on to the end of the journey. The set of boxes nearest the fore-end of the carriage is used by the officer who deals with the registered letters. This set can be closed by means of a revolving shutter, which is fitted with a lock and key; so that, should the registered-letter officer have to quit his post for any purpose, he can secure the contents of his boxes, and so feel satisfied that they are in a safe place. This officer also disposes of all the letter-bills on which the addresses of the registered letters are advised.

The set of boxes into which the newspapers and book packets are sorted is about twice the size of an ordinary letter set, and occupies the centre part of the whole box arrangement. This space is assigned to the newspaper boxes for two reasons: the set is exactly opposite the doorway through which the bags are taken in at the stopping station, so that they lie on the floor behind the sorter who opens them; he has therefore simply to turn round and pick them up one by one as he requires them, thereby saving both time and labour. Again, as the bags are opened, the bundles of letters which are labelled No. 1 and No. 2 respectively, in accordance with the list supplied to postmasters for their guidance, have to be distributed to the letter-sorters—No. 1 bundles to the left, No. 2 to the right; and this distribution could not be so conveniently performed with the newspaper or bag-opening table placed in a different position. Most of the newspaper boxes, as we have said, are about twice the size of a letter box; some, however, such as those used for large towns like Liverpool, Manchester, Birmingham, &c., are four times the size; and the necessity for this can be readily understood.

We will now look at the other side of the carriage—or that nearest the platform. Along the whole length of that side, strong iron pegs are fixed about an inch apart, and on these pegs the bags to be made up and despatched on the way are hung. Most of the bags used in the Travelling Post-office are of one size—three feet six inches long, and two feet four inches wide; but for the large towns, bags of greater dimensions are required. Each bag is distinctly marked on both sides with the name of the town to which it is to be forwarded, the letters forming the name being an inch and a quarter in length. The name is also stencilled inside the mouth of the bag, so that the sorter has it immediately before his eyes when putting the letters, &c., away. On reaching its destination the bag is emptied of its contents, is turned inside out, and then the name of the Travelling Post-office from which it was received appears in view. The bag is then folded up and kept ready for the return despatch on the following night. In this way it passes and repasses until it is worn out, when it is withdrawn, and a new one takes its place.

We will now assume the train is fairly on its way, and that we are approaching Harrow, the first station at which the mail-bags are received by means of the apparatus. As the machinery constituting the apparatus is of great importance in the system of working, we shall here endeavour to describe it.

We may say that the apparatus in the Special Mail is worked in a separate carriage which runs immediately behind the one to which we have referred in the preceding details. A large and very strong net is firmly fixed on the side of the carriage on the near end, and the woodwork being cut away, an aperture is formed through which the pouches containing the bags are taken into the carriage. The net is raised or lowered by pressing down a lever very similar in structure and appearance to the levers which are seen in a signalman's cabin. When the net is lowered, a strong rope is seen to stretch across from the fore-part, and this rope, being held in position by a chain attached to the back-part of the net, forms what is called a detaching line in the shape of the letter V placed thus, <; and as the carriage travels along, the rope at the point forming the angle strikes the suspended pouch, and detaches it from the standard, when it falls into the net, and is removed by the officer attending to the apparatus. The machinery is also arranged so that a bag can be despatched as well as received. A man doing this work should possess keen eyes, steady nerves, and a full average amount of strength. On a dark or foggy night it is difficult to see the objects which serve as guides to the whereabouts of the train, and which are technically known in the office as 'marks.'

The net is now lowered for the receipt at Harrow. In a second or two, a tremendous thud is heard, and a large pouch comes crashing into the carriage through the aperture, the men meanwhile keeping a respectful distance. I should perhaps explain that in the Special Mail a new form of net is used. The bottom of it is flush with the carriage floor, and as the lower portion is constructed with an angle of about forty-five degrees, the pouches roll into the carriage by their own weight.

We will now see what the pouch from Harrow contains. It is quickly unstrapped; the bags are taken out; and it is then laid aside, to be used for despatch at a subsequent station. There are three bags for the Travelling Post-office received in this pouch—two containing correspondence for England and Scotland, and one for Ireland. The bags are immediately opened by the proper officers. The first duty is to find the letter-bill; and if there are any registered letters, to compare them with the entries on the bill, when, if correct, the bill is signed and passed over, together with the registered letters, to the officer who disposes of that class of correspondence, and by whom an acknowledgment of the receipt of the letters is at once given to the bag-opener. It is in this way that a hand-to-hand check is established which ensures the practical safety of such letters.

The bag-opener then proceeds to pick out from amongst the mass of correspondence the bundles of ordinary letters, and to pass them to the right or left according as they are labelled No. 1 or No. 2. These bundles are cut open by the respective sorters who work at the several sets of boxes, the letters being laid in a row on the desk, and the men then proceed to sort them in accordance with the addresses they bear. As the boxes (each of which will hold about one hundred and fifty) become full, the letters are tied up securely in bundles, and the sorters, turning round, drop them into the bags which hang along the other side of the carriage. And so the work goes on in the same way throughout the entire journey.

Let us now try to show to how great an extent the Travelling Post-office has contributed to the acceleration of correspondence from place to place. On an examination of the letters received from Harrow, it is found that there are three for Aberdeen; and a similar number for that city will be received from the several towns between London and Rugby, and so on. Of course, the number of letters mentioned would not be sufficient for a direct bag between each of these places and Aberdeen; but the small numbers referred to being brought together in the Travelling Post-office, it is found that when the train arrives at Carlisle a sufficient amount of correspondence for the northern city has been received to fill a large bag. This bag is therefore closed at that point, and a fresh one hung up, to contain the correspondence for that city received northwards of Carlisle. The same may be said of the other large towns in Scotland. Now, if there were no Travelling Post-office, how would the few letters for Aberdeen emanating from the various towns in England be dealt with? In the first place, they would have to be picked up by a stopping train, and even if this train ran direct to Aberdeen, there would be a difference in the time of arrival of at least eight hours. But the letters could not go direct in such a case, as that would mean the making-up of separate bags at each place; and we have already shown that the letters are too few in number to justify such an arrangement. They would have to be collected at some central office, say at Birmingham, where they would of necessity be detained some time; so that altogether it is probable they would not arrive at their destination early enough to be delivered on the day following that of posting. What, however, is the case now? Thanks to the Travelling Post-office with its mail-bag apparatus, the letters are whirled along at close upon fifty miles an hour without intermission, thus admitting of the delivery of letters from London at so remote a place as Aberdeen long before noon on the following day.

We will now assume that the train has arrived at Rugby—the distance eighty-four miles. At this station mails for Coventry, Birmingham, &c., are left to be forwarded by a branch train. After a stop of four minutes, the train again speeds on its way, the next stopping-place being Tamworth. Here a large number of mail-bags are despatched, including those for the Midland Travelling Post-office, going north to Newcastle-on-Tyne, which serves Derbyshire, Yorkshire, and the whole country-side bordering on the north-east coast; for the Shrewsbury mail-train, which serves the whole of Mid-Wales; and for the Lincoln mail-train, which serves Nottinghamshire and Lincolnshire.

The next halt is at Crewe, where formerly a large exchange of bags took place, having been passed without stopping. Crewe is, for Travelling Post-office purposes, by far the most important junction in the kingdom. Within three hours—that is, between half-past eleven at night and half-past two in the morning—over a dozen mail-trains, each with sorting-carriages attached, arrive and depart; whilst the weight of mails exchanged here within the hours mentioned is not less than twenty tons. A great amount of labour is involved in receiving and delivering such an immense weight of bags, the work being all done by hand, and the mail-porters have to exercise great care in keeping them in proper course for the respective trains. Nevertheless, these responsible duties are remarkably well performed, mistakes very rarely occurring.

The Irish mail which runs from London to Holyhead, and in which correspondence for Ireland is almost exclusively dealt with, branches off at Crewe, the remainder of the journey being run by way of Chester and North Wales.

Leaving Warrington, the next stoppage is at Wigan. Here the mails for Liverpool are despatched, and the receipt includes bags which have been brought through a long line of country, stretching from Newcastle-on-Tyne through York, Normanton, and Stalybridge, and thence to Wigan. The mails for Preston and East Lancashire are left at Preston, and, running through Lancaster, Carnforth is soon reached. At this station the mails for North-west Lancashire and West Cumberland are despatched, and this is the last stopping-place before arriving at Carlisle, which is the terminal point of the North-Western Railway.

Mention should be made of the noteworthy despatch of mails by apparatus at Oxenholme, the junction for Kendal, Windermere, and the Lake District. It is the largest despatch by that method in the kingdom, as many as nine pouches being delivered into two nets. Each pouch at this station weighs on an average fifty pounds, so that altogether four hundred and fifty pounds of mail-matter is despatched at this one station — no inconsiderable feat.

At Carlisle the mails for the Waverley route country and for the whole of the south-west of Scotland, including Ayrshire, are left. There is another long run over the Caledonian Railway—about seventy-eight miles—without a stop, the apparatus being worked seven times in that distance until Carstairs is reached. Here, one of the sorting-carriages is detached, and proceeds to Edinburgh; and a few miles farther on three more are detached, and proceed to Glasgow from Holytown Junction. From that point, therefore, only two sorting-carriages remain in the train, and these go on to Aberdeen.

The next stop is at Stirling, where the bags for the Western Highlands are left; and we then run on to Perth.

At Perth, the mails for Dundee and the northern Highlands are despatched, the latter being forwarded by a mail-train which runs on the Highland Railway *viâ* Inverness. Again the Special Mail starts on its way, there being only one stop—at Forfar—before arriving at Aberdeen, where the journey ends. Here the last bags are despatched. The carriage is clear. The sorting-boxes are carefully searched, to see that no letters have been left in them; and the carriage is then taken charge of by the railway officials, to be thoroughly cleansed and made ready for the return journey on the following day. The duties on the way to London are performed in a precisely similar manner to those on the journey northwards.

EARLY TELEGRAPHS.

THE ancient Greeks and Romans practised telegraphy with the help of pots filled with straw and twigs saturated in oil, which, being placed in rows, expressed certain letters according to the order in which they were lighted; but the only one of their contrivances that merits a detailed description was that invented by a Grecian general named Æneas, who flourished in the time of Aristotle, intended for communication between the generals of an army. It consisted of two exactly similar earthen vessels, filled with water, each provided with a cock that would discharge an equal quantity of water in a given time, so that the whole or any part of the contents would escape in precisely the same period from both vessels. On the surface of each floated a piece of cork supporting an upright, marked off into divisions, each division having a certain sentence inscribed upon it. One of the vessels was placed at each station; and when either party desired to communicate, he lighted a torch, which he held aloft until the other did the same, as a sign that he was all attention. On the sender of the message lowering or extinguishing his torch, each party immediately opened the cock of his vessel, and so left it until the sender relighted his torch, when it was at once closed. The receiver then read the sentence on the division of the upright that was level with the mouth of the vessel, and which, if everything had been executed with exactness, corresponded with that of the sender, and so conveyed the desired intimation.

We must here pause a moment to point out one great advantage that this contrivance, simple as it undoubtedly was, will be seen to possess over the more scientific ones that follow, and that was, its equal efficacy in any sort of country and in any position, whether on a plain, on the summit of a hill, or in a sequestered valley.

To descend to more modern times. Kessler in his *Concealed Arts* advised the cutting out of characters in the bottom of casks, which would appear luminous when a light was placed inside. In the *Spectator* of December 6, 1711, there is an extract from Strada, an Italian historian, who published his *Prolusiones Academicæ* in 1617. In the passage referred to, the modern system of telegraphy is curiously indicated. It is as follows: 'Strada, in one of his Prolusions, gives an account of a chimerical correspondence between two friends by the help of a certain loadstone, which had such virtue in it, that if it touched two several needles, when one of the needles so touched began to move, the other, though at never so great a distance, moved at the same time and in the same manner. He tells us that the two friends, being each of them possessed of one of these needles, made a kind of dial-plate, inscribing it with the four-and-twenty letters, in the same manner as the hours of the day are marked upon the ordinary dial-plate. They then fixed one of the needles on each of these plates in such a manner that it could move round without impediment so as to touch any of the four-and-twenty letters. Upon their separating from one another into distant countries, they agreed to withdraw themselves punctually into their closets at a certain hour of the day, and to converse with one another by means of this their invention. Accordingly, when they were some hundred miles asunder, each of them shut himself up in his closet at the time appointed, and immediately cast his eye upon his dial-plate. If he had a mind to write anything to his friend, he directed his needle to every letter that formed the words which he had occasion for, making a little pause at the end of every word or sentence, to avoid confusion. The friend, in the meanwhile, saw his own sympathetic needle moving of itself to every letter which that of his correspondent pointed at. By this means they talked together across a whole continent, and conveyed their thoughts to one another in an instant over cities or mountains, seas or deserts.

It was not till near the close of the seventeenth century that a really practical system of visual signalling from hill to hill was introduced by Dr Hooke, whose attention had been turned to the subject at the siege of Vienna by the Turks. He erected on the top of several hills having a sky-line background three high poles or masts, connected at their upper ends by a cross-piece. The space between two of these poles was filled in with timbers to form a screen, behind which the various letters were hung in order on lines, and, by means of pulleys, run out into the clear space between the other two, when they stood out clear against the sky-line. The letters were thus run out and back again in the required order of spelling, and were divided into day and night letters—the former being made of deals, the latter with the addition of links or lights; besides which there were certain conventional characters to represent such sentences as, 'I am ready to communicate,' 'I am ready to receive.' In his description of the device, read before the Royal Society on the 21st of May 1684, Dr Hooke, after claiming for it the power of transmitting messages to a station thirty or forty miles distant, said: 'For the performance of this we must be beholden to a late invention, which we do not find any of the ancients knew; that is, the eye must be assisted with telescopes, that whatever characters are exposed at one station may be made plain and distinguishable at the other.' A cipher code was subsequently added by an ingenious Frenchman named Amontons.

In 1767 we find Mr Richard L. Edgeworth, the father of Maria Edgeworth, employing the sails of a common windmill for communicating intelligence, by an arranged system of signals according to the different positions of the arms. The signals were made to denote numbers, the corresponding parties being each provided with a dictionary in which the words were numbered—the system in vogue for our army-signalling till 1871, when the Morse alphabet was substituted for it.

A great stride was made in 1793 by M. Chappe, a citizen of Paris, when the French Revolution directed all the energies of that nation to the improvement of the art of war; reporting on whose machine to the French Convention in August of the following year, Barère remarked: 'By this invention, remoteness and distance almost disappear, and all the communications of correspondence are effected with the rapidity of the twinkling of an eye.' It consisted of a strong wooden mast some twenty-five feet high, with a cross-beam twelve feet by nine inches jointed on to its top, so as to be movable about its centre like a scale-beam, and could thus be placed horizontally, vertically, or anyhow inclined by means of cords. To each end of this cross-beam was affixed a short vertical indicator about four feet long, which likewise turned on pivots by means of cords, and to the end of each was attached a counterweight, almost invisible at a distance, to balance the weight of it. This machine could be made to assume certain positions which represented or were symbolical of letters of the alphabet. In working, nothing depended on the operator's manual skill, as the movements were regulated mechanically. The time taken up for each movement was twenty seconds, of which the actual motion occupied four; during the other sixteen, the telegraph was kept stationary, to allow of its being distinctly observed and the letter written down by those at the next station. All the parts were painted dark brown, that they might stand out well against the sky; and three persons were required at each station, one to manipulate the machine, another to read the messages through a telescope, and the third to transfer them to paper, or repeat them to No. 1 to send on. The first machine of this kind was erected on the roof of the Paris Louvre, to communicate with the army which was then stationed near Lille, between which places intermediate ones from nine to twelve miles apart were erected, the second being at Montmartre. The different limbs were furnished with argand lamps for night-work.

Shortly after this, our own government set up lines of communication from the Admiralty to Deal, Portsmouth, and other points on the coast, which we find thus reported in the *Annual Register* for 1796:

March 28th. 'A telegraph was this day erected over the Admiralty, which is to be the point of communication with all the different sea-ports in the kingdom. The nearest telegraph to London has hitherto been in St George's Fields; and to such perfection has this ingenious and useful contrivance been already brought, that one day last week information was conveyed from Dover to London in the space of only seven minutes. The plan proposed to be adopted in respect to telegraphs is yet only carried into effect between London and Dover; but it is intended to extend all over the kingdom. The importance of this speedy communication must be evident to every one; and it has this advantage, that the information conveyed is known only to the person who sends and to him who receives it. The intermediate posts have only to answer and convey the signals.'

The machines used consisted of three masts connected by a top-piece. The spaces between the masts were divided into three horizontally, and in each partition a large wooden octagon was fixed, poised upon a horizontal axis across its centre, so that it could be made to present either its surface or its edge to the observer. The octagons were turned by means of cranks upon the ends of the axles, from which cords descended into a cabin below. By the changes in the position of these six octagonal boards, thirty-six changes were easily exhibited, and the signal to represent any letter or number made: thus, one board being turned into a horizontal position so as to expose its edge, while the other five remained shut or in a vertical position, might stand for A, two of them only in a horizontal position for B, three for C, and so on. It was, however, found that the octagons were less evident to the eye at a distance than the indicators of Chappe's machine, requiring the stations to be closer together; nor could this telegraph be made to change its direction, so that it could only be seen from one particular point, which necessitated having a separate machine at the Admiralty for each line, as well as an additional one at every branch-point. It was, moreover, too bulky and of a form unsuitable for illumination at night.

Here we may notice that in 1801 Mr John Boaz of Glasgow obtained a patent for a telegraph which effected the signal by means of twenty-five lamps arranged in five rows of five each, so as to form a square. Each lamp was provided with a blind, with which its light could be obscured, so that they could be made to exhibit letters and figures by leaving such lamps only visible as were necessary to form the character.

The next improvement again came from France, in 1806, when an entirely new set of telegraphs on the following principle was established along the whole extent of the coast of the French empire. A single upright pole was provided with three arms, each movable about an axis at one end—one near the head, the other two at points lower down, all painted black, with their counterpoises white, so as to be invisible a short way off. Each arm could assume six different positions—one straight out on either side of the pole, two at an angle of forty-five degrees above this line, and two at forty-five degrees below it. The arm near the head could be made to exhibit seven positions, the seventh being the vertical; but as this might have been mistaken for part of the pole, it was not employed. The number of combinations or different signals that could be rendered by this machine, employing only three objects, was consequently three hundred and forty-two against sixty-three by that of our Admiralty just described, and which employed six objects.

It was not long, however, before we copied the advancement of our neighbours across the Channel, and in some respects improved upon it, the main differences being that only two arms were employed—one at the top, the other half-way down, and that the mast was made to revolve on a vertical axis, so that the arms could be rendered visible from any desired quarter. Its mechanism, the invention of Sir Home Popham, enabled the arms to be moved by means of endless screws worked by iron spindles from below, a vast improvement on the old cords, the more so as they worked inside the mast, which was hollow, hexagonal in section, and framed of six boards bound together by iron hoops, and were thus protected from the weather. Inside the cabin he erected two dials, one for each arm, each having an index finger that worked simultaneously with its corresponding arm above, on the same principle as the little semaphore models to be seen nowadays in our railway signal cabins.

We have now described the most prominent of the numerous contrivances which, prior to the application of electricity to that end, were devised and made use of for telegraphic communication, all of which, unlike that subtle power that is not afraid of the dark and can travel in all weathers, possessed a common weakness in their liability to failure through atmospheric causes, fog, mist, and haze. To us who live in this age of electrical marvels, when that particular science more than all others progresses by leaps and bounds, it appears passing strange and almost incredible that so many years were allowed to elapse before the parents of the electric telegraph, the electrical machine and magnetic compass, were joined in wedlock to produce their amazing progeny, which now enables all mankind, however distant, to hold rapid, soft, and easy converse.

THE TELEGRAPH OF TO-DAY.

A veil of mystery still hangs around the first plan for an electric telegraph, communicated to the *Scots Magazine* for 1753 by one 'C. M.' of Renfrew. Even the name of this obscure and modest genius is doubtful; but it is probable that he was Charles Morrison, a native of Greenock, who was trained as a surgeon. At this period only the electricity developed by friction was available for the purpose, and being of a refractory nature, there was no practical result.

But after Volta had invented the chemical generator or voltaic pile in the first year of our century, and Oersted, in 1820, had discovered the influence of the electric current on a magnetic needle, the illustrious Laplace suggested to Ampère, the famous electrician, that a working telegraph might be produced if currents were conveyed to a distance by wires, and made to deflect magnetic needles, one for every letter of the alphabet. This was in the year 1820; but it was not until sixteen years later that the idea was put in practice. In 1836 Mr William Fothergill Cooke, an officer of the Madras army, at home on furlough, was travelling in Germany, and chanced to see at the university of Heidelberg, in the early part of March, an experimental telegraph, fitted up between the study and the lecture theatre of the Professor of Natural Philosophy. It was based on the principle of Laplace and Ampère, and consisted of two electric circuits and a pair of magnetic needles which responded to the interruptions of the current. Mr Cooke was struck with this device; but it was only during his journey from Heidelberg to Frankfort on the 17th of the month, while reading Mrs Mary Somerville's book on the *Correlation of the Physical Sciences*, that the notion of his practical telegraph flashed upon his mind. Sanguine of success, he abandoned his earlier pursuits and devoted all his energies to realise his invention.

The following year he associated himself with Professor Wheatstone; a joint patent was procured; and the Cooke and Wheatstone needle telegraph was erected between the Euston Square and Camden Town stations of the London and Birmingham Railway. To test the working of the instruments through a longer distance, several miles of wire were suspended in the carriage-shed at Euston, and included in the circuit. All being ready, the trial was made on the evening of the 25th of July 1837, a memorable date. Some friends of the inventors were present, including Mr George Stephenson and Mr Isambard Brunel, the celebrated engineers. Mr Cooke, with these, was stationed at Camden Town, and Mr Wheatstone at Euston Square. The latter struck the key and signalled the first message. Instantly the answer came on the vibrating needles, and their hopes were realised. 'Never,' said Professor Wheatstone—'never did I feel such a tumultuous sensation before, as when, all alone in the still room, I heard the needles click; and as I spelled the words I felt all the magnitude of the invention, now proved to be practical beyond cavil or dispute.'

It was in 1832, during a voyage from Havre to New York in the packet *Sully*, that Mr S. F. B. Morse, then an artist, conceived the idea of the electro-magnetic marking telegraph, and drew a design for it in his sketch-book.

But it was not until the beginning of 1838 that he and his colleague, Mr Alfred Vail, succeeded in getting the apparatus to work. Judge Vail, the father of Alfred, and proprietor of the Speedwell ironworks, had found the money for the experiments; but as time went on and no result was achieved, he became disheartened, and perhaps annoyed at the sarcasms of his neighbours, so that the inventors were afraid to meet him. 'I recall vividly,' says Mr Baxter, 'even after the lapse of so many years, the proud moment when Alfred said to me, "William, go up to the house and invite father to come down and see the telegraph-machine work." I did not stop to don my coat, although it was the 6th of January, but ran in my shop-clothes as fast as I possibly could. It was just after dinner when I knocked at the door of the house, and was ushered into the sitting-room. The judge had on his broad-brimmed hat and surtout, as if prepared to go out; but he sat before the fireplace, leaning his head on his cane, apparently in deep meditation. As I entered his room he looked up and said, "Well, William?" and I answered: "Mr Alfred and Mr Morse sent me to invite you to come down to the room and see the telegraph-machine work." He started up, as if the importance of the message impressed him deeply; and in a few minutes we were standing in the experimental room. After a short explanation, he called for a piece of paper, and writing upon it the words, "A patient waiter is no loser," he handed it to Alfred, saying, "If you can send this, and Mr Morse can read it at the other end, I shall be convinced." The message was received by Morse at the other end, and handed to the judge, who, at this unexpected triumph, was overcome by his emotions.' The practical value of the invention was soon realised; by 1840 telegraph lines were being made in civilised countries, and ere long extended into the network of lines which now encircle the globe and bring the remotest ends of the earth into direct and immediate communication.

ATLANTIC CABLES.

A year or two before the first attempt to lay an Atlantic cable, there were only eighty-seven nautical miles of submarine cables laid; now, the total length of these wonderful message-carriers under the waves is over 160,500 English statute miles. There are now fourteen cables crossing the Atlantic, which are owned by six different companies.

The charter which Mr Cyrus W. Field obtained for the New York, Newfoundland, and London Telegraph Company was granted in the year 1854. It constructed the land-line telegraph in Newfoundland, and laid a cable across the Gulf of St Lawrence; but this was only the commencement of the work. Soundings of the sea were needed; electricians had to devise forms of cable most suitable; engineers to consider the methods of carrying and of laying the cable; and capitalists had to be convinced that the scheme was practicable, and likely to be remunerative; whilst governments were appealed to for aid. Great Britain readily promised aid; but the United States Senate passed the needful Bill by a majority of one.

But when the first Atlantic cable expedition left the coast of Kerry, it was a stately squadron of British and American ships of war, such as the *Niagara* and the *Agamemnon*, and of merchant steamships. The Lord-lieutenant of Ireland, Directors of the Atlantic Telegraph Company, and of British railways, were there, with representatives of several nations; and when the shore-end had been landed at Valentia, the expedition left the Irish coast in August 1857. When 335 miles of the cable had been laid, it parted, and high hopes were buried many fathoms below the surface.

The first expedition of 1858 also failed; the second one was successful; and on the 16th of August in that year, Queen Victoria congratulated the President of the United States 'upon the successful completion of this great international work;' and President Buchanan replied, trusting that the telegraph might 'prove to be a bond of perpetual peace and friendship between the kindred nations.' But after a few weeks' work, the cable gave its last throb, and was silent.

Not until 1865 was another attempt made, and then the cable was broken after 1200 miles had been successfully laid. Then, at the suggestion of Mr (afterwards Sir) Daniel Gooch, the Anglo-American Telegraph Company was formed; and on 13th July 1866 another expedition left Ireland; and towards the end of the month, the *Great Eastern* glided calmly into Heart's Content, 'dropping her anchor in front of the telegraph house, having trailed behind her a chain of two thousand miles, to bind the Old World to the New.'

But the success of the year was more than the mere laying of a cable: the *Great Eastern* was able, in the words of the late Lord Iddesleigh, to complete the 'laying of the cable of 1866, and the recovering that of 1865.' The Queen conferred the honour of knighthood on Captain Anderson, on Professor Thomson, and on Messrs Glass and Channing; whilst Mr Gooch, M.P., was made a baronet. The charge for a limited message was then twenty pounds; and it was not long before a rival company was begun, to share in the rich harvest looked for; and thus another cable was laid, leading ultimately to an amalgamation between its ordinary company and the original Anglo-American Telegraph Company.

Then, shortly afterwards, the Direct United States Cable

The *Great Eastern* paying out the Atlantic Cable.

Company came into being, and laid a cable; a French company followed suit; the great Western Union Telegraph Company of America entered into the Atlantic trade, and had two cables constructed and laid. The commencement of ocean telegraphy by each of these companies led to competition, and reduced rates for a time with the original company, ending in what is known as a pool or joint purse agreement, under which the total receipts were divided in allotted proportions to the companies. These companies have now eight cables usually operative; and it was stated by Sir J. Pender that these eight cables 'are capable of carrying over forty million words per annum.'

In addition to the cables of the associated companies, the Commercial Cable Company own two modern cables; and one of the two additional ones was laid by this company—the other by the original—the Anglo-American Company. But the work is simple now to what it was thirty years ago. Then, there were only one or two cable-ships; now, Mr Preece enumerates thirty-seven, of which five belong to the greatest of our telegraph companies, the Eastern. The authority we have just named says that 'the form of cable has practically remained unaltered since the original Calais cable was laid in 1851;' its weight has been increased; and there have been additions to it to enable it to resist insidious submarine enemies. The gear of the steamships used in the service has been improved; whilst the 'picking-up gear' of one of the best known of these cable-ships is 'capable of lifting thirty tons at a speed of one knot per hour.' And there has been a wide knowledge gained of the ocean, its depth, its mountains, and its valleys, so that the task of cable-laying is much more of an exact science than it was. When the first attempt was made to lay an Atlantic cable, 'the manufacture of sea-cables' had been only recently begun; now, 140,000 knots are at work in the sea, and yearly the area is being enlarged. When, in 1856, Mr Thackeray subscribed to the Atlantic Telegraph Company, its share capital was £350,000—that being the estimated cost of the cable between Newfoundland and Ireland; now, five companies have a capital of over £12,500,000 invested in the Atlantic telegraph trade. The largest portion of the capital is that of the Anglo-American Telegraph Company, which has a capital of £7,000,000, and which represents the Atlantic Telegraph Company, the New York, and Newfoundland, and the French Atlantic Companies of old.

Though the traffic fluctuates greatly, in some degree according to the charge per word (for in one year of lowest charges the number of words carried by the associated companies increased by 133 per cent., whilst the receipts decreased about 49 per cent.), yet it does not occupy fully the carrying capacity of the cables. But their 'life' and service is finite, and thus it becomes needful from time to time to renew these great and costly carriers under the Atlantic.

THE STATE AND THE TELEGRAPHS.

Since the telegraphs of the United Kingdom passed into the hands of the State, the changes which have taken place during that period in the volume of the business transacted, the rapidity in the transit of messages, and the charges made for sending telegrams, are little short of marvellous. It was in the year 1852 that the acquisition of the telegraph system by the State was first suggested, but not until late in the year 1867, when Mr Disraeli was Chancellor of the Exchequer, did the government definitely determine to take the matter up. At that time, as Mr Baines, C.B., tells us in his book, *Forty Years at the Post-office:* 'Five powerful telegraph companies were in existence—The Electric and International, the British and Irish Magnetic, the United Kingdom, the Universal Private, and the London and Provincial Companies. There were others of less importance. Terms had to be made with all of them. The railway interest had to be considered, and the submarine companies to be thought of, though not bought.' With strong and well-organised interests like these fighting hard to secure for themselves the very best possible terms, the government had not unnaturally to submit to a hard bargain before they could obtain from Parliament the powers which they required. However, after a severe struggle, the necessary Bill was successfully passed, and the consequent Money Bill became law in the following session. As the result of this action, the telegraphs became the property of the State upon the 29th of January 1870, and upon the 5th of the following month the actual transfer took place. The step seems to have been taken none too soon, for under the companies the telegraphs had been worked in a manner far from satisfactory to the public. Many districts had been completely neglected, and even between important centres the service had been quite inadequate. Moreover, charges had been high, and exasperating delays of frequent occurrence.

Six million pounds was the sum first voted by Parliament for the purchase of the telegraphs, and this was practically all swallowed up in compensation. The Electric and International Company received £2,938,826; the Magnetic Company, £1,243,536; Reuter's Telegram Company, £726,000; the United Kingdom Company, £562,264; the Universal Private Company, £184,421; and the London and Provincial Company, £60,000. But large as these amounts were, they only made up about one-half of the expenditure which the government had to incur, and the total cost ultimately reached the enormous sum of eleven millions. Some idea of the manner in which the extra five millions was expended may be gathered from the fact that between October 1869 and October 1870, about 15,000 miles of iron wire, nearly 2000 miles of gutta-percha-covered copper wire, about 100,000 poles, and 1,000,000 other fittings were purchased and fixed in position, 3500 telegraph instruments and 15,000 batteries were acquired, and about 2400 new telegraphists and temporary assistants were trained. The total expenditure was so vast that the Treasury eventually took fright, and in 1875 a committee was appointed 'to investigate the causes of the increased cost of the telegraph service since the acquisition of the telegraphs by the State.'

This committee found that the following were the three main causes of the increase: The salaries of all the officials of the telegraph companies had been largely increased after their entry into the government service; the supervising staff maintained by the State was much more costly than that formerly employed by the companies; and a large additional outlay had been forced upon the government in connection with the maintenance of the telegraph lines. 'It would not,' they say in their report, 'be possible, in our opinion, for various reasons, for the government to work at so cheap a rate as the telegraph companies, but . . . a reasonable expectation might be entertained that the working expenses could be kept within seventy or seventy-five per cent. of the gross revenue, and the responsible officers of the Postoffice telegraph service should be urged to work up to that standard. Such a result would cover the cost of working, and the sum necessary for payment of interest on the debt incurred in the purchase of the telegraphs.' In regard to this question of cost, Mr Baines most truly remarks that the real stumbling-block of the Department was, and still is, 'the interest payable on £11,000,000 capital outlay, equal at, say, three per cent. to a charge of £330,000 a year.'

The transfer of the telegraphs to the State was immediately followed by a startling increase in the number of messages sent. In fact, the public, attracted by the shilling rate, poured in telegrams so fast, and were so well supported by the news-agencies, who took full advantage of the reduced scale, that there was at first some danger of a collapse. Fortunately, however, the staff was equal to the emergency, and after the first rush was over, everything worked with perfect smoothness.

During the next four years the enlargement of business was simply extraordinary. In 1875 the rate of increase was not maintained at quite so high a level, but nevertheless nearly 1,650,000 more messages were dealt with than during the previous year. The quantity of matter transmitted for Press purposes was also much greater than it had ever been before, and amounted to more than 220,000,000 words.

In 1895 the number of telegraph offices at post-offices was 7409, in addition to 2252 at railway stations, or a grand total of 9661. The number of ordinary inland messages sent during the year was 71,589,064.

In regard to the great increase of pace in the transmission of telegraphic messages, Mr Baines tells us that, 'looking back fifty years, we see wires working at the rate of eight words a minute, or an average of four words per wire per minute, over relatively short distances. Now, there is a potentiality of 400 words—nay, even 600 or 700 words—per wire per minute, over very long distances. As the invention of duplex working has been supplemented by the contrivances for multiplex working (one line sufficing to connect several different offices in one part of the country with one or more offices in another part), it is almost impossible to put a limit to the carrying capacity of a single wire.' In 1866 the time occupied in sending a telegram between London and Bournemouth was two hours, and between Manchester and Bolton, two hours and a quarter; while in 1893 the times occupied were ten minutes and five minutes respectively.

Press telegrams have enormously increased in number and length since the purchase of the telegraph system by the State. When the companies owned the wires, the news service from London to the provinces was ordinarily not more than a column of print a night. At the present time the news service of the Press Association alone over the Post-office wires to papers outside the metropolis averages fully 500 columns nightly. Since 1870 this Association has paid the Post-office £750,000 for telegraphic charges, and in addition to this, very large sums have been paid by the London and provincial daily papers for the independent transmission of news, and by the principal journals in the country for the exclusive use, during certain hours, of 'special wires.' Some of the leading papers in the provinces receive ten or more columns of specially telegraphed news on nights when important matters are under discussion in Parliament; and from this some idea may be formed of the amount of business now transacted between the Press and the Telegraph Department.

THE TELEPHONE.

So much have times altered in the last fifty years, that the electric telegraph itself, which now reaches its thin arms into more than six thousand offices, is threatened in its turn with serious rivalry at the hands of a youthful but vigorous competitor, the telephone. Its advantages are such that its ultimate popularity cannot be a matter of doubt. It is no small benefit to be able to recognise voices, to transact business with promptitude by word of mouth, to get a reply, 'Yes' or 'No,' on the spot, instead of having to rush to the nearest telegraph office.

Great inventions are often conceived a long time before they are realised in practice. Sometimes the original idea occurs to the man who subsequently works it out; and sometimes it comes as a happy thought to one who is either in advance of his age, or who is prevented by adverse circumstances from following it up, and who yet lives to see the day when some more fortunate individual gives it a material shape, and so achieves the fame which was denied to him. Such is the case of M. Charles Bourselle, who in 1854 proposed a form of speaking-telephone, which, although not practicable in its first crude condition, might have led its originator to a more successful instrument if he had pursued the subject further.

The telephone is an instrument designed to reproduce sounds at a distance by means of electricity. It was believed by most people, and even by eminent electricians, that the speaking-telephone had never been dreamed of by any one before Professor Graham Bell introduced his marvellous little apparatus to the scientific world. But that was a mistake. More than one person had thought of such a thing, Bourselle among the number. Philip Reis, a German electrician, had even constructed an electric telephone in 1864, which transmitted words with some degree of perfection; and the assistant of Reis asserts that it was designed to carry music as well as words. Professor Bell, in devising his telephone, copied the human ear with its vibrating drum. The first iron plate he used as a vibrator was a little piece of clock-spring glued to a parchment diaphragm, and on saying to the spring on the telephone at one end of the line : ' Do you understand what I say ? ' the answer from his assistant at the other end came back immediately : ' Yes ; I understand you perfectly.' The sounds were feeble, and he had to hold his ear close to the little piece of iron on the parchment, but they were distinct ; and though Reis had transmitted certain single words some ten years before, Bell was the first to make a piece of matter utter sentences. Reis gave the electric wire a tongue so that it could mumble like an infant ; but Bell taught it to speak.

The next step is attributed to Mr Elisha Gray of Chicago, who sent successions of electrical current of varying strength as well as of varying frequency into the circuit, and thus enabled the relative loudness as well as the pitch of sounds to be transmitted ; and who afterwards took the important step of using the variations of a steady current. These variations, positive and negative, are capable of representing all the back-and-fore variations of position of a particle of air, however irregular these may be : and he secured them by making the sound-waves set a diaphragm in vibration. This diaphragm carried a metallic point which dipped in dilute sulphuric acid ; the deeper it dipped the less was the resistance to a current passing through the acid, and *vice versâ :* so that every variation in the position of the diaphragm produced a corresponding variation in the intensity of the current : and the varying current acted upon a distant electro-magnet, which accordingly fluctuated in strength, and in its attraction for a piece of soft iron suspended on a flexible diaphragm : this piece of soft iron accordingly oscillated, pulling the flexible diaphragm with it ; and the variations of pressure in the air acted upon by the diaphragm produced waves, reproducing the characteristics of the original sound-waves, and perceived by the ear as reproducing the original sound or voice. Mr Gray lodged a *caveat* for this contrivance in the United States Patent Office on 14th February 1876; but on the same day Professor Alexander Graham Bell filed a specification and drawings of the original Bell telephone.

Bell's telephone was first exhibited in America at the Centennial Exhibition in Philadelphia in 1876; and in England, at the Glasgow meeting of the British Association in September of that year. On that occasion, Sir William Thomson (now Lord Kelvin) pronounced it, with enthusiasm, to be the 'greatest of all the marvels of the electric telegraph.' The surprise created by its first appearance was, however, nothing to the astonishment and delight which it aroused in this country when Professor Bell, the following year, himself exhibited it in London to the Society of Telegraph Engineers. Since then, its introduction as a valuable aid to social life has been very rapid, and the telephone is now to be found in use from China to Peru.

THOMAS ALVA EDISON AND THE PHONOGRAPH.

The Phonograph is an instrument for mechanically recording and reproducing articulate human speech, song, &c. It was invented by Mr T. A. Edison in the spring of 1877, at his Menlo Park Laboratory, New Jersey, and came into existence as the result of one of the many lines of experiment he was then engaged upon.

Thomas Alva Edison, this notable American inventor, was born at Milan, Ohio, 11th February 1847, but his early years were spent at Port Huron, Michigan. His father was of Dutch, and his mother of Scotch descent; the latter, having been a teacher, gave him what schooling he received. Edison was a great reader in his youth, and

Edison with his Phonograph.

at the age of twelve he became a newsboy on the Grand Trunk Line running into Detroit, and began to experiment in chemistry. Gaining the exclusive right of selling newspapers on this line, and purchasing some old type, with the aid of four assistants he printed and issued the *Grand Trunk Herald*, the first newspaper printed in a railway train. A station-master, in gratitude for his having saved his child from the front of an advancing train, taught him telegraphy, in which he had previously been greatly interested; and thenceforward he concentrated the energies of a very versatile mind chiefly upon electrical studies.

Edison invented an automatic repeater, by means of which messages could be sent from one wire to another without the intervention of the operator. His system of duplex telegraphy was perfected while a telegraph operator in Boston, but was not entirely successful until 1872. In 1871 he became superintendent of the New York Gold and Stock Company, and here invented the printing-telegraph for gold and stock quotations, for the manufacture of which he established a workshop at Newark, N.J., continuing there till his removal to Menlo Park, N.J., in 1876. Ten years later he settled at Orange, at the foot of the Orange Mountains, his large premises at Menlo Park having grown too small for him.

His inventive faculties now getting full play, he took out over fifty patents in connection with improvements in telegraphy, including the duplex, quadruplex, and sextuplex system; the carbon telephone transmitter; microtasimeter; aerophone, for amplifying sound; the megaphone, for magnifying sound. Thence also emanated his phonograph, a form of telephone, and various practical adaptations of the electric light. His kinetoscope (1894) is a development of the Zoetrope, in which the continuous picture is obtained from a swift succession of instantaneous photographs (taken 46 or more in a second), and printed on a strip of celluloid. Of late he has devoted himself to improving metallurgic methods. He has taken out some 500 patents, and founded many companies at home and in Europe.

Following up some of his telegraphic inventions, he had developed a machine which, by reason of the indentations made on paper, would transfer a message in Morse characters from one circuit to another automatically, through the agency of a tracing-point connected with a circuit-closing device. Upon revolving with rapidity the cylinder that carried the indented or embossed paper Mr Edison found that the indentations could be reproduced with immense rapidity through the vibration of the tracing-point. He at once saw that he could vibrate a diaphragm by the sound-waves of the voice, and, by means of a stylus attached to the diaphragm, make them record themselves upon an impressible substance placed on the revolving cylinder. The record being made thus, the diaphragm would, when the stylus again traversed the cylinder, be thrown into the same vibrations as before, and the actual reproduction of human speech, or any other sound, would be the result. The invention thought out in this manner was at once tried, with paraffined paper as the receiving material, and afterwards with tinfoil, the experiment proving a remarkable success, despite the crudity of the apparatus. In 1878 Mr Edison made a number of phonographs, which were exhibited in America and Europe, and attracted universal attention. The records were made in these on soft tinfoil sheets fastened around metal cylinders. For a while Mr Edison was compelled to suspend work on this invention, but soon returned to it and worked out the machine as it exists practically to-day. It occupies about the same space as a hand sewing-machine. A light tube of wax to slide on and off the cylinder is substituted for the tinfoil, which had been wrapped round it, and the indenting stylus is replaced by a minute engraving point. Under the varying pressure of the sound-waves, this point or knife cuts into the tube almost imperceptibly, the wax chiselled away wreathing off in very fine spirals before the edge of the little blade, as the cylinder travels under it. Each cylinder will receive about a thousand words. In the improved machine Mr Edison at first employed two diaphragms in 'spectacle' form, one to receive and the other to reproduce; but he has since combined these in a single efficient attachment. The wax cylinders can be used several hundred times, the machine being fitted with a small paring tool which will shave off the record previously made, leaving a smooth new surface. The machine has also been supplemented by the inventor with an ingenious little electric motor with delicate governing mechanism, so that the phonograph can be operated at any chosen rate of speed, uniformly. This motor derives its energising current either from an Edison-Lalande primary battery, a storage battery, or an electric-light circuit.

The new and perfected Edison phonograph has already gone into very general use, and many thousands are distributed in American business offices, where they facilitate correspondence in a variety of ways. They are also employed by stenographers as a help in the transcription of their shorthand notes. Heretofore these notes have been slowly dictated to amanuenses, but they are now frequently read off to a phonograph, and then written out at leisure. The phonograph is, however, being used for direct stenograph work, and it reported verbatim 40,000 words of discussion at one convention held in 1890, the words being quietly repeated into the machine by the reporter as quickly as they were uttered by the various speakers. A large number of machines are in use by actors, clergymen, musicians, reciters, and others, to improve their elocution and singing. Automatic phonographs are also to be found in many places of public resort, equipped with musical or elocutionary cylinders, which can be heard upon the insertion of a small coin; and miniature phonographs have been applied to dolls and toys. The value of the phonograph in the preservation of dying languages has been perceived too, and records have already been secured of the speech, songs, war-cries, and folklore of American tribes now becoming extinct. It is also worthy of note that several voice records remain of distinguished men, who 'being dead yet speak.' Their tones can now be renewed at will, and their very utterances, faithful in accent and individuality, can be heard again and again through all time.

Improvements are being made in the wholesale reproduction of phonographic cylinders, by electrotyping and other processes; and the machine, in a more or less modified form, is being introduced as a means of furnishing a record of communications through the telephone. Phonographic clocks, books, and other devices have also been invented by Mr Edison, whose discovery is evidently of a generic nature, opening up a large and entirely new field in the arts and sciences.

THE END.

Edinburgh:
Printed by W. & R. Chambers, Limited.

BOOKS COMPILED BY
ROBERT COCHRANE

PUBLISHED BY
W. & R. CHAMBERS, Limited.

ADVENTURE AND ADVENTURERS. Being True Tales of Daring, Peril, and Heroism. Illustrated.   2/6

GOOD AND GREAT WOMEN. Lives of Queen Victoria, Florence Nightingale, Jenny Lind, &c. Illustrated.   2/6

BENEFICENT AND USEFUL LIVES. Lives of Lord Shaftesbury, George Peabody, Sir W. Besant, Samuel Morley, Sir J. Y. Simpson, &c. Illustrated.   2/6

GREAT THINKERS AND WORKERS. Lives of Thomas Carlyle, Lord Armstrong, Lord Tennyson, Charles Dickens, W. M. Thackeray, Sir H. Bessemer, James Nasmyth, &c. Illustrated.   2/6

RECENT TRAVEL AND ADVENTURE. Travels of H. M. Stanley, Lieutenant Greely, Joseph Thomson, Dr Livingstone, Lady Brassey, Arminius Vambéry, Sir Richard Burton, &c. Illustrated.   2/6

GREAT HISTORIC EVENTS. Indian Mutiny, French Revolution, the Crusades, Conquest of Mexico, &c. Illustrated.   2/6

London and Edinburgh.

www.ingramcontent.com/pod-product-compliance
Lightning Source LLC
Chambersburg PA
CBHW032056220426
43664CB00008B/1027